MAKING SENSE OF PHONICS

Also from Isabel L. Beck

Bringing Words to Life, Second Edition:
Robust Vocabulary Instruction
*Isabel L. Beck, Margaret G. McKeown,
and Linda Kucan*

Creating Robust Vocabulary:
Frequently Asked Questions and Extended Examples
*Isabel L. Beck, Margaret G. McKeown,
and Linda Kucan*

Making Sense of Phonics

THE HOWS AND WHYS

SECOND EDITION

ISABEL L. BECK
MARK E. BECK

THE GUILFORD PRESS
New York   London

© 2013 The Guilford Press
A Division of Guilford Publications, Inc.
370 Seventh Avenue, Suite 1200, New York, NY 10001
www.guilford.com

Printed in the United States of America

This book is printed on acid-free paper.

Last digit is print number: 9   8   7   6

Library of Congress Cataloging-in-Publication Data

Beck, Isabel L.
  Making sense of phonics : the hows and whys / Isabel L. Beck, Mark E. Beck. — Second ed.
    pages cm
  Includes bibliographical references and index.
  ISBN 978-1-4625-1199-0 (pbk.) — ISBN 978-1-4625-1205-8 (hardcover)
  1. Reading—Phonetic method.   2. Reading (Elementary).   I. Title.
  LB1573.3.B43 2013
  372.46′5—dc23
                                                                2013011133

To Ethan Carl Beck,
who reads and rocks

About the Authors

Isabel L. Beck, PhD, is Professor Emerita in the School of Education at the University of Pittsburgh. Before starting her career at the University, she was a public school teacher, and has taught most elementary grades. Dr. Beck's work has been acknowledged by awards from the International Reading Association, the National Reading Conference, and the American Federation of Teachers, among others. Most recently she was elected to the National Academy of Education.

Mark E. Beck, MEd, JD, is a reading specialist at Manchester Academic Charter School in Pittsburgh, where he works with children in grades K–5. After practicing law for 14 years, Mr. Beck changed careers, obtaining his Pennsylvania elementary teaching certification and working as a classroom teacher. Subsequently he obtained his reading specialist certification. He has also been a part-time instructor in the Reading Department in the School of Education at the University of Pittsburgh.

Preface

Isabel's Prologue

Writing the second edition of this book has been a unique and exceedingly gratifying experience, owing to the collaboration of my coauthor, Mark, who is my son. Few parents have the opportunity to work closely with an adult who happens to be their child on a topic about which they both are passionate.

Mark is the reading specialist at an urban school in Pittsburgh, the Manchester Academic Charter School, where he works with struggling readers as well as skilled readers. Mark had a successful career as a lawyer before he decided to change professions and do what he had always wanted to do—be a teacher. So after more than a dozen years as a practicing attorney, he went back to school, got his elementary teaching certification, taught, went back to school again, and got his master's degree and reading specialist certification. Mark loves what he does and talks and talks and talks about it, especially to me. And therein lies the motivation for this book.

Thanks to Mark, I have been in the unique position of listening to the details and ongoing experiences of a highly skilled practitioner about how the instructional strategies I offered in the first edition of *Making Sense of Phonics* worked. Generally, Mark is a fan of those strategies, and he has shared many stories about the children who benefited from them. He also told me about aspects of those strategies that he's had to modify, those that were too hard to manage or that were only partially understood by some teachers because they were not fully explained, and the like.

Several years ago, when Mark and I were having an animated conversation—we think it was about multisyllabic words—it all came together, and almost simultaneously we said something about writing a book together. And here it is!

Introducing the Second Edition

This second edition of *Making Sense of Phonics* has been expanded considerably from the first—our revised book is almost twice as long as the original. The increased length comes from the inclusion of completely new topics, as well as the further development of topics that had been discussed more briefly in the first edition. The original book had six chapters; the second edition has 12 chapters, plus five appendices, a glossary, and three sets of online resources. We briefly describe each of these next.

Chapter 1, "Situating Phonics Instruction," is completely new. It describes the theoretical background and history underlying reading instruction, focusing on the last hundred years. We deal briefly with phonics, whole-word instruction, and whole language. We include the firsthand comments of educators in the 1920s and 1930s, who watched a swing from phonics instruction to a whole-word emphasis. Similarly, we include the firsthand comments of educators in the 1980s and 1990s, who commented on the swing back from whole word to phonics. Along the way, we take a brief look at some of the more interesting pieces of research from this period.

Chapter 2, "The Alphabetic Principle and Phonics," includes much from the first edition, but even more that is new. Chapter 2 in the first edition contained 2,242 words; the revised version is more than twice as long, with 5,650 words. The new material includes greater discussion of the alphabetic principle, several examples and case studies that describe where students go awry early on with respect to the alphabetic principle, and an interesting summary of a decade of rigorous research that turned some conventional wisdom upside down.

Chapter 3, "Phonemic Awareness: A Bit of a Different Take," is largely new, although it borrows some ideas from the old book. The importance of phonemic awareness is discussed, as are several theories regarding the relationship between phonemic awareness and decoding. Additionally, we present an activity involving phonemic awareness through the use of letter cards.

Chapter 4, "The Phonics Landscape," is completely new. We describe the primary phonics categories taught typically around K–2. We also suggest some ideas for the ordering of letter–sound instruction. To a large extent, the organizational structure of this chapter is aligned with the phonics activities and assessments presented later in Chapters 7 and 8.

Chapter 5, "Teaching Children the Sounds That Letters Represent," includes most of the content of Chapter 3 from the first edition, along with a few new ideas about letter–sound instruction.

Chapter 6, "Blending," combines most of the material from Chapter 4 from the first edition with several new ideas, such as discussions of short-term-memory issues and how to apply the blending strategy to words with initial-consonant blends.

Chapter 7, "Word Building," includes much of the material from Chapter 5 of the first edition. In addition, the chapter provides a discussion of the importance of decodable text and an explanation of the difficulty some children experience in discriminating among phonic units. We also introduce what we call Silly Questions, in which words from Word Building sequences are used. Students read and answer the questions, and the nature of the questions seems to encourage creative answers.

Chapter 8, "Assessment," is entirely new. We have created a new assessment, the Specific Phonics Assessment (SPA), to determine how proficient students are in reading words containing eight different groups of phonics patterns. Sample SPA results are provided, along with discussion about how to interpret them and how these results may inform instruction and intervention.

We have taken the ideas from Chapter 6 in the first edition and divided them into two chapters, 9 and 10. Chapter 9, "Multisyllabic Words," lays out some of the principles of reading multisyllabic words. In the new edition, more examples of students correctly and incorrectly reading multisyllabic words are analyzed. We then provide an extensive discussion of how to decode longer words through three steps: analysis, pronunciation, and synthesis. The chapter also includes demonstrations of how much students' knowledge of single-syllable words can support their ability to decode multisyllable words.

Chapter 10, "Syllasearch," presents the directions for engaging in Syllasearch, an activity to support decoding multisyllabic words. The original material from the first edition reappears, along with some modifications.

New to this edition is Chapter 11, "Orthography: A Sticking Point in Word Recognition," which describes the importance of understanding orthography in reading words and offers some activities designed to promote understanding of and engagement with orthography.

Chapter 12, "Automaticity," also new to this edition, deals with the importance of reading words automatically and not just accurately. Repeated readings, along with other ideas about how to increase repetition and reading volume, are dealt with in some detail.

The Appendices

Appendix 1 contains the Word Building lists, which have been expanded and clarified from the first edition. The organization of the Word Building lists largely follows from the Phonics Landscape described in Chapter 4. For every list, there are two Silly Questions to be asked and answered at the end of the word-building process.

Appendix 2 provides the new SPAs, along with guidelines for administering and scoring them. There are eight SPAs, which are aligned with each of the eight word-building sequences from Appendix 1. Each SPA contains a Student Page for students to read and a Teacher Page to mark up and score.

Appendix 3 provides the Syllasearch lists, which have been somewhat revised from the first edition. There are now four sequences in the new edition, and they have a bit more of a systematic nature to them. A new sequence involves the open–closed syllable rule to help students distinguish between the pronunciation of long vowels in open syllables and short vowels in closed syllables. Additionally, we have inserted new teaching tips into the first two sequences to alert teachers to upcoming content.

Appendix 4 presents instructions and materials for the Word Pocket activity that was included in the first edition, and Appendix 5 offers a full list of the online teaching resources that are a new feature of the second edition, as described next.

Online Teaching Resources

As a means of assisting teachers in conducting the assessments and Syllasearch activities, this new edition also provides the following online resources:

1. *SPA word lists.* As an alternative to having students read words from Appendix 2, they can read the SPA words directly on the computer, one word at a time. We have found that often students are more engaged reading the words from a computer screen than from a paper.

2. *Syllasearch word and syllable cards.* Syllasearch requires displaying a number of word and syllable cards so that every student can see them. To reduce the time it takes to make the cards, we have provided enlarged versions of every word and every syllable in 35 separate files that match the 35 Syllasearch lessons. All teachers need to do is access the appropriate lists of words and syllables, and then print and display them for use. Printing them on card stock or laminating them enables repeated use of the same cards.

3. *Syllasearch stories.* We also provide 35 short stories, one for each of the 35 Syllasearch lessons, that include most of the words in each Syllasearch list. These stories can be printed out and read in class at the end of every Syllasearch lesson.

Common Core State Standards

We want to emphasize that the content presented in this second edition of *Making Sense of Phonics* is directly related to the Common Core State Standards (CCSS), particularly those standards for kindergarten through grade 2 (National Governors Association Center for Best Practices and Council of Chief State School Officers, 2010). Virtually all of the Standards under the heading Phonics and Word Recognition for K–2 address content and skills that we examine in this book. For example, kindergarten students are expected to understand vowel sounds, recognize common high-frequency words, and identify sounds of letters that differ when comparing two words. Grade 1 students are expected to know about consonant digraphs, words with long vowels, and certain issues involving syllables. Grade 2 students are also expected to know about long vowels, two-syllable words, and irregularly spelled words. A brief review of the chapters in this new edition will show that all of these issues addressed in the Standards are covered in depth.

Fluency is a separate heading of its own in the CCSS. Grade 1 and 2 students are expected to read with "sufficient accuracy and fluency" (pp. 16–17). Chapter 11 of this edition deals with orthography, the writing (spelling) system of language. Knowledge of orthography has been shown to influence reading fluency and is sometimes described as "a sticking point" in achieving fluency. Similarly, Chapter 12 addresses issues at the core of automatic and fluent reading. In summary, the materials, strategies, and resources provided in *Making Sense of Phonics, Second Edition*, will be very helpful to teachers as they support students in meeting the Standards.

Final Comment

Our goal in preparing this edition was to support teachers in building their specialized knowledge for phonics instruction, as well as to provide them with specific instructional approaches and resources to use with their students. Our hope is that teachers will find our book useful and that they will measure its usefulness by the progress of their students.

ISABEL L. BECK
MARK E. BECK

Acknowledgments

We want to acknowledge and thank the Manchester Academic Charter School (MACS) community—the administration, the teachers, the staff, the parents, the board, and especially the students, who teach us so much about teaching reading. We are fortunate to be associated with MACS, a children-first, academically focused, friendly, and happy school.

We also want to acknowledge and thank Linda Kucan, Isabel's friend and colleague and Mark's friend and former teacher, who once again was our first and best reader and editor. She fixed our punctuation, made suggestions to clarify our descriptions and explanations, and offered a "bravo" for a chapter just when we needed it.

I (Isabel) want to express my gratitude to Shelley Tavis, who for years and years has produced my manuscripts, checked everything twice, solved problems, and remained cheerful, even when most people would not have. My appreciation for Shelley's role in my success as an academic is profound.

I (Mark) want to acknowledge my wife, Marsha, for her patience and support during the long hours that I worked on the book.

Finally, we want to mention how much the other authors in our family have modeled and inspired us—those who have come before us, the one that left us too soon, and those who are with us. We mention the publication date only of each author's first book: Carl Beck (1904), Edward F. W. Beck (1954), Carl Beck (1974), and Elizabeth L. Beck (2007).

Contents

An extensive set of supplemental teaching resources to accompany this book is available from *www.guilford.com/beck10-materials*.

Additionally, purchasers of this book can download copies of the reproducible materials herein from *www.guilford.com/beck10-forms*.

Situating Phonics Instruction

Prelude

• •

Some years ago, I (Isabel) was chatting with a first-grade teacher who was in her third year of teaching in a public school. The teacher—let's call her Ms. James (all teacher and student names in this book are pseudonyms)—had gone to a small state college and had taken two literacy courses—the state requirement. At the time she and I spoke, Ms. James was enrolled in a master's in reading program. Our conversation quickly turned to reading when Ms. James asked a question about sight words. In the back-and-forth of our chat, Ms. James mentioned that she had seen a reference to the "look–say" method of teaching reading and didn't know what that was.

Hmm, I wondered. After two literacy courses and current enrollment in a master's program, was not knowing about "look–say" the tip of an iceberg? And was the iceberg that perhaps younger teachers were not informed about the underpinnings of the instructional strategies that they used in their classrooms? Given that the reading field has been known for swinging back and forth between instructional approaches for teaching beginning reading, the classic remark "Those who ignore history are bound to repeat it" came to mind. So I thought we might start this book with a little background about instructional approaches to reading. To make sure that this was the way to begin, I asked a perfect informant—my coauthor, Mark. Over the last several years, Mark has taught reading methods courses to university students who were just entering education after they had received their undergraduate degrees.

I (Mark) was sure that a little history about reading instruction was a good way to start our book because I soon learned that students taking their first reading course entered the program as tabulae rasae. When I brought up a topic, I frequently had to go back and fill in information. This is not to disparage the students; they were wonderful students, but they knew very little about reading instruction. However, why should they? They were just starting.

Introduction

We are going to start our historical overview at the beginning of the 20th century. However, we want to point out that, from the Colonial American period on, there are references in the historical literature to sentence methods, experience methods, word methods, and phonics methods. Nevertheless, although various methods appeared in the professional literature from time to time, phonics was the prevailing approach to teaching beginning reading from the Colonial period into the 1920s (Smith, 2002).

In more recent times, the teaching of beginning reading has been among the most controversial topics in American education. Across the decades, questions have been raised about most facets of beginning reading: *When* should children be taught to read? *Where* should they be taught to read? *How* should they be taught to read? *How* children should be taught to read—that is, the appropriate instructional strategies for beginning reading—has received the lion's share of attention.

The kinds of instructional strategies used in beginning reading are represented in commercially available reading programs—in particular, the large K–8 basal reading programs. There used to be about 10 or 12 such programs, but most smaller companies went out of business, partly because they couldn't compete with the editorial and marketing resources available to large companies. To the best of our knowledge, presently there are three large publishing companies that publish comprehensive basal programs.

Two Families of Approaches to Teaching Beginning Reading

In her landmark book, Chall (1967, 1987) sorted commercially available materials into two general families of instructional approaches: meaning-emphasis methods and code-emphasis methods. Although variations exist within these two families, the categories are quite useful because they allow discussion of distinctions between philosophies and about instructional methods.

Proponents of various meaning-emphasis approaches stress the communication aspects of reading from the beginning of instruction. To a large extent, they believe that initial reading instruction should be arranged to put learners into a position in which they emulate skilled reading performance as closely as possible. Meaning-emphasis approaches therefore emphasize that because skilled readers appear to process units such as words and sentences, so should beginning readers, even if they can manage only a few words and sentences.

By contrast, code-emphasis approaches assume that the fundamental task of initial reading is to learn the relationships between written letter sequences and speech. Proponents of various code-emphasis approaches do not see initial reading instruction as primarily concerned with arranging conditions for the beginning reader to behave as a miniature skilled reader. They find it appropriate to engage beginning readers in behaviors that are not comparable to skilled performance, such as systematic analysis of the relationship between written letters and their sounds in speech.

An important distinction in practice between the two general families is which major strategy is provided to learners about what clues to use when decoding an unknown word. The meaning-emphasis programs stress the use of context and picture clues. The code-emphasis programs stress the letter–sound correspondences of major phonic elements.

Given that there are systematic relationships between letters and sounds in an alphabetic language such as English, it stands to reason that those who are responsible for teaching initial reading would consider telling beginners directly what those relationships are, which translates into explicit phonics instruction. As noted, until about about 80 or 90 years ago, this is what most teachers did. However, a major point that will be emphasized in this chapter is that there are better and worse ways to tell children about the relationships between print and speech. Toward that end, we take a broad and brief look at about the last 100 years of beginning reading instruction.

Phonics: The Past

In discussing phonics, it is important to recognize that it is not a single approach. Under the phonics label, one can find a variety of instructional strategies for teaching the relationship between letters and sounds. It appears, however, that the kind of phonics practiced through the first decades of the 20th century was an elongated, elaborated, drill-and-more-drill method. Diederich (1973), a doctoral student in education, described the scene: "Initial instruction in letter–sound relationships and pronunciation rules was done to death . . . children had to learn so much abstract material by rote before doing any significant amount of reading" (p. 7).

To illustrate more concretely what Diederich was describing, picture the following: It is October 1921, and 40 first graders are seated at rows of desks. The teacher stands at the front of the class and points with a long wooden pointer to a wall chart that contains columns of letters and letter combinations. As she points to a column of short vowel and consonant *b* combinations, the class responds with the sound of each combination—/ab/, /eb/, /ib/, /ob/, /ub/—and then the reverse—/ba/, /be/, and so forth. Then the teacher asks, "What's the rule?" The children respond in unison, "In a one-syllable word, in which there is a single vowel followed by a consonant. . . . " And so it went day after day with letter–sound relationships and pronunciation rules done to death.

It is no wonder that educators as prominent as William S. Gray described this kind of phonics as "heartless drudgery." In the late 1920s, Gray urged that it (the heartless drudgery) be replaced with the look–say approach, subsequently also called the whole-word method, as well as the sight-word method.

The Look–Say/Whole-Word/Sight-Word Method

The three labels in the preceding heading refer to the same method. The idea behind the look–say approach was that children could learn to recognize words through repeated exposure without direct attention to subword parts. The relief from extended drill with letter sounds, their synthesis into often meaningless syllables, and the recitation of rules of pronunciation is evident in Diederich's own response to the look–say method when he first saw it as a graduate student in education at the University of Chicago. According to Diederich (1973):

> When [this] writer began his graduate study of education in 1928 . . . no less an authority than Walter Dearborn had to send his students to observe several classes that were learning to read by the new "look–say" method before they would believe that it was possible. (p. 7)

The whole-word method, as exemplified in the major publishing houses' basal materials (e.g., Scott Foresman's "Dick and Jane" materials), continued virtually unchallenged from the 1930s until the 1950s. Two important features of these programs were the kind of vocabulary used in the materials and the repetition of vocabulary. Specifically, stories were written using high-frequency words that were likely to be in young children's listening and speaking vocabulary. Many of the words did not follow regular phonics patterns (e.g., *said, talk, who, friend*). Therefore, there was no opportunity to teach predictable patterns in a systematic way. Rather, the words were gradually introduced as whole units and repeated often.

The Whole-Word Method Is Criticized

In the 1950s, the prevailing whole-word approach was challenged from two quarters—the academic world and the public sector. The academic challenge was launched by linguists who revived the notions Bloomfield (1942) had discussed several decades earlier. The linguists argued that the whole-word approach as exemplified in the basal readers of the period made it difficult for the child to figure out the systematic relationship between written and spoken language. That is, because the words for the basals were chosen for their frequency in the language and their meaningfulness to the young child, they were not of the sort that displayed the regularity of the written code. For example, the following words could have appeared early and in close proximity to each other: *come, hot, stove, coat, store.* Notice the various speech sounds for *o* in these words. The academic challengers pointed out that, when the words used in the early stages of learning to read include many of the complexities of our writing system, the task of learning to read is made unnecessarily difficult. They urged that instructional materials be arranged to expose beginning readers to words that maximize the regularities of print-to-sound mapping (e.g., *man, pan*; *men, pen*; *met, pet*) rather than to those that exacerbate the complexities.

In the public sector, Rudolph Flesch, in his best-selling book *Why Johnny Can't Read* (1955), vehemently attacked the prevailing method of reading instruction and demanded a return to phonics. Although the general public and press reacted favorably to Flesch's book, reviewers of educational journals rejected it partly because he made a rhetorical argument rather than a carefully reasoned presentation of evidence.

Phonics: From about the Mid-1960s to Mid-1980s

The public fuss and the linguists' logic did not go unheeded by publishing companies, and two trends appeared in the commercial reading programs of the day. First, houses that published meaning-emphasis programs (i.e., extended whole-word instruction before phonics instruction) began to incorporate substantial phonics instruction very early in the instructional sequences of their newer editions (Popp, 1975).

So now that phonics was available, educators had the appropriate tools for teaching reading. Right? Not really. The reason has to do with the extent to which the kind of phonics employed by the major look–say basal programs was helpful. Toward unpacking that issue, we need to consider kinds of phonics. Approaches to phonics instruction can generally be described by one of two terms: explicit phonics and implicit phonics. These terms refer to the explicitness with which letter sounds are taught in a given approach.

In explicit phonics, children are directly told the sounds of individual letters and other subword units (e.g., the letter *m* stands for /m/ in *man*). In implicit phonics, children are expected to induce the sounds that correspond to letters from accumulated auditory and visual exposure to words containing those letters (e.g., induce /m/ from hearing the teacher read *man, make, mother* as she identifies the words on the chalkboard). There is strong evidence that many young children cannot extract a phoneme (an individual sound) from hearing it within a word (see Chapter 3). Therefore, implicit phonics presupposes an ability that many beginning readers don't yet have.

The Relationship between Phonics and Materials Children Read

A problem that Diederich (1973) pointed to in the way phonics was presented in the past was that "children had to learn so much abstract material [i.e., letter–sound relationships] by rote before doing any significant amount of reading" (p. 7). This "abstractness" problem can be reduced by recognizing that instruction is inadequate when it does not give students opportunities to apply what they are learning. In reading, that means reading. That is, very early in the learning-to-read process, children need a lot of experience reading meaningful material that includes many words that exemplify the letter–sound patterns or the whole words that are being introduced. Both approaches, the more meaning-oriented and the more code-oriented, did provide such materials. But the content of the materials was very different.

Reading programs of the period under discussion (mid-1960s to mid-1980s) chose the words used in their early text selections on the basis of one of the two criteria noted earlier: (1) high-frequency words that are likely to be in young children's listening and speaking vocabularies or (2) words that exemplify the letter–sound relationships being introduced in phonics instruction. The two criteria produce a very different relationship between what children were learning—be they whole words or letter–sound patterns—and the words in the text material they were supposed to read.

To illustrate the differences, *Becoming a Nation of Readers* (Anderson, Hiebert, Scott, & Wilkinson, 1985) presented excerpts from two programs that exemplified the two relationships. Both excerpts came from material that would be read approximately in November of first grade, when both programs have introduced about 30 letter–sound relationships.

The following excerpt comes from a program in which the relationship between the letter–sound patterns that children were learning in their phonics and the materials they read was very low.

> "We have come, Grandma," said Ana.
> "We have come to work with you."
> "Come in," Grandma said.
> "Look in the book," said Grandma.
> "Mix this and this."

In the 26-word excerpt from the low-relationship program, there were 17 different words, and "of these 17, only 4 (or 24 percent) could be decoded entirely on the basis of letter–sound relationships that have been introduced in the program's phonics lessons" (Anderson et al., 1985, p. 45).

Now consider the following few sentences of a story from a high-relationship program that would also be read in about November of first grade.

> Ray loads the boat.
> He says, "I'll row."
> Neal says, "We'll both row."
> They leave, and Eve rides home alone.

This excerpt from the high-relationship program showed that 13 of the 18 different words in the excerpt, or 72%, "could be decoded entirely on the basis of letter–sound relationships that students should know from the program's phonics lessons" (Anderson et al., 1985, p. 46). The two excerpts are reflective of the findings of an analysis of eight beginning reading programs (Beck, 1981).

Show Me the Evidence

The evidence in support of advantages for approaches to beginning reading instruction that emphasize the code is quite strong. In the following we simply cite several researchers' conclusions about this advantage. It should be noted that those we cite spent years poring over original studies, and, as such, the conclusions are based on patterns of evidence from numerous individual studies.

In 1967, Chall's conclusion pointed to benefits from those programs that include early and systematic phonics: "My review of the research . . . from 1912 to 1965 indicates that a code-emphasis method . . . produces better results. . . ." The advantage continued to be found in the 1970s and early 1980s. (See, e.g., Barr, 1972, 1974, 1974–1975; DeLawter, 1970; Elder, 1971; Evans & Carr, 1983; Guthrie et al., 1976; Johnson & Baumann, 1984). In 1987, when Chall updated her book, she pointed out that "the research support [in favor of a code-emphasis] seems to be even stronger than it was in 1967" (p. 43). The same conclusion was noted in 1990 in Marilyn Adams's prizewinning book:

> Collectively . . . studies suggest, with impressive consistency, that programs including systematic instruction on letter-to-sound correspondences lead to higher achievement in both word recognition and spelling, at least in the early grades and especially for slower or economically disadvantaged students. (Adams, 1990, p. 32)

In the mid-1980s, the kind of evidence noted here was taken seriously by the National Commission on Reading, comprising a range of representatives from the research community (and sponsored in part by the National Institute of Education). The commission developed *Becoming a Nation of Readers* (Anderson et al., 1985), which concluded that early and systematic phonics was essential. Instead of moving in directions supported by research, however, many in the reading field embraced *whole language*.

Whole Language

The *whole-language movement*, with its related literature-based approach to reading instruction, probably began its widest sweep across the nation about the time that California published its English/Language Arts Framework in 1986. The enormity of the whole-language movement's impact on the reading field and the speed with which it gained momentum was captured by Pearson (1989):

> Never have I witnessed anything like the rapid spread of the whole-language movement. Pick your metaphor—an epidemic, wildfire, manna from heaven— whole language has spread so rapidly throughout North America that it is a fact of life in literacy curriculum and research. (p. 231)

Given its impact, it is important that we look at whole language. At this point in a discussion it would be incumbent on authors to define and explain what whole language is. Our review of dozens of articles about whole language showed that none of the authors of those articles provided a definition. Bergeron (1990) attempted to develop a definition of whole language from an extensive review of journal articles in which the term *whole language* had appeared. However, she concluded that she could not develop a "concise definition" because whole language represented different things to various people. She did indicate, however, that certain characteristics appeared in more than half the articles she analyzed, and she identified those characteristics. They are: (1) construction of meaning, wherein an emphasis is placed on comprehending what is read; (2) functional language, or language that has purpose and relevance to the learner; (3) the use of literature in a variety of forms; (4) the writing process through which learners write, revise, and edit written works; (5) cooperative student work; and (6) an emphasis on affective aspects of the students' learning experiences, such as motivation, enthusiasm, and interest (Bergeron, 1990, p. 319). Notice that there is no suggestion of how students can be taught to recognize words. However, whole-language proponents do assert that the way words can be recognized is through the use of the three-cueing system, which we take up in the next section.

The Three-Cueing System

The three-cueing system suggests that there are three types of cues that support word recognition—the semantic, the syntactic, and the graphophonic. That is, as a student reads text, he uses information from one or all of the cues to help him identify words. For example, a student may use semantic or meaning cues to determine what a word is. For instance, in the course of reading a story about a musical band, say a student encounters the word *piccolo*. Semantic support in the story would point to a musical instrument as a cue to the identification of *piccolo*. In addition, a student may use syntax, the grammar and structure of a sentence, to help him read a word. For example, consider the sentence "After the applause died down everyone knew that the saxophone player was a phenomenal musician." A student would at minimum know that *phenomenal* was a positive description of the musician. Finally, a student may rely on graphophonic information, that is, the printed letters and their relationship to sounds in spoken words to help identify words.

The three-cueing system is in harmony with whole-language principles because use of the principles of the alphabetic code and letter–sound relationships is given a low priority. In contrast, Perfetti (1985) made the point that

> the main failing of this approach [the three-cueing system] to reading is that it does not recognize that one of the "cueing systems" is more central than the others. A child who learns the code has knowledge that can enable him to read, no matter how the semantic, syntactic, and pragmatic cues might conspire against him. (p. 239)

Learning to Read Is Not Like Learning to Talk

A major underlying premise of whole language is that learning to read should be as natural as learning to talk. The notion is that because children learn to talk in authentic communicative environments, reading could be similarly acquired through authentic literacy acts. The problem with this notion is that it is well established that there is a biological predisposition to oral language acquisition that is *not* the case for written language acquisition. That is, humans are "hard wired" to acquire oral language; this is not the case with written language. Perfetti's (1991) no-nonsense summary points out that

> learning to read is not like acquiring one's native language; no matter how much someone wishes it were so. Natural language is acquired quickly with a large biological contribution. It is universal among human communities. By contrast literacy is a cultural invention. It is far from universal. (p. 75)

To go forward to where we now are in the second decade in the 21st century, we think it will be helpful to summarize what was going on in the 1980s. During that time there were two conflicting strands. Both have been mentioned before, but let us spotlight them. First, lots of evidence of positive effects from a code approach were brought forward with the conclusion that early and systematic phonics was essential. Second, the field did not move in directions supported by research. Unexpectedly, the field moved quite far away from the research evidence and embraced whole language.

Reaction to the Whole-Language Movement

In the 1989 article mentioned earlier, Pearson predicted that whole language would have staying power. "Unlike the open school movement of the early 1970s, [whole language] is not likely to die at an early age" (p. 231). Isabel's prediction was similar (Beck, 1993). However, in the middle of the 1990s, it appeared that the predicted longevity of whole language had not been correct.

Since the initial predictions and popularity of whole language, some things changed. Specifically, what changed was the public sector's response to whole language and teachers' concerns. To provide a sense of what was going on, let's consider just a few examples.

In his 1994 *Atlantic Monthly* article, "The Great Debate Revisited," Art Levin focused on the notion that "there's little hard evidence to back up [some whole-language] claims across the board . . . and good reason to be concerned about the whole-language method when it's used to the exclusion of other approaches."

California newspapers were full of dismay about the state's reading scores. As an example, a September 18, 1995, editorial in the *Sacramento Bee* stated that "that shift [to whole language] reflected in the state's classrooms, has almost certainly been a factor in the dismally low reading scores among California's primary-school children" ("Toward Better Teaching," 1995).

The summer 1995 issue of the *American Educator*, a publication of the American Federation of Teachers, featured three articles that provided some of the scientific bases for reading and their instructional implications. In the editor's introduction, Elizabeth McPike (1995b) synthesized the issues developed in those articles and suggested that "to the extent that [whole language] has reduced decoding to an incidental place in the reading curriculum, it has done a terrible disservice to the children whose lives depend on mastery of that skill" (p. 6).

In the subsequent fall 1995 issue, the letters section of the *American Educator* contained the following editor's note (McPike, 1995a):

> We have been inundated with requests for thousands and thousands of extra copies of our summer 1995 issue on Learning to Read: "I have to have one to give to my principal"; "to send to the school board"; "for my neighbor, whose child is having a problem" . . . and on and on. . . . It is notable that of the countless comments we have received, only four or five have disagreed with the point of view expressed in the articles or found fault with the research presented. (p. 6)

The wave of dissatisfaction with how reading was being taught in the primary grades contributed to the creation of the National Reading Panel, which we consider next.

The National Reading Panel

The National Reading Panel (NRP) was created in 1997 at the request of Congress to examine scientific research that could contribute to primary-grades reading instruction. In 2000 the panel reported findings in five areas, one of which was phonics. From an initial examination of more than 1,000 studies that dealt with phonics, 38 studies were found that met specific research criteria. From the 38 studies, 66 treatment–control group comparisons were derived, and those data were entered into a meta-analysis. The panel concluded that phonics was the most successful way to teach reading and that instruction that included phonics was more effective than instruction that included little or no phonics (NRP, 2000). But the panel went further. Phonics instruction needed to be systematic and explicit. Systematic phonics instruction involves teaching letter–sound patterns in a logical order. Explicit phonics instruction points to the teaching of letter–sound patterns directly.

With the report of the NRP in the background, in 2001 Congress enacted the No Child Left Behind Act, which included a program known as the Reading First initiative (U.S. Department of Education, 2002). Materials and resources throughout the country, many of them funded by Reading First, helped to advance systematic and explicit phonics instruction. Commercial reading series, many of which are still used today, moved sharply in the direction of teaching systematic and explicit phonics. Note that this was profoundly different from the commercial whole-word programs of a quarter of a century earlier, as well as the commercial literature-based programs toward the end of the 20th century. As we write today, explicit phonics instruction seems to have the upper hand in primary basal reading series and in reading instruction used in many, if not most, schools in the United States.

Where We Are Now

To the best of our knowledge, most basal programs in the editions of the late 1990s and early 2000s provided explicit, systematic phonics instruction, although from our cursory review of several, there is variation in the quality of that instruction. There is, however, no formal evidence of where phonics is in this second decade of the 21st century. We had hoped we could say more; however, more is not available. So we came up with the idea that we might get a sense of what was in going on in practice beyond our firsthand local knowledge by asking some colleagues in different parts of the country to weigh in on the present status of phonics.

We sent e-mails to some colleagues explaining that we were writing a second edition of *Making Sense of Phonics* and simply asked "What do you see as the present status of phonics in reading instruction?" We selected colleagues who were in positions that took them to schools, who interacted with teachers and administrators, who taught inservice teachers. We also asked them to forward our question to folks they knew who might have some insight. Two did so. We received answers from 18 individuals, about two-thirds of whom were teachers and central office literacy directors. The remaining one-third were university faculty members plus an educational consultant who travels constantly to schools across the country and another individual who is the director of language arts from a large publishing company.

We handled the responses by reading and identifying categories of comments. It was not difficult to identify the categories, which we discuss shortly. But first, a strong word of caution: our little e-mail attempt to get a sense of where phonics instruction is currently was merely our attempt to get a tiny taste of instruction. Although it is needless to say that our little survey was far from a scientific endeavor, we nevertheless remind you that it is only what 18 people in the field from around the country think. However, perhaps what they said is worth paying attention to in that it provides some data points.

The Common Core State Standards (CCSS) in association with phonics was on half of the respondents' minds. Mostly they were concerned about where teachers were going to get the time to do everything required. They worried that because more time was needed to adhere to the numerous standards, time would be taken from phonics instruction. Others thought that the standards would have little influence on phonics instruction, as current phonics instruction already covered what CCSS called for. In contrast, a somewhat edgy comment pointed to the omission of blending in primary-grades phonics foundational skills. The respondent asked in somewhat strong language why CCSS had not included blending, given that blending had been emphasized as an especially important feature of phonics instruction by two national panels (the 1985 panel that developed *Becoming a Nation of Readers* [Anderson et al., 1985] and, 15 years later, the National Reading Panel, which published *Teaching Children to Read: An Evidence-Based Assessment of the Scientific Literature on Reading and Its Implication for Reading Instruction* [NRP, 2000]).

There were four comments from our e-mail respondents about whole language. One respondent titled her remarks "Whole Language Revisited." According to this respondent, central office literacy directors, "many of whom had gained that position because of their earlier excellence as whole-language teachers, were relieved with the end of Reading First. The result—softer phonics." Another take on whole language comprised three comments directed toward inadequate teacher preparation. All three indicated that those leaving college had little to no instruction outside of whole language. For example, "Even here [an area in which explicit phonics is strong], general educators are immersed in whole language."

As a teacher educator, that makes me (Isabel) sad for my profession and anxious for children. When asked, teachers say that years back children simply did not make it with whole language. From this little sample (18 individuals), it seems that those in the practicing part of our field, teachers and coaches, know the research better than three teacher educators.

There were five comments suggesting that phonics was not going away. For example, "Teachers are having success teaching phonics . . . and I do not see them changing what is working for their students." And another: "The body of research [that supports phonics instruction] is such a part of the culture now, I do not foresee it being easily unseated by any trend or fashion that will insinuate itself as part of the CC [CCSS]."

Of course we were happy that no one said phonics had gone away or was going away. But even more pleasing were those comments that suggested that the field seems to have come away from the reading wars.

> "Phonics seems to be less and less of a forbidden term and is becoming more acceptable."
> "I don't see phonics being dismissed wholesale or demonized as I used to, even at a small scale."
> "The variables that might be making the difference [between an old view of phonics and the present view] are: brain research, accountability and RTI (response to instruction)."

Perhaps the comments that phonics was no longer disdained were particularly gratifying because they put phonics in its place. That is, phonics is merely an important and useful strategy, nothing more and nothing less. For those of us who have seen firsthand several iterations of phonics being practiced and not being practiced, it could be that the field has matured and that discussions will be based on evidence and not on rhetoric. But just in case, we'll keep our fingers crossed.

In the next chapter, we look at the foundation of our written language, the alphabetic principle, and how that principle is learned. We provide examples of children having difficulty engaging the principle and briefly suggest intervention.

The Alphabetic Principle and Phonics

I (Isabel) used to start a graduate course I taught, titled Psychological Theory and Research in Reading, with the following little survey: What do you think is the greater invention or discovery in the social history of humankind in each of the following pairs: (1) the invention of the wheel or the discovery of relativity theory, (2) fire or the alphabet, (3) the method of expressing all numbers by means of 10 symbols or the Industrial Revolution, and sometimes a few other pairs. I read a question and two potential choices and asked students to write their choices on a scrap of paper. The point of the little exercise was to prime discussion, and indeed it did so, sometimes in a very animated fashion.

My use of the survey developed from some previous experience I had when I provided classes with a little background about language and literacy. I was usually disappointed with students' reactions to my statement "the alphabet is among the greatest inventions of humankind," which seemed to make little impression. Even after I explained it and students seemed to understand, reactions were still rather muted. That was disappointing because many of us who study literacy stand in awe of the invention of the alphabet.

In the class discussion that followed the little survey, several members of the class suggested that one important criterion for deciding what makes something greater than something else was which one had had the greater influence on human development. That point prompted thinking about where the world would be without the alphabet and eventually became the major reason that the class unanimously choose development of the alphabet as the greatest invention.

Speaking, Writing, and the Alphabet

There is no way to know for sure, but humans are estimated to have developed speech at least 100,000 years ago. Spoken language, however, has a strong biological component. "It is generally agreed that the ability to speak was the result of an evolutionary change in the brain. Certain areas of the human brain associated with speech are markedly larger than in the ape brain" (Raynor & Pollatsek, 1989, p. 36). Another argument for the biological influence on the development of language is that all human societies have developed oral language, but even today there are many societies that have not developed a writing system.

Writing and the Alphabet

The development of literacy starts with the development of writing, which was not biologically but culturally driven. Writing artifacts from about 5,000 years ago were uncovered in Mesopotamia. Over time, writing moved from drawings to pictograms to logograms to syllabaries and eventually to representations of sounds in some words. Depending on the source, the crown jewel in written language—the alphabet—was developed about 2,500–3,000 years ago. Most sources point to the Phoenicians as the first to develop an alphabet, noting that the Phoenicians adapted Greek letters. The beauty of an alphabet is that it can represent in writing all spoken language. A remarkable characteristic is that from 21 to 30 letters can capture the individual sounds that comprise every spoken word in a given language's word reservoir. So if someone said, "The wheat is high," the precise words could be written. There would be no need to draw a hand raised high above a drawing of wheat, or above a standard symbol of wheat, or eventually a symbol combined with the first sound in the spoken *wheat*.

Implications of the Alphabet

The importance of the alphabet cannot be understated. Speech is temporary; whatever anyone says goes away. The alphabet allows speech and thought to become permanent. Thus a culture can pass on its views, discoveries, problems, reflections, and the like to later cultures. Before the alphabet, the writing systems that had been developed were far too complicated and incomplete to represent all of spoken language, in particular abstract thought. Thus, with an alphabet, cultures could pass on to the next generations what they knew. Without an alphabet, subsequent cultures could not benefit much from earlier knowledge.

The Phoneme Is Key

The feature of an alphabet that enables the faithful representation of spoken language in writing is the identification of the smallest sound within words—the phoneme—and the ability to represent those sounds with a manageable number of written symbols. As such, phonemes are the keystone to the alphabetic principle; that is, spoken words comprise individual sounds that are separable and can be represented in writing. The written representations of phonemes are called graphemes. In a perfect alphabet, there would be a one-to-one relationship between each phoneme and a grapheme. Spanish gets close to a perfect alphabet, but English does not. It is generally agreed that there are 42 phonemes in English, but there are only 26 graphemes to represent them. Thus English is said to have a deep orthography, or writing system, because several graphemes can represent more than one phoneme: for instance, the letter *c* can represent /k/ or /s/.

Although it is likely easier to learn to read with an alphabet in which every phoneme is associated with one grapheme, English "rules" are more consistent than some have asserted. If knowledge of several layers of English were input into a computer, the computer would be able to recognize 90% of input words (Moats, 2000).

Children need to understand the alphabetic principle, and the general understanding is not usually hard to grasp. But in order to apply the general understanding, the specifics of one's language need to be learned. That is, phonemes within words need to be learned so they can be associated with the written representation of these phonemes—graphemes. Those specifics require time and are sometimes hard for some children to learn. We take up those issues next.

Phonics

Some years ago, I (Isabel) was in a line at the post office and overheard two mothers in conversation. I moved to full-fledged eavesdropping when I recognized that the conversation was about their 6-year-old boys and how they were learning to read in different schools. Early in the conversation, one of the mothers asked the other whether her child was learning phonics, and the other asked what she meant. Both of these young women were clearly intelligent and educated, so it may surprise those of you who are reading this book that some people don't know what phonics is.

As it turned out, the first mother's reply to the second mother was right on: "[Phonics] is about the relationship between letters and their sounds." The NRP (2000) defined phonics as an instructional strategy that teaches letter–sound associations and their application through spelling and reading words. That, indeed, is what phonics is, and phonics is the instructional approach that supports learning how the alphabetic principle is applied in one's language. What can get hard and require time is teaching children the details of that principle (e.g., that the phoneme /r/ is represented by the written letter *r*, the phoneme /th/ is represented by the two letters *th*). So how does that knowledge get learned? As straightforward as the task of learning the letter–sound correspondences may be for some children, other children have difficulty. Whatever the difficulty is, it needs to be identified and immediate intervention provided. Let's look at several children who had difficulty learning letter–sound correspondences.

Examples of What Can Go Awry

Theresa's Story

Lisa, a student in a master's-level university reading course, had been anxiously telling me (Isabel) about Theresa, a child in her second grade with strange word recognition problems: strange because she could read a lot of words that were harder than many she missed. Lisa was particularly concerned that, in the middle of Theresa's second-grade year, the percentage of words she read incorrectly seemed to be increasing. Lisa brought the results of Theresa's performance on some word recognition tests to class, and we tried to analyze her problems. Following are selected words from several word recognition lists that Lisa had administered to Theresa. The words in **bold** are those that Theresa did not read correctly.

an	he
and	here
are	hot
bat	**me**
be	men
boy	off
but	on
can	tree
cut	with
down	work
go	yellow

Another presentation of Theresa's misreadings helps illustrate her difficulty more obviously. The words she read correctly are in the first column, and the words she read incorrectly are in the second column.

Words known	Words not known
and	an
bat	but
cut	me
he	not
hot	
mom	
no	

Notice that Theresa could read *and*, but she could not delete the *d* and read *an*. She was able to read *bat* and *cut*, but she apparently was not able to use the *b* and *t* in *bat* and the *u* (or the *ut*) in *cut* to read *but*. Theresa could read *mom* and *he* but couldn't use the appropriate phonemes from those words to read *me*. Finally, she was unable to read *not*, even though she was able to read *hot* and *no*.

Theresa is a quintessential example of a child who has virtually no understanding of the alphabetic principle. That principle is that the sounds within spoken words are represented in writing by letters and that those letters represent the sounds rather consistently.

Although Theresa's instructional experiences had included only superficial phonics, a question of interest is how a bright child (and Theresa was bright) could still not have figured out the alphabetic principle. Many of her classmates had, even though, like Theresa, they were not directly taught to do so. Why not Theresa? The answer is that some people just don't. Some interesting evidence associated with the "some folks just don't" notion comes from the work of Bishop (1964).

The Bishop Study

Bishop (1964) conducted a study with students from a prestigious university in which she simulated the beginning reading experience by teaching some students to read some Arabic words. Eight Arabic words used in the experiment included twelve letters for which there were perfect letter–sound correspondences.

Two groups were established. One group was taught a set of words, all of which included the twelve Arabic letters, through a whole-word approach (seeing and hearing a word until it was remembered). The other group was taught the phonemes that were associated with each of the twelve letters. The groups were then compared on their ability to read a set of transfer words (i.e., words that were not used in instruction but that contained the letter–sound correspondences that had been taught and used in instructional words).

The results of a transfer test showed that the letter–sound group performed best. Of more interest was that 12 of the 20 members of the whole-word group obtained scores similar to those of the letter–sound group. When asked how they read the words, they reported that they had tried to figure out the letter sounds within the words presented in instruction and thus had been able to extrapolate the letter–sound correspondences from the training words. As such, these adults used the alphabetic principle. This is far from surprising given that they were college students who read English well.

What is of greatest interest is that 8 of the 20 adult participants in the word group did not attempt to use the alphabetic principle and instead attempted to memorize the words. We can only speculate why the 8 college students did not call up the alphabetic principle. Perhaps they were not such good readers and in particular slow decoders; perhaps they were not good spellers—both possibilities could suggest that although knowledge of the alphabetic principle is available to them, they are not facile with it. How could not-so-good readers be at a prestigious university? There *are* poor readers who are highly intelligent. We only know that intelligent college students did not use the alphabetic principle, even though the phonemes in this study could have been easily derived. So it should not be too surprising that some 7-year-olds will not figure out the alphabetic principle.

Back to Theresa

So what do we do about Theresa? Lisa believed that Theresa needed drill on the words that she did not read correctly. Lisa's suggestion of what to do about the child's problem reminded me of how much I would have agreed with her in the earlier days of my public school teaching career. In fact, flash card drill was exactly what I did with my first graders who were having difficulty. But both Lisa and I were wrong! Theresa's large sight vocabulary had masked her lack of phonics knowledge.

A misleading phenomenon for both Lisa and the earlier Isabel is that repeated word drills can produce a result. In fact, I would guess that if Lisa had done flash card drills on the words that Theresa had not read correctly in the preceding examples and on other words that Theresa didn't know, there would have been improvement on those words. That is, with her apparently good visual memory, Theresa probably would have learned some more sight words. But Theresa would have "hit the wall" sooner or later because of her astonishing lack of understanding of the alphabetic principle. Notice how much the following comment by Share and Stanovich (1995) captures Lisa's experience with Theresa.

> An analytic processing stance towards words . . . is probably not the "natural" processing set adopted by most children and some children have extreme difficulty in adopting an analytic processing set. The latter group will, as a result, have considerable difficulty building up knowledge of sub-word spelling–sound correspondences. (p. 153)

What Theresa clearly needed was phonics, which was perfectly defined by the first mother in the anecdote at the start of this chapter: "the relationship between letters and sounds." Lisa did provide Theresa with some phonics. She taught Theresa some letter–sound correspondences and how to blend those sounds. Actually, Lisa used procedures similar to the ones provided in this book, although not as complete for letter–sound and blending instruction. But Lisa's initiation of phonics with Theresa did not go easily at first. Theresa objected to the procedures. In fact, she actually asked Lisa to teach her the words she didn't know but not to do it with the sounds. Figuring out words through their sounds slowed Theresa down and was not satisfying. She just wanted to read the words.

But Lisa persisted with some motivational devices. Eventually Theresa loved decoding words she hadn't been able to read, and her reading took off. My point in telling the story is not to show what phonics can do but rather to indicate that if a teacher knows why she is doing something—in conversations with me and through readings that I provided in the course, Lisa came to understand Theresa's problems at a deep level—she can have confidence in what she is doing, in spite of some less-than-smooth lessons.

Rasheed's Story

As mentioned, Theresa's large sight vocabulary had masked her lack of phonics knowledge, and it took some digging to uncover her problem. The results of a pseudoword test given in March to Rasheed, a first grader who was not making progress in reading, follow. The teacher knew Rasheed had decoding problems but didn't know the extent of it or what to do about it.

Pseudoword	Child's response
kot	ka
swip	s
gan	ga
dree	da . . . er
shub	ser
doy	ba
flate	fa
meep	mech
dut	da . . . u
pog	pa . . . u . . . ch
nack	na

The results suggest that Rasheed had some knowledge of the first sound in a syllable but was virtually unable to decode the vowel and final phoneme. The called-for remediation was teaching vowel sounds and how to blend all the sounds into a word. Rasheed's story had, at least, a short-term positive outcome. That is, through 3 months of special small-group instruction with emphasis on vowels and blending, his pseudoword results, as well as normal reading, improved. We do not know what happened later, but it seemed that he had made an important inroad; he applied the alphabetic principle from the beginning through the end of a word. Of course, that is not enough, and Rasheed will probably need extra support, but at least at the end of first grade, his reading was in the ballpark.

Derek's Story

Theresa had almost no appreciation for the alphabetic principle, and Rasheed had some letter–sound, or grapheme–phoneme, correspondence knowledge, but he was able to apply it only to the initial grapheme in a word, generally a consonant. Derek's problem is a little different from Theresa's or Rasheed's. The results of an assessment, this time using real words, is particularly revealing:

Word	Child's response
cold	could
wear	war
figure	finger
certain	curtur
mineral	material
paragraph	photograph
describe	decided
century	country

Notice that the first two word pairs on the test contain single-syllable words and that the remaining six word pairs have two- or three-syllable words. In either case, Derek is mostly accurate decoding the first and last grapheme but falls apart on the interior of words, whether the interior is one or two graphemes or the larger portion of a syllable. To handle the problem, Derek seems to have developed an interesting strategy. He seems to figure out the beginning and final phonemes, finds some letters in the interior of the target word, and transports those letters into a word he knows. It is interesting that he tends to keep the shape of the internal portion of the response word close to the target words. So the target word *figure* becomes *finger*, with *f, i,* and *g,* a match with the target letters in *figure*.

Derek knows a lot. He knows he has to represent the phonemes across a word, but the letters in the interior become a muddle. So he finds a word in memory that shares similar orthography, or spelling, with the target word and offers that word. What he doesn't know is how to put the sounds together. Word Building and blending is a perfect intervention for Derek. But we don't know Derek, so we don't know whether and what kind of intervention was offered.

Anisha's Story

Anisha's story is different from the preceding stories. Anisha did learn most of the letter–sound correspondences in kindergarten, albeit a little more slowly than most of her peers. On many occasions, Anisha had demonstrated that she was able to sound out consonant–vowel–consonant (CVC) words and was quite accurate, although again slower. However, when Anisha was reading aloud, she got to some words and blurted out a word that had no orthographic resemblance to the printed word. It was not a matter of missing one letter or sound; the entire word she pronounced was nowhere in the ballpark. A sentence might be, "The pets are in the pen," but she might read "The pets are in the cage" or "The animals are in the cage."

Anisha and I (Mark) had an interesting conversation near the middle of kindergarten, which I remember as if it were yesterday. I asked her to read a decodable story with a lot of predictable CVC words. I noticed that she tended to be distracted by the pictures, so I covered up a picture and asked her to read the text. She replied, "I can't." I found that puzzling because I knew that, at least in the past, she could. I asked her why not, and she said, "I can't read it because you covered up the pictures." I challenged her on that point, but she clung to her position that I had made it impossible for her to read the words when there were no pictures for her to look at. Of course, I wondered, if she can decode much of the time, why not today? I now know the answer: Sometimes Anisha didn't try to work out the pronunciation of words because decoding was so hard for her. Up until she made a substitution, I could see her lips moving in an attempt to figure out a pronunciation. It seemed that when she resorted to substitution, she was tired of the work she had been doing; she had kind of "had it" and changed to an easier way.

Anisha is fairly typical of a certain subgroup of early struggling readers. She actually has an appreciation of the alphabetic principle, and she knows many letter–sound correspondences. It is tenuous, but it is much better than the three children we discussed earlier. Unfortunately, other forces compete with the alphabetic principle. In Anisha's case, using the story context and pictures at times wins out over the alphabetic principle. Why? Because it is easier for her to "read" that way. Like most humans, she takes the easier path. It has been our experience that this type of "reading" is among the early signals that things are going awry. I have witnessed students as late as third grade blurt out words that have nothing to do with the spelling of the word in front of them. Such a tendency should be picked up early and intervention begun immediately. In Anisha's case, it was noticed in the middle of kindergarten.

The intervention that was most helpful for Anisha was one-on-one reading of decodable text with redirection every time she pronounced words that were not on the page. Gradually, Anisha got the message that she had to do the hard work of connecting graphemes to phonemes, blending, and pronouncing the word that was on the page. Within a few months, Anisha's decoding took off. She had placed at the very bottom of her class in January on a pseudoword test. By the end of the school year in May, she improved dramatically on the same assessment, placing within the top half of her class. Most professionals would probably not consider her a struggling reader anymore. With lots of practice and insistence that she read the words that were on a page, Anisha didn't substitute words as often as she had. But interventions to help her become a more facile decoder were essential. Decoding had been given at least a fighting chance, whereas before it had been a severe underdog. This is not to say, however, that Anisha did not continue to guess from time to time.

Kurt's Story

Consider examples of a first grader reading "A Lost Button," a story from the popular *Frog and Toad Are Friends* series (Lobel, 1970). In the story, Toad discovers that a button from his jacket is missing. Toad, a complainer, is upset, and Frog, a kind creature, looks for the button. Frog and other forest friends find many buttons. The buttons are brought to Toad, but each is not the lost button. Frog eventually finds the correct button, but Toad is annoyed that all the wrong buttons are cluttering his floor. Overnight, Frog sews all the discarded buttons on Toad's jacket, and when Toad sees his jacket, he is delighted. Following are four of the miscues Kurt made. Each word that Kurt substituted for is in italics, and the words he substituted are in parentheses.

They walked across a large *meadow* (woods).

The turtle and the lizards and the snake and the dragonflies and the field mouse all sat on the *riverbank* (lake).

That button is thin. My button is *thick* (fat).

Toad thought that it [the jacket with lots of buttons on it] was *beautiful* (fantastic).

In consideration of Kurt's substitutions, we developed some reasonable speculation about what Kurt may have perceived about each target word in resorting to substitutions and what clues enabled him to insert meaningful words. We offer the following notions.

In the case of substituting *woods* for *meadow*, there are two features of the word that could have been problematic: he could not decode *meadow* because the *ea* represented an infrequent phoneme for Kurt, and it would not be unlikely that the meaning of *meadow* was unknown to a second grader. As to the clues for the use of *woods*, many pictures suggested it could be woods. The two creatures are shown among very tall grasses, and relative to the size of Frog and Toad, they could be trees. Moreover, if Kurt had known that a *meadow* had flat topography with few if any trees, he couldn't have identified a *meadow* from the pictures because the animals are shown in the midst of tall vegetation.

In substituting *lake* for *riverbank*, we first note that *riverbank* is a three-syllable word, likely difficult for Kurt to decode. Furthermore, the picture associated with the text shows more of an open area of water, like a lake, rather than water flowing in one direction, like a river. So the target word is a compound word with three syllables, the water in the picture does not look like a river, and this urban child likely has never been close to a riverbank and has not heard it in conversation. *Lake* is a perfect solution!

When Kurt read, "My button is fat," *fat* may have been a more natural opposite for *thin* in his mind than *thick*. Also, *thick* contains two consonant digraphs, which may have presented enough of a temporary hurdle to decoding that he chose to avoid it and instead used *fat*.

Finally, Kurt read that a jacket on which Frog has sewn a lot of buttons was *fantastic* rather than *beautiful*, the word on the page. Both are fairly long words, so judging just from length, *fantastic* was one of several appropriate choices. More substantively, Kurt may have been looking to describe that Toad wanted to show appreciation for what Frog had done. In that sense, *fantastic* may have been a more appropriate way to respond to what Frog had done.

One might ask how all those considerations could have happened in the short time it took to pronounce any of the substituted words. The answer is that reading happens as quickly as the blink of an eye. For example the average response time of third graders reading words from a list is about 680 milliseconds (Perfetti, Goldman, & Hogaboam, 1979, p. 275). A millisecond is one one-thousandth of a second.

We worried about Kurt, but two prominent academics, Frank Smith (1973, p. 190, cited in Stanovich, 2000, p. 6) and Ken Goodman (1976, p. 504, cited in Stanovich, 2000, p. 6), would not have worried about Kurt's substitutions. Indeed, they would have praised him because his substitutions made sense. We assert that Smith and Goodman would respond as we just suggested because they view reading as proceeding top-down. That is, a reader uses ideas about the meaning of a text to develop hypotheses about information on a page, and, as the reader goes along, she confirms or revises her hypotheses by sampling the graphic information (the words). In fact, Goodman called reading a psycholinguistic guessing game (Goodman, 1967). Smith claimed that good readers "were particularly good at developing hypotheses about upcoming words, and were able to confirm the identity of a word by sampling only a few features in the visual array" (1971, p. 5). The position endorsed by Goodman and Smith holds that good readers rely more on context and less on graphic information than less skilled readers. As it turns out, many, many research studies show clearly that that is not the case. Let's look at some of those findings.

A Short Tale about a Long Scientific Effort

Early in their careers, cognitive psychologists Keith Stanovich and Richard West held a view of reading that was in agreement with Smith's and Goodman's top-down model. So in an early research project, Stanovich and West (1989) initiated a program of research to bring data to Smith and Goodman's theories, as they had never been tested. Stanovich and West's rigorous studies used reaction-time techniques to test their hypotheses.

A few words about how these reaction-time (often called *latency*) techniques work. The general setup is that a word or a sentence appears on a screen. The time it takes between the appearance of a word to the instant a participant starts to say the word is called the response time. The resultant data is in milliseconds. Response-time techniques have been shown to be reliable and valid measures.

In the development of their studies, Stanovich (2000) describes how he and West adopted Smith and Goodman's own positions, as they expressed them, as hypotheses to the test:

- As the child develops reading skill and speed, he uses increasingly fewer graphic cues, that is, mostly words on a page (Goodman, 1976, p. 504).
- The more difficulty a reader has with reading, the more he relies on visual information (Smith, 1971, p. 221).
- One difference between good readers and the one heading for trouble lies in the overreliance on visual information that inefficient—or improperly taught—beginning readers tend to show at the expense of sense (Smith, 1973, p. 190).

Those statements were the target of Stanovich and West's investigations. We use Stanovich's own words to tell you how their studies turned out, which we found fascinating. According to Stanovich (2000):

> These were the predictions [the three stated above] that Rich West and I went on to test with reaction-time techniques derived from cognitive psychology. To our surprise, all of our research results pointed in the opposite direction, it was the poorer readers, not the more skilled readers, who were more reliant on context to facilitate word recognitions. I say surprised because we embarked on these studies fully expecting to confirm Smith's (1971) views. The history of our work in this area is thus deeply ironic. We *did* [original emphasis] start out with a theoretical bias, one consistent with the top down view. But in real science one is eventually influenced by the evidence, regardless of one's initial bias, and the consistency of our findings led us away from the top down view. (p. 6)

In the same time period, Charles Perfetti from the University of Pittsburgh was finding the same thing (see, e.g., Perfetti et al., 1979; Perfetti & Hogaboam, 1975; Perfetti & Roth, 1981). We present the essence of what Perfetti and his colleagues and students found across at least a dozen rigorous word recognition studies. Keep in mind that the variable being measured is speed, so the shorter the latency, the better the participant's performance.

High-Skilled Readers Recognize Words Faster Than Low-Skilled Readers

Both low-skilled readers and high-skilled readers say words faster in supportive context in comparison with reading words in isolation. However, high-skilled readers are still faster than low-skilled readers.

Both low- and high-skilled students are negatively affected by *anomalous* context but low-skilled readers are more negatively affected. For example, "Bill wrapped his laundry in a curtain." The essence, then, is that fast, context-free word recognition enables a reader to reserve much of her attention capacity to attend to the higher order processes involved in comprehension.

In summary, let's answer a critical question: What do children need to know and be able to do to read words? They need to:

- Understand the alphabetic principle: that words are composed of separable sounds that are represented consistently by symbols.
- Know that the speech sounds are represented in writing by letters of the alphabet.
- Know which speech sounds correspond with which written letters.
- Know how to put those sounds together to form a pronounceable word.
- Have a strong sense of English orthography.
- Recognize words rapidly.

We deal with each of those components in the chapters that follow.

Mark's First Encounter with Learning to Read

I (Mark) clearly remember an incident that somewhat connects with Theresa's initial resistance to learning letter–sound correspondences. When I was about 4, I asked my mother to teach me to read. I remember sitting at our kitchen table and being very excited at the prospect of being able to read. After some preliminaries, Mom held out a letter card and told me that the letter *a* stands for the /a/ sound. She then told me to pronounce the /a/ sound. I diligently complied. We went through this routine several times. Then I told her, "Actually, I want to do the kind of reading that everyone else does with the words on the pages!"[1] Mom explained that I needed to do this first and that in 2 days I would be able to read some words. She continued with several other letters, and when 2 more days had passed, I did read several words. I was very excited. My mother had earned credibility, and I listened and became a good reader early on. Looking back, I could clearly identify with Theresa's impatience.

• • • • • • • • • • • YOUR TURN • • • • • • • • • •

It may help set the backdrop for this book if you would reflect a few moments about some of the students in your class.

---

[1]The story is not unlike my practicing tennis with my 6-year-old son. We went out to the court and struggled to keep the ball going over the net for more than one or two volleys. After several such attempts, he told me, "Dad, I want to do the type of tennis where the ball goes back and forth over the net a lot."

- Make a list of several of your best readers and several of your weakest readers. Turn each of the six preceding statements into a question. For example, Does (student's name) know the sounds represented by the letters and letter combinations?

- For each question, rate each student as high, medium, or low for the six bulleted statements. Note that the six statements can be asked at first grade and higher grades, as the components are needed at all grade levels, albeit for increasingly complex words.

- Look at the results and determine the extent to which there is a different profile for the strong and weak readers. You may want to keep younger or weaker students in mind as the instructional strategies in this book are presented.

CHAPTER 3

Phonemic Awareness
A Bit of a Different Take

Over the last 25 years or so, researchers have developed a strong consensus that one of the best predictors of early reading success is phonemic awareness, the understanding that spoken words are composed of individual sounds, or phonemes. The NRP (2000), highlighted phonemic awareness by naming it one of the five most important components of reading.

In this chapter, we review some commonly accepted notions about phonemic awareness, discuss the inherent difficulties of developing phonemic awareness, and demonstrate that phonemic awareness can be taught. We then review three perspectives on the relationship between phonemic awareness and decoding, and finally we suggest phonemic awareness activities that can be considered at the juncture of pure phonemic awareness and phonics instruction.

Phonemic Awareness Can Be Hard for Young Children

There is a general sequence of phonemic awareness tasks that make up a continuum that starts with easier activities, such as rhyming and identifying a word that does not start like several others. Additional phonemic awareness tasks target individual phonemes and include synthesis activities such as blending: "What word is made up of the sounds /s/ /a/ /t/?" Harder yet is segmentation: "What are the sounds in the word *rip*?" Most difficult of all are various manipulations, such as "Change the /p/ in *map* to the /t/ sound and say the word." Manipulations can take a variety of forms, but they all require students to isolate a phoneme, delete a phoneme, or change one of the phonemes in a word to another phoneme.

The first major problem in the identification of phonemes within words is that a child does not perceive subsounds in a word. What the child hears is the whole word. She knows that words communicate, tell stories, and the like, but she knows nothing of the structure of words. And why would she? A phoneme is an abstraction that even some adults have difficulty identifying, including bright undergraduate students (Perfetti, Beck, Bell, & Hughes, 1987). The anecdote about Linda at the end of this chapter is a great example of a young child not perceiving subword units.

Now we're going to say a word and ask you to say the number of phonemes. Ready? How many phonemes are in the word *speech*? Did you do it? The word *speech* has six letters but only four phonemes. The two *e* letters represent one phoneme, the long-*e* sound; the *ch* represents the /ch/. Try it with one more word. Ready? How many phonemes are in *table*? There are four phonemes in *table*: /t/ /a/(long) /b/ /l/.

A second reason phoneme segmentation is hard is that phonemes often overlap in speech production. They are coarticulated. Consider the word *speech*. As one is pronouncing the phoneme /s/, one's mouth, tongue, and lips are already getting in position to pronounce the phoneme /p/. So it is inherently difficult to perceive where one phoneme ends and the next one begins.

Another reason that segmentation is difficult for young children who have not yet learned to read is that they do not have much knowledge of English orthography, which is the essence of spelling. To demonstrate how important orthographic knowledge is in analytic phonemic tasks, we are going to ask you to engage in the most difficult analytic tasks. Ready? Say *black*. Now, say *black* without the /l/. How did you get to *back*? It is very likely that you saw *black* in your mind's eye and then were able to remove the letter that represented the /l/ and thus say *back*. According to Perfetti (1985), phoneme segmentation may be an even more cognitively demanding process than reading. In fact, it is likely that, when engaging in phoneme segmentation activities, children are doing something that is harder for them than decoding simple CVC words (*cat, hit, pet*). Our solution is to teach phonemic awareness and early decoding in parallel, in a reciprocal supporting relationship.

Teaching Phonemic Awareness

There is evidence that phonemic awareness can be taught to young children and that such teaching can have positive effects on early reading acquisition (see, e.g., Blachman, Ball, Black, & Tangel, 1994; Lundberg, Frost, & Petersen, 1988). I (Mark) have direct evidence of this phenomenon from a group of kindergarten students that I worked with. Several years ago, an entire kindergarten class had not been directly taught phonemic awareness for the first few months into the school year. In January, the teacher made a decision to teach phonemic awareness for a few minutes almost every day. To assess the effectiveness of instruction, as a baseline measure we used a popular phoneme segmentation assessment in which the administrator pronounces a word and asks the students to pronounce all the sounds in the word separately. The score is the number of phonemes, or chunks in some cases, pronounced in 1 minute. As is customary for this type of assessment, the assessment is given midyear and again at the end of the year. Students generally show some improvement during the intervening months.

In the kindergarten case I mentioned, however, the improvement, with the initiation of instruction in phonemic awareness in January, was unusually dramatic. A review of the 10 lowest scores in January and the increase through May is shown here.

January	May	Increase
11	75	+ 64
9	49	+ 49
9	57	+ 46
9	54	+ 45
16	54	+ 38
11	47	+ 36
18	54	+ 36
19	53	+ 34
13	46	+ 33
9	34	+ 25

The scores are shown from the highest to the lowest increase, with increases ranging from 25 to 64. Increases of this magnitude are well above average for the 4-month period. We found this quite compelling evidence for the impact of explicit instruction for the purpose of supporting students' phonemic awareness.

Perspectives on the Relationship between Phonemic Awareness and Decoding

In thinking about the role of phonemic awareness in learning to decode, three perspectives on the relationship between phonemic awareness and decoding are important to consider: the prerequisite perspective, the byproduct perspective, and the reciprocal perspective.

One perspective has it that phonemic awareness is a prerequisite to learning to decode (Liberman & Shankweiler, 1979). The idea is that decoding instruction will move along better if children start it with phonemic awareness capability. A strict prerequisite position would assert that some degree of phonemic awareness prior to decoding instruction was essential.

A second perspective is that phonemic awareness is actually a byproduct of learning to decode (e.g., Morais, Cary, Alegria, & Bertelson, 1979). From this perspective, simply learning to decode will result in phonemic awareness, even though phonemic awareness is not explicitly taught. In the Morais and colleagues (1979) work, adult illiterates who did not have phonemic awareness gained it when taught to read. As such, proponents of the byproduct view suggest that phonemic awareness activities are unnecessary.

I (Isabel) was intrigued by the Morais et al. finding that reading instruction in itself resulted in phonemic awareness. The reason is that I think I sensed something similar when I taught Army sergeants who had not achieved third-grade reading equivalent scores. In those days, I had not heard of phonemic awareness, and I don't think it was only because I was young and inexperienced. I just don't think the notions were present in the field. Anyway, I eventually had some success in teaching the sergeants some phonics, and they did learn how to figure out the pronunciations of not-too-complex words by producing the phonemes of the letters in a word. My sense that these men were acquiring phonemic awareness came from incidents such as a man who finally decoded *tent*, looking up and saying something like, "Oh yeah, *tent* has four sounds." Another man noticed that *tents* had "one more sound than *tent*." Certainly such distant and anecdotal evidence is at best merely a vague impression, but that impression came to mind when I read about the Morais work. A strict byproduct orientation would assert that teaching phonemic awareness is unnecessary.

The third perspective, and the one we find the most convincing case for, captures elements of both the prerequisite perspective and the byproduct perspective. According to this perspective, phonemic awareness supports decoding, as is commonly accepted, but also decoding instruction supports phonemic awareness. In fact, it is the case that explicit decoding instruction does enhance phonemic awareness (Blachman et al., 1994). Decoding instruction does not need to wait for a requisite level of phonemic awareness; they can both be taught and can support and reinforce each other.

Research tells us that, at least with respect to analytic activities, phonemic awareness is promoted by learning to decode. We can add our experience to that assertion in that neither of us can recall knowing a child who was able to engage in consistent segmentation, deletion/elision, or manipulation tasks without knowing some letter–sound correspondences. The more complex manifestations of phonemic awareness (i.e., knowing that *sit* has three distinctive sounds) and being able to manipulate phonemes—"Say *sit* without the /s/"—develops along with reading instruction. Perfetti and colleagues (1987) and others have identified the reciprocal relationship between phonemic awareness and reading. Phonemic awareness enhances the acquisition of reading, and reading enhances the acquisition of phonemic awareness.

A Demonstration of the Reciprocal Nature of Phonemic Awareness and Decoding Instruction

Results of a study by McCandliss, Beck, Sandak, and Perfetti (2003) demonstrated the reciprocal nature of phonemic awareness and reading instruction. The study involved an intervention with students who had completed at least the first grade but who demonstrated reading difficulties. Students were randomly assigned to an experimental group or to a wait-list control group. The parents of the students in the control group were provided with books and other literacy materials that they could use during the wait time for participation in the experimental condition in the next semester.

Students in the experimental group participated in a summer intervention in which Word Building (Beck, 2006) was implemented. Tutors, trained undergraduate students, provided the instruction in one-on-one situations. In each lesson, students were given a small set of letter cards from which they were directed by the tutor to form and read an initial word and then directed to form new words by exchanging, deleting, or inserting one letter. As such, a chain of words that differed by only one letter from the previous word was built. For example, a chain that students could develop in a fairly early lesson might be *pat, pet, set, sat, mat, man, pan, pen, ten*. After the first word, *pat*, was formed, as can be seen from the chain, the tutor's next direction was to change the *a* letter card to the *e* letter card and read the resultant word, then to change *p* to *s* and read the word, and so on. A later lesson might look like this: *chin, in, inch, in, pin, pinch, pin, shin, ship, shop, chop, pop*. Beyond developing a word chain, students read some "Silly Sentences" that included a fair number of the words in a given sequence. There was no other kind of instruction involved in the experimental intervention. (Word Building is fully discussed in Chapter 7.) Here our purpose is to provide some interesting findings about the reciprocal nature of decoding instruction and phonemic awareness.

In McCandliss and his colleagues' (2003) study, among the tests given to the students were three phonemic awareness and one pseudoword reading test. These provided pre- and posttest comparisons that point to the reciprocal nature of decoding and phonemic awareness. The three phonemic awareness tests that were administered—Blending Words, Blending Nonwords, and Elision subtests— were taken from a prototype version of the Comprehensive Test of Phonological Processing (Wagner, Torgesen, & Rashotte, 1994). In the Blending Words test, children listened to segments of words on a tape recorder and were asked to blend them together into a word pronunciation. The Blending Nonwords test followed the same procedures, but the segments combined to form pronounceable pseudowords. In the Elision test, the experimenter read a word and then asked the child what real word would be made if a particular phoneme were removed (e.g., "Say *brake*; now say it without saying /r/"). In addition to the three phonemic awareness tests, students were asked read aloud a list of 128 pseudowords.

All results reported here were obtained in the context of no direct phonemic awareness activities. Students in the experimental group engaged only in Word Building activities and reading of some text material (sentences) that included words from the Word Building activities. Results of the two blending tests, Blending Words and Blending Nonwords, tell different stories. On the Blending Word subset, both the experimental and control groups showed improvement. Although the experimental gains were larger than for the control group, they did not approach significance. As such, the data indicate that the intervention did not directly support gains in blending words. However, the results of the Blending Nonwords test showed that the experimental groups' improvements were significantly larger than the control group's improvements. Why the difference? The suggestion is that blending nonwords increases the need for phonological competence since one cannot determine whether the results of blending nonwords are correct as they are not part of the English word stock.

Additionally, students in the control group failed to demonstrate significant improvements on the Elision task. This suggests that deficits that were demonstrated in pretest measures were rather persistent and that whatever accounted for the increases in their performance at blending words did not lead to improvements on more demanding phonemic awareness tasks.

Use of Letters with Phonemic Awareness Activities

Over the years a mnemonic emerged to help preservice teachers distinguish the difference between phonemic awareness and phonics. If an activity could be conducted with the lights off, it was phonemic awareness because it was auditory only; if the activity required that the lights be on, it was phonics because phonics involves seeing letters. It is easy to see that most of the phonemic awareness studies in the literature have involved tasks that could be done with the lights off (see, e.g., Bradley & Bryant, 1978; Stanovich, Cunningham, & Cramer, 1984). Presumably, most, if not all, of instructional practice of phonemic awareness, as seen in widely used reading programs, consists of purely oral activities.

An emerging consensus, however, suggests that, beyond preschool, phonemic awareness instruction is most effective when such instruction is imparted through the use of printed letters (Bus & van IJzendoorn, 1999; National Reading Panel, 2000). Once letters are used, we have discarded the more common view of phonemic awareness as a purely auditory task in favor of phonics, which additionally includes the visual system. We believe that decoding can be taught with the inclusion of phonemic awareness and that phonemic awareness can be taught by incorporating letters (see Chapter 5). Beyond easier phonemic awareness speech-only activities ("What word do you get when you blend /s/ /a/ /t/?"), our experience is that there is much to be gained in using letters to create activities that support letter-sound knowledge and phonemic awareness.

We present two activities, the first of which involves one letter and the second of which involves two letters. We have partly scripted the directions for the activities, as that form is parsimonious in terms of our ability to save words in communicating with our readers and teachers' abilities to save time when planning lessons. Where potential words are given for use in a lesson, the teacher, of course, may decrease or increase the number of words as she sees how students are progressing through the activities.

Example of a One-Letter Phonemic Awareness Activity

Initial Position

1. Teacher provides an *m* letter card to each student. Teacher says *man* and asks students to repeat *man*.
2. Teacher tells student, "I am going to say a word. If the word has the /m/ sound at the beginning, touch the *m* card. If the word does not have the /m/ sound at the beginning, put your hand behind your back."
   - Possible words: *mat, sat, rat, mat, mike, mop, stop, top.*
   - Use same tasks with other consonants in the initial position once those consonants have been taught.

Final Position

1. Repeat the preceding instructions. However, instruct the student to decide whether a target phoneme, in this case *m*, is at the end of a word.
   - Possible words: *Sam, ram, rat, sat, Tim, tip, rip, rim, ram.*
   - Use the same task with other consonants in the final position once those consonants have been taught.

Medial Position

1. Teacher gives the student an *a* card. Teacher then says, "I am going to say a word. If the word has the /a/ sound in the middle, touch the *a* card. If the word does not have the /a/ sound in the middle, put your hand behind your back."
   - Possible words: *cat, cap, hip, sip, sap, rip, rot, map, mop, fit, pat.*
   - Use the same task with other vowels in the medial position once those vowels have been taught.

Example of a Two-Letter Phonemic Awareness Activity

Initial Position

1. Teacher provides the *m* and *p* letter cards to each child. Teacher says *man* and asks students to repeat *man*. Then teacher says *pet* and asks students to repeat *pet*.

2. Teacher tells student, "Now you will say words that might begin with the /m/ sound or the /p/ sound. I am going to say a word. If the word has the /m/ sound at the beginning, touch the *m* card. If the word has the /p/ sound at the beginning, touch the *p* card.

   "For example, if I say *man*, show me the letter card you will touch. If I say *pet*, show me the card you will touch." (Confirm by saying something like the word *man* has the /m/ sound at the beginning and the word *pet* has the /p/ sound at the beginning.)

   ▪ Possible words: *pat, mat, mark, park, ran, pack, pick, mid, mud.*

Final Position

1. The instructions are the same as the preceding. However, the student is instructed to listen to which of two phonemes, in this case /m/ or /p/, is heard at the end of a word.

   ▪ Possible words: *cap, rap, rip, rim, Sam, sap, lap, lip, Tim, dim, dip.*

Medial Position

1. Teacher provides the *a* and *i* letter cards to each child. "Now, I will say words that might have the /a/ sound in the middle or the /i/ sound in the middle. I'm going to say a word. If the word has the /a/ sound in the middle, touch the *a* card. If the word has the /i/ sound in the middle, touch the *i* card.

   ▪ Possible words: *sip, sap, lap, lip, lid, rid, rap, tip, tap, map, mat, kid.*

What do you think? Are these activities letter-sound instruction or phonemic awareness instruction? We see them as primarily phonemic awareness instruction, but with letter support. In one-on-one situations, I (Mark) have been able to observe closely what some students do during these activities. After I pronounce a word, I can notice a child's lips moving or quietly whispering the word and trying to strip the target phoneme from the word. And often when a child has made the decision which card to touch, I've seen some do so triumphantly.

On the other hand, as many of us have experienced, things can always go awry. Consider the example of Laura, a PreK student with whom I worked briefly:

MARK: What's the name of this letter [pointing to the *m* letter card]?

LAURA: *m*.

MARK: Right. The letter *m* stands for the /m/ sound. Say it with me: /m/.

LAURA: /m/.

MARK: *Monkey* is a word that starts with the /m/ sound. Let's say *monkey* together.

MARK AND LAURA: Monkey.

(Mark offers several more words that begin with /m/ and Laura repeats them.)

MARK: Now, can you think of a word that begins with /m/? [pause] I've got one, *meat*. *Meat* begins with /m/. You say *meat*.

LAURA: *Meat*.

MARK: Do you hear that /m/ sound at the beginning of *meat*?

LAURA: Yes.

MARK: Now you say a word that begins with /m/.

LAURA: *Chicken*!

A Caveat

To reiterate, research tells us that phonemic awareness helps predict decoding and overall reading achievement, but we offer this caveat: phonemic awareness is a means to an end (decoding words). It is important for students to have a sufficient amount of phonemic awareness only to the extent that it helps them decode words. Once a student has demonstrated an ability to decode words, phonemic awareness takes on much less importance. We mention this as we need to share a concern that, in the instructional domain, phonemic awareness may be taking on more of a life of its own than is useful. For example, several reading coaches have told us about some second- and third-grade teachers who have students whose decoding is limited in that they make too many mistakes, about 30–40%. The teachers asked the coach for materials that they could use to provide more phonemic awareness instruction to those students.

The coach indicated that the children could successfully engage in relatively easy phonemic awareness tasks, such as oral blending and identifying words that begin with the same sounds. With the skills they have, these children have enough phonemic awareness competency to support decoding instruction, and the appropriate instructional recommendation is that they receive more intense decoding instruction rather than phonemic awareness instruction. There is no evidence that trying to improve reading by asking such children to engage in sophisticated speech-only tasks (e.g., say *splash* without the /p/) will improve decoding. In fact, what might enable them to say *splash* without the /p/ is letter-sound and blending instruction with a healthy dose of writing.

A Young Child Demonstrates a Major Point

Jen, a graduate student in a master's-level reading course that I (Isabel) had taught, became intrigued with phonemic awareness. Toward the end of the semester, at the beginning of a class, she could hardly wait to talk about an experience that she had with her 4½-year-old niece, Linda. Jen reported that she had engaged Linda in some early phonemic awareness activities—"Which word doesn't start like the other two: *met, cap, man?*"—and the child had done well. So Jen skipped way ahead in the phonemic awareness sequence to see what would happen and asked the child "How many sounds do you hear in the word *baby?*" The child looked at her in puzzlement, so Jen gave her some simple examples (the word *man* has three sounds, etc.). But the examples weren't taking. So Jen tried again: "Just tell me the sounds you hear when I say *baby, baabee.*" Linda wrinkled her forehead. Later, Jen tried again, "Linda, let's just try one more time. How many sounds do you hear in the word *baby?*" With annoyance in her tone, the child said, "How many times do I have to tell you, the sound I hear is **baby!**"

• • • • • • • • • • • YOUR TURN • • • • • • • • • •

If you would like to "see" the differences in young children's abilities to engage in the continuum of phonemic awareness activities, you could do a little study by borrowing children from kindergarten and first grade.

Phonemic awareness activity	Example	Comments
1. Matching sound	Which word doesn't belong with the others? a. Beginning sounds: *cat, hat, can* b. Ending sounds: *ten, pen, bed*	Develop several additional examples. If a child gets three correct in both beginning and ending sounds, move on to #2. If a child is not correct on two or three items in each category, still move on to #2.

| 2. Blending | What word do you get if you put together the sounds I say: /r/ /a/ /t/ /m/ /o/ /p/ /s/ /i/ /p/? | Develop several additional examples. |
| 3. Segmenting | How many sounds do you hear in the word *cat* . . . in the word *pot*? | Develop several additional examples. |

CHAPTER 4

The Phonics Landscape

When in graduate school, I (Mark) worked with a closely knit group of about 20 fellow students. Our spring semester involved mostly student teaching at various school sites, but we did take one class together. At our sites, we used a variety of basal reading series and taught in a variety of grade levels. My student teaching placement was in a first-grade classroom in a city public school. Before our weekly class, I once overheard two fellow students, also student teaching in first grade in two other school districts, discussing their lesson plans. As they compared their lessons, one of the students showed some surprise when he noticed that they were teaching the same letter-sound pattern (I think it was *ee/ea*) at about the same time despite using different basal reading programs. With this epiphany the first student said to the other, "Look, it seems there's an accepted order in which we teach these patterns in first grade." The other student glanced at the two lesson plans and responded with something like, "Right. I can see it. I didn't know that."

I did know it, but while I was growing up with my mother, teaching materials associated with reading were always around our home. I recognized that there was really no reason why my fellow students should have known about the general letter-sound teaching sequence. A review of current commercial reading programs continues to show overall consistency of the phonics elements *taught*. And that is what we consider in this chapter—the general *teaching* landscape.

What Is the Content of Beginning Reading?

It has been suggested that reading, unlike mathematics and science and other content area subjects, is really not a content area. It is not a body of knowledge; rather, it is a skill—a process in which people engage. In this regard noted psychologist and linguist John Carroll (1964) suggested that, if there is subject-matter content in reading, "that content is the relationship between the structure of spoken messages and the system of marks or symbols used to represent these messages" (p. 339).[1] A less abstract way of expressing the same idea is that the content of reading is the relationship between written letters and the sounds they represent in speech, be they individual letters or in words.

Overview of Major Phonics Content

The table below covers much of the content usually presented as students are learning to read.

Phonics Categories and Examples

	Category	Examples
1.	Individual consonants	b, c, d, f, g, h, j, k, l, m, n, p, q, r, s, t, v, w, x, y, z
2.	Short vowels	a (c<u>a</u>t), o (m<u>o</u>p), i (s<u>i</u>t), e (p<u>e</u>t), u (r<u>u</u>b)
3.	Consonant blends (examples)	st (<u>st</u>op), sl (<u>sl</u>ip), tr (<u>tr</u>ap), br (<u>br</u>ick) -nd (a<u>nd</u>), -st (be<u>st</u>)
4.	Consonant digraphs	-ck (ba<u>ck</u>) th (<u>th</u>at, ba<u>th</u>) sh (<u>sh</u>op, ma<u>sh</u>) ch/-tch (<u>ch</u>ip, ba<u>tch</u>)
5.	Long vowels in CVCe words	c<u>a</u>ke, r<u>i</u>ce, h<u>o</u>pe, r<u>u</u>de
6.	Long vowels in CVVC words	ai/ay (r<u>ai</u>n, m<u>ay</u>) ea/ee (b<u>ea</u>n, s<u>ee</u>p) oa/ow (b<u>oa</u>t, r<u>ow</u>) ie (p<u>ie</u>) ui, ue, ew (s<u>ui</u>t, bl<u>ue</u>, st<u>ew</u>)

---

[1]Others may not accept this narrow description. They would note that the content of early reading is far broader, for example, knowledge of how stories are usually structured, knowledge of various genres, awareness of certain authors' aspects of the craft, and more. These objections are legitimate, and we agree. We use the narrow description to put the focus on phonics, which, of course, is the topic of this book.

7.	*R*-controlled vowels	ar (b<u>ar</u>k) or (c<u>or</u>n) er/ur/ir (h<u>er</u>d, b<u>ur</u>n, st<u>ir</u>)
8.	Diphthongs and other vowel patterns	oi/oy (j<u>oi</u>n, b<u>oy</u>) ou/ow (r<u>ou</u>nd, c<u>ow</u>) aw/augh (str<u>aw</u>, t<u>augh</u>t) oo [long] (sp<u>oo</u>n), oo [short] (f<u>oo</u>t)

The eight categories shown in the first column start with content that is seen as easier to learn and moves down through categories that are more complex, such as *r*-controlled words (*car, stir*), and finally to diphthongs (*join, cow*). The second column provides all or most of the content in a category. The order in which the examples are presented does not imply an instructional order. For instance, the consonants in the table are presented in alphabetical order. That does not mean that that is the order in which they are or should be taught. Next, we make some comments about each category that include definitions of terms.

Consonants

In many dictionaries as well as other resources, the first definition of a consonant is that it is "a letter that is not a vowel." Along with what it is not, various resources will tell you that the phoneme of a consonant grapheme is a class of speech sounds that is pronounced with partial obstruction of the airway.

Short Vowels

Every word and every syllable requires a vowel. Although we've seen vowels defined as letters that are not consonants, that description does not appear nearly as often as the parallel consonant description, that is, that consonants are not vowels. Vowel phonemes are characterized as phonemes that are pronounced with no obstruction in the airway. With knowledge of the grapheme–phoneme correspondences for one short vowel and several consonants, children are able to decode (read) and encode (write) a surprisingly large number of CVC words. For example, knowing the consonants *m, s,* and *t* and the vowel *a* allows us to read or write: *sat, Sam, mat, mast.*

Consonant Blends/Clusters

A consonant blend (sometimes referred to as a consonant cluster) is composed of two or more adjacent consonants, with each grapheme retaining its original phonemic quality when uttered. (Say *step* and you will hear that /s/ and /t/ are both pronounced.) Consonant blends are found at the beginning (*stop, trip*) or at the end of words (*rest, limp*). When consonant blends are first introduced to students, the blends can be a challenge. (Chapter 6 suggests a strategy that supports reading words with consonant blends.)

Consonant Digraphs

A consonant digraph (e.g., *ch*ip) includes two or more adjacent consonants that combine to form one new phoneme, which is a different sound from either of the sounds associated with the individual consonants. Some common digraphs are *ck, ch, th, sh*. Even though the grapheme for a consonant digraph includes two letters, it is a single grapheme because it is the written representation of a single phoneme. Consonant digraphs can be found at the beginning or end of a word. The digraph *ck* is only found at the end of a word, and the digraph *ch* usually becomes *tch* when at the end of a word. In our experiences, students do not seem to find consonant digraphs particularly difficult to learn.

CVCe Words

In a typical CVC*e* word, such as *made*, the *a* is pronounced as a long *a*, in contrast to *mad*, in which the *a* is pronounced as a short *a*. The vernacular explanation is that the *e* at the end is silent, but it changes the sound of the vowel to a long vowel. The more sophisticated expression is that the final *e* is a marker to the pronunciation of the vowel. The CVC*e* pattern is often, but not always, the first exposure to long vowels that students encounter, and learning it provides a challenge for many students. Students who struggle with the overall alphabetic code often struggle even more with CVC*e* words. The difficulty is probably related to the position of the silent *e*. That is, when decoding from left to right, there is no information that the *a* is long because the reader has not yet encountered the silent *e*, two positions to the right of the vowel. Words with the CVC*e* pattern often take some time getting used to.

CVVC Words

CVVC words are often called words with vowel teams or vowel digraphs. CVVC words include two medial vowels. Usually, the first vowel is pronounced long and the second vowel is silent (*boat, seat*). CVVC words present less difficulty for students when compared with CVC*e* words. Perhaps the reason is that students need no subsequent distant marker to pronounce the *oa* grapheme. When they see it they can decode it from left to right. Often the graphemes *ow, ew*, and *ay* are included among CVVC words despite *w* and *y* sometimes functioning as consonants.

R-Controlled Vowels

An *r*-controlled word can look like a CVC word, but in an *r*-controlled word, such as *far*, the vowel combines with the *r* to form a single phoneme, which is not identical to the more common short vowel sound in CVC words (e.g., *her* vs. *hem*). The graphemes *er, ir,* and *ur,* as in *her, sir,* and *fur,* all represent the same /er/ phoneme. Teachers note that a problem arises when a student is asked to spell those *r*-controlled words. For instance, how does a child learn to spell *her* as *h-e-r* and not *h-i-r*? It must be done by memorizing the spelling of those words and encountering them in text. A bit less challenging are the graphemes *ar,* which represents the /ar/ sound, as in *far,* and the grapheme *or,* which represents the /or/ sound, as in *fork*.

Diphthongs

Diphthongs are two adjacent vowels, which speech professionals refer to as gliding vowels (*boy, cow*) because, when pronounced, there is a change within the sound. Try saying /oy/ slowly. Did you sense the two sounds? The change from the first sound to the second is subtle because the first sound glides right into the second sound. Some major diphthongs are *ow, ou, oy,* and *oi*.

The elements just discussed provide a large portion of the content of early reading. We look next to how some of that content is sequenced for instruction.

Sequencing Phonic Elements for Instruction

Developing a sequence for the introduction of grapheme–phoneme correspondences requires making decisions about the order in which graphemes should be introduced. The most important decisions are those about the sequencing of the early correspondences because it makes sense to arrange them in ways that may facilitate, or at least not confuse, the early months of childrens' literacy journeys. We point to some potential confusions and suggest ways to reduce them. Consideration will also be given to several issues related to providing a productive sequence, one in which children are able to decode words early. Among the reasons for especially arranging conditions that support smooth progress in the early part of learning to read is evidence that children who do not catch on to decoding early—in a typical time frame—are likely on the path to reading difficulties. There is, in fact, persuasive evidence that children who get off to a slow start rarely become strong readers (Juel, 1988; Stanovich, 1986). Thus the earliest instructional conditions should be given the greatest consideration.

We hastily emphasize that all phases of learning to read are important, that students can get into trouble in later phases of learning to read, and that thoughtful instruction, including sequencing of later correspondences, matters a lot.

Given that grapheme–phoneme correspondences are the keystone to learning to read, let's consider a couple of decisions. Assuming that letter names are introduced in alphabetical order, should phonemes be taught simultaneously with the introduction of the letter names? Or after the letter names are under control, is it sensible to go back to *a* and teach the phonemes in alphabetical order? Our assertion is that teaching the phonemes in alphabetical order is a poor practice. Being able to utter /a/, /b/, /k/, /d/, /e/, and so forth in isolation has no purpose beyond accomplishing such a questionable feat. The purpose of learning phonemes is to be able to figure out the pronunciation of words. And teaching some phonemes to do so must be done sooner rather than later.

One problem with using alphabetical order to teach phonemes is that it limits when and how many real words can be created from several phonemes. Consider the first four letters of the alphabet (*a, b, c, d*) and see how many words those correspondences would allow. We came up with four: *bad, dad, cab, dab*. Except for *dad*, the other three words are far from exciting. Reading a *meaningful* unit approximates real reading. And blending sounds that result in a word is a prideful accomplishment. Both of us have seen the pleasure that emerges when a child recognizes that he has actually figured out the way to read a word by himself.

I (Isabel) remember sitting with a first grader, having asked him to blend three letters that were on cards on his desk. When the child got through the sequence for blending, he turned to me and said, "Did you see that? I read *ten*!"

Having rejected alphabetical order for teaching phonemes, what should be considered? We turn to that issue next.

Is There Any Research That Can Help?

There is a smidgen of research that might bear on the question. Coleman (1970) reported some research in terms of the relative ease with which letter–sound correspondences are learned. In his study, he determined the rank ordering of 35 letters and letter combinations according to the ease with which preschool children learned them. He suggested that sequences be developed that are based on a continuum from easier-to-learn to harder-to-learn correspondences.

A listing follows of Coleman's 15 easiest-to-learn grapheme–phoneme correspondences (the graphemes are presented here with a word to illustrate the phoneme each represents):

1. s   as in s<u>ee</u>

2. i e   as in r<u>ide</u>

3. o e   as in n<u>ose</u>

4. z   as in <u>zoo</u>

5. sh   as in <u>sh</u>ut

6. o   as in h<u>o</u>t

7. ow   as in h<u>ow</u>

8. m   as in <u>m</u>e

9. ue   as in d<u>ue</u>

10. k   as in <u>k</u>it

11. oo   as in b<u>oo</u>t

12. f   as in <u>f</u>an

13. th   as in <u>th</u>e (voiced)
             and <u>th</u>ank (unvoiced)

14. v   as in <u>v</u>est

15. ee   as in s<u>ee</u>

On the basis of ease of learning alone, Coleman's notion could not be ignored. However, our second criterion for ordering correspondences is that they produce words that are meaningful to young children very early in the process of learning to read. Words that can be generated from Coleman's 15 easiest correspondences include *fee, five, mime, mom, moss, see, size, sow, sue, thee, those, vow,* and *zoom.* The words *five, mom, see, size, those,* and *zoom* would likely be in the vocabularies of our target population, but the others most likely would not. Considering one aspect of a developmental sequence independent of other aspects can result in an inadequate picture.

Let's Not Repeat the Mistakes of the Past

In 1973, Diederich suggested that a major weakness in the phonics approaches used in the 1930s was the abstract material to which beginning readers were exposed before any real reading occurred. (Recall the phonics exercises described in Chapter 1.) Like the child described earlier who seemed to be elated when he read *ten*, it is vital for the beginning reader to realize when he has read a word. Thus the words that children are asked to read should be words whose meanings they know from oral language. To us, meaning is implicit in the decoding stage of reading because without meaning the process is recoding (i.e., going from one code to another). We suggest that the recognition of meaning would not likely occur with the words *fee, thee, sue, sow, vow, mime,* and *moss*.

So it is the case that the two variables in sequencing letter–sounds—the ease of learning correspondences and their use in the production of meaningful words—cannot be considered independently. Those features and several other features are taken up in the context of the table that follows, which shows the order for teaching letter–sound correspondences in three current, widely used commercial basal reading programs. We have given each program a number, which we use to refer to them.

1.	m	s	r	t	n	p	c	a	d	i	g	f	b	k	o	l	h	w	x	e	v	j	y	z	u	q
2.	m	a	s	p	t	i	n	c	o	f	h	d	r	e	b	l	k	u	g	w	x	v	j	q	y	z
3.	m	a	s	d	t	p	c	r	n	i	f	b	h	k	o	g	l	e	v	j	u	q	w	x	y	z

Where in a Sequence Should the First Short Vowel Be Placed?

Because we have stressed the importance of enabling beginning students to be able to read words early in the course of learning to read, the placement of vowels is of utmost importance. In order to make comparisons among programs, the vowels are shown against a shaded background. Looking across the sequences, it can seen that the order of the vowels is the same across the three program sequences, *a, i, o, e, u.*

We see that in Programs 2 and 3, the *a* is the second letter introduced, but in Program 1, introduction of *a* does not occur until the eighth position in its sequence. Notice that after the *a* has been introduced, Programs 2 and 3 enable the *a* and *m* to be blended and *am* read. We acknowledge that *am* in isolation is barely a word; however, programs and many teachers introduce the pronoun *I* in conjunction with *am*, so *I am* can be read. After the *s*, the words *as* and *Sam* become available, and after the *p* in Program 2 is taught, the CVCs *map, sap, Pam*, and *can* come into play. The addition of *d* in Program 3 enables *mad, sad*, and *dad*. And so it goes. With each new consonant, more and more words become available, and a little window may be opening for children into how sounds and letters work in reading words. This is not the case for Program 1; it is not until the eighth position that children in Program 1 can read words. That is almost a third of the way through the sequence.

Where in a Sequence Should the Second Vowel Be Placed?

The answer to this question is that the Goldilocks position holds: the second vowel should not be too close to nor should it be too far away from the first vowel. There should be enough distance between the *a* and the next vowel so that enough practice decoding words with the *a* has enabled children to develop a strong /a/ response before the *i* enters the scene and muddles things up.

The muddle comes from the fact that the phonemes for each of the five short vowels are articulated very close to each other. As a result, it is not uncommon for some children to confuse the correct phoneme for a short vowel with another short vowel. For example, a student might say *hat* for *hot*, or *sit* for *set*. The reason is that the vocalizations for each of the five short vowel phonemes are not distinctly different from each other. The utterance of a phoneme has to do with where in the mouth the phoneme is produced. For the five short vowel phonemes there are *not* a lot of differences in the position of the lips and tongue. Each utterance of a phoneme is close to another. You can observe the point by inserting the phoneme for each short vowel in the middle of b__t and saying the resultant five words while looking in the mirror. Notice that the position of your lips and tongue do not change much. To reduce the problem, there should be some distance between the introductions of each vowel. Again, the reason is to provide time for practice and repetition of the vowels already introduced so that children's representations of them in memory are strong.

Given that learning letter–sound correspondences is associative learning, Holland and Doran (1973) point out:

> The principal problem in learning associations is interference among new associations. . . . Similarity between elements is a major variable leading to interferences among the elements. Spaced practice decreases such interference and hence becomes important when many associations must be learned. (p. 299)

In the case of the short vowels, it is the phonemes of each vowel grapheme that are similar. Even with research providing support for spaced presentations, decisions are rarely based on just one variable. For example, we just called for distance between the introduction of the short vowels, especially the first two. But if there is too much distance in terms of elapsed time and intervening elements between the first and second vowels, let's say *a* and *i*, an unintended message that the /a/ is always the phoneme in the middle of words might be internalized. We've seen it many times. Our judgment, then, is that the introduction of the *i* in Program 1 is too close to where the *a* was introduced, and the introduction of the *i* in Program 3 may be too far away. On this feature Program 2 seems to be just right.

Visually Similar Graphemes

Let's consider one more feature, the order of introduction among the three programs of visually similar graphemes. The research we discuss here notes that both similarity of response and visually similar stimuli lead to interference. There are several pairs of letters that are visually similar, but none more than the *b* and the *d*, which we assert most kindergarten and first-grade teachers would testify to with certainty. There is also empirical evidence that, from a letter recognition standpoint, they are the most difficult letter pair to discriminate (Popp, 1964). The reason the *b* and *d* are difficult is that this is the first time that children have encountered something that becomes something else when its orientation is changed. Up to now that has not been their experience—a spoon is a spoon when it is flipped around, moved from a vertical orientation to a horizontal one, balanced on your palm, whatever—a spoon is a spoon. This is not the case for the *b* because when it is flipped to the left it becomes a *d*, just as when the *d* is flipped to the right, it becomes a *b*.

Thus we would like to see *b* and *d* introduced at a distance from each other. In the chart of the programs' sequences, we have placed the *d* and *b* on a dotted background. Each program has chosen to introduce the *d* before the *b*, but it doesn't matter, except to the extent that the letter choice, in combination with previous correspondences, enables some useful words. In Program 1, there are three intervening letter between *d* and *b*; in Program 2, two intervening letters; and in Program 3, seven intervening letters. We far prefer Program 3, given the high incidence of confusion between *b* and *d*.

The first two categories on the chart given earlier in the chapter, consonants and short vowels, comprise all the letters in the alphabet. In time, students will learn words with more complex graphemes, described in Programs 3–8 of the chart. Examples of such words include *boat, paid, chuck, fresh, cow, round*, and *spend*. A variety of considerations enter into the sequencing of those phonic elements as well.

Not All Grapheme–Phoneme Correspondences Are Created Equal

One issue here is the equality of instructional time spent on a given grapheme–phoneme correspondence. Commercial reading series are often divided into a 30-week cycle, with 1 week scheduled for every correspondence. Toward the end of programs' sequences, when the correspondences are less frequent (e.g., *q, v, x, y, z*), two correspondences may be introduced in a week. The 30-week cycle can give the misleading impression that all grapheme–phoneme correspondences taught in each of the 30 weeks are of equal importance. This is not the case.

One commercial reading series in second grade allows exactly 1 week to review the CVC*e* pattern very early during the school year. The CVC*e* pattern had been taught in first grade, but it can be tricky from a decoding standpoint. One week is also the amount of time that is devoted to other patterns, such as *air/are*. The number of one-syllable words one can read if one is proficient with CVC*e* words is too large to list here. The list of words we came up with that contain *air* and *are* include *bare, care, dare, hare, mare, rare, fair, hair, pair, stair, spare, stare, chair*. That's not an insignificant number, yet it's nowhere near the number of CVC*e* words one could come up with. We submit that the number of words a student will be able to read once he has mastered the CVC*e* pattern is considerably more than those he could read if he mastered the graphemes *air* and *are*. It is critical to always remember that word recognition is the goal. We are not suggesting that explicit instruction about *air/are* is wasted, but a weighing of priorities would tilt strongly toward spending time reviewing CVC*es*.

The general issue is that some correspondences are easier to learn than others. Treiman, Broderick, Tincoff, and Rodriguez (1998) pointed to the issues when they noted that results of a study in which they engaged

> shed doubt on the practice, common in United States, of spending the same amount of time on each letter–sound pair. . . . [For instance,] spending the same amount of time teaching the sound of *b* as the sound of *w*. Given that the former is easier for children to learn than the latter. (p. 1538)

Teachers need to use their knowledge of what children tend to have difficulty with and override the basal's distribution of time.

All phoneme–grapheme relationships do not need to be taught. For example, the CVC*e* pattern for the long *e* is of less than trivial use. The only *e* examples we could think of are *these, Crete, Eve, Pete*. On the other hand, the CVC*e* rule involving the long vowels *a, i, o*, and *u* are more common. Less frequent patterns can be brought up when encountered in context. For instance, *ar* usually stands for the /ar/ sound as in *car*. There is, however, an idiosyncratic rule that *ar* preceded by the letter *w* actually stands for the /or/ sound most of the time (*warm, war, ward, wart*). It's worth mentioning when such a word is encountered, but that is enough.

There are 40 to 44 phonemes in English.[2] The 26 letters and combinations of those letters represent the 44 phonemes. However, many of those phonemes can be spelled differently. (Notice the spellings for the long *o* in b*oa*t, h*o*p*e*, sl*ow*, t*oe*.) Hanna, Hanna, Hodges, and Rudorf (1966) identified the number of occurrences of different sound spellings for single phonemes in a corpus of 17,000 most frequent words. For example, /n/ is spelled *n*, as in *neat* (97 %), and also *knife, gnome, inn* (3%).

Godfrey Dewey (1970) identified 561 ways that 42 English phonemes could be spelled! In contrast, Moats (2000) suggested that there are "over 250 spellings" of 44 phonemes. Not only would attempting to teach 250 spellings directly be foolish, with an expenditure of an enormous amount of time, but also the success rate for children would be off the bottom of the chart. The good news is that they do not all need to be taught. Most of the low-frequency spellings will be picked up when reading and in environmental print.

So how much of the 250–561 sound spellings should be taught? The preceding points to a little being better than too much. And, most important, when too much is provided explicitly, the assumption has to be that nothing can be learned without direct explicit instruction. That is not the case. Think of how much you have picked up without being taught, think of how much your students pick up without

---

[2] The discrepancy is a result of researchers using different criteria to identify phonemes.

being taught. The theoretical notion points to self-learning, which has been mentioned in an earlier chapter, a lot of which occurs in the course of other learning.

We now consider irregular words, those English words that do not adhere to the general rules of spelling.

Words That Break the Rules

Given our emphasis on children being able to read real words in the early phases of learning to read, it follows that we also stress the importance of children being able to read connected text near the beginning of reading instruction. There are several reasons. Sentences carry more meaning than individual words, and meaning is the point of reading. Second, engaging with connected texts (sentences, paragraphs, little stories) in which there are a number of words that correspond with what children are learning in phonics is a high-value practice. Among the reasons it is of high value is that there is some content—a sentence, paragraph, story has to be about something—that the teacher and students can discuss. The standard reading fare at this point might be something like the following: "The cat did not sit on the hat. The cat did not sit on the pan. The cat sat on the can." To check on comprehension, as well as providing a model of how to deal with what a text is saying, the teacher could ask, "Where did the cat decide to sit?"[3] To provide a prompt for a little bit of discussion, the teacher could ask, "Why do you think the cat made that decision?" Dealing with content that has been read is a major aspect of comprehension.

Now comes the problem of how connected text can be written given the need for irregular, high-frequency words that do not follow the English rules of pronunciation. And many high-frequency words are function words (e.g., *the*, *of*, *are*). Such function words serve as the glue that ties words together in connected text.

How are irregular words taught? They need to be memorized, so repetition is essential. And repetition in a variety of ways, particularly game-like repetition, is called for, such as reading connected texts such as the previous one. Indeed, connected text cannot be written without some irregular words. And connected text supports sight-word learning. Most kindergarten curricula call for teaching children some sight words. So as they are learning to sound out regular words, they are also being asked to memorize some words. What follows is a suggested procedure for teaching students irregular high-frequency words:

---

[3] *The Cat in the Hat* and similar stories have been criticized by some, who say they make no sense, that they are a poor model for what good stories are about, and that children don't like them. Our experience, and many of our teacher friends, say that isn't the case. Children enjoy, like, even love and laugh at such stories. But of course children should experience the many delightful real stories in trade books through read-alouds. And of course children who can read better stories should be reading better stories.

- Say the target word and tell children that it is one of the rule breakers.
- Display a sentence in which the target word appears.
- Read and reread the sentence aloud.
- Indicate the target word and read it aloud. Ask the students to read it aloud several times.
- Point to each letter and ask the students to spell the word aloud. It is a good idea to occasionally ask students to write the words, saying each letter.[4]

At a very early phase, students are taught to accept certain contradictions: Words can be read by applying consistent patterns—except when they do not follow regular patterns. But the significant majority of words do follow regular patterns. We have found it useful to be explicit about the contradictions and to tell the students that there are two types of words: sound-out words and rule breakers. I (Mark) typically go into kindergarten classrooms at midyear and engage students in activities to distinguish sound-out words from rule breakers. Once, after a couple of sessions I entered a room and wrote *who* on the board. Without blinking an eye, one child yelled out, "That's one of those law breakers."

Isabel's Anecdote

In the course of teaching first grade for several years, having friends who are first-grade and kindergarten teachers, and knowing many first-grade teachers in classes at the university, I have been privy to many "kids say the funniest things." They come to mind occasionally when some topic that is under discussion triggers a memory. When thinking about the phonics landscape, I remembered several.

A student, who was a first-grade teacher in a master's class, told us about Joey. Joey was fully aware that he had a lot of difficulty writing words with *b* and *d*—a rather common phenomenon. In the course of going over a paper with Joey, I pointed to a *b* (written like a *d*) and two *d*'s written like *b*'s. Joey gritted his teeth and kind of growled, narrowed his eyes, and with a menacing expression said, "I'd like to get the guy who made the *b* and *d* that way!" Sometime later, when Joey had conquered the *b* and *d*, I asked him if he still would want to get the guy. He replied, "You bet!"

When I was in California, a first-grade teacher friend, Lilly, told me she didn't know where it came from, but the idea that, at 26 letters, we had too many letters to spread among the children. Lilly told the children that there were other languages that had about 26 letters but that Russian had 33, seven more than we had. "Poor Russians." "I feel sorry for the Russas [sic]." "I'm never going to Russia." Then she told the children that the Hawaiian language had only 13 letters. Immediately, one child said, "No wonder so many people go to Hawaii." Indeed, the child had it half right: lots of people who live in California go to Hawaii!

---

[4]The reason to spell irregular words is that it provides a bit of a support for memorizing these words.

And finally Randolph, a bright, talkative, talented, funny child, decided to come to my rescue when my class was to perform for the kindergarten, which included singing and acting out the alphabet song. When we were practicing and I got ready to start the song, Randolph said, "Ms. B, Let me start it, you are a good teacher, but not a good singer." As well as saying the funniest things, kids often get to the core of a matter.

● ● ● ● ● ● ● ● ● ● ● ●YOUR TURN● ● ● ● ● ● ● ● ● ●

- You may want to get a sense of the different speech mechanisms involved in pronouncing consonants and short vowels by uttering phonemes for several items in each category and paying attention to where your lips are and what you are doing with your breath. Say *b* and *k*. Where are your lips? Now say the short vowel sound for short *a* and *o*. Where are your lips? This time, say the sounds of /b/ and /a/. Say the pair several times. What is the difference between where your lips are for each sound? Again say /b/ and /a/ several times and notice what you are doing with your breath. When you say /b/, notice that you cut off the sound at the end. Now say /a/. Notice that you do not stop the sound; you could extend it as long as you like.

- If you want to get a sense of the differences in the speech mechanisms for uttering long and short vowels, say short *a* and long *a*. Try it again. Say the short *i* and long *i*.

- Some folks find it enlightening and fun to identify the words that could be made from, let's say, the first third of a sequence. We suggest Program 3. Make the table as shown below.

m, a, s, d	mad, dad, sad, Sam, dam
t	
p	
c	
r	
n	
i	

CHAPTER 5

Teaching Children the Sounds That Letters Represent

In this chapter, we build on the concepts of the alphabetic principle (Chapter 2) and the phonics landscape (Chapter 4). We discuss the role of knowing the letter names, especially in terms of supporting letter-sound instruction. Learning the phonemes represented by letters is the competency that is essential for learning to read, but it can be difficult to learn. Thus the major part of this chapter deals with introducing and maintaining letter–sound relationships for consonants, vowels, and phonemes represented by more than one letter. But first we discuss issues related to letter names.

Learning Letter Names

In the United States, many children learn or begin to learn the letter names before they enter school (Mason, 1980). The alphabet song is virtually universal and is often a child's initiation to the alphabet. *Sesame Street* has certainly contributed to children's letter-name knowledge, as have other, more recent TV programs targeted to young children. Parents and grandparents have confidence that they are doing the right thing when they point out letter names in the environment. Although many children enter school knowing all or some of the letter names, other children do not. All children need to know the names of the letters, and the schools are responsible for making sure that they do. Research shows that not knowing the letter names is strongly related to having serious difficulty learning the sounds that are associated with letters (Ehri & Wilce, 1979).

The question about letter names that researchers have been most interested in is whether knowing the letter names influences learning the letter sounds. Some find that it does not, and others find that it does. Gibson and Levin (1975) were among the first who viewed letter naming as unimportant to subsequent reading success. Feitelson (1988) pointed to several studies that had not found causal connections between letter-name knowledge and decoding. But most researchers who have conducted empirical studies concluded that knowledge of letter names facilitated learning letter sounds (see, e.g., Hohn & Ehri, 1983; McBride-Chang, 1999; McGuinness, 1997; Treiman, Tincoff, Rodriguez, Mouzaki, & Francis, 1998).

Researchers offer several reasons for the facilitative effects of knowing letter names. One is that most letter names include letter-sound information. Say the names of the letters *b*, *f*, and *k* and listen for sound information. Notice how much /b/ you hear in *be*, /f/ in *ef*, /k/ in *kay*. Another reason that researchers find letter names facilitative of learning letter sounds is that to learn a letter sound, it needs to be paired with something. The sound /b/ could, we suppose, be paired with a picture of a boat—/b/ is the first sound in *boat*—but that is arbitrary; /b/ could just as well be paired with *ball*. McGuinness (1997) describes the "sound picture" that was developed for the Phono-Graphix™ in which letters are called "sound pictures," so /b/ doesn't stand for the letter *b*—rather, /b/ stands for this sound picture *b*. The avoidance of the letter name is done because some view it as getting in the way of learning the letter sound. Although both of us have occasionally encountered a few children who, when first being taught the letter sound after having learned the letter names, say the letter name when asked for the letter sound, it took little time or effort to clear the confusion. Perhaps it is because we took care to label the letter *b* as the letter name and /b/ as the letter sound. Thus we think that pairing the letter sound with the letter name is the most natural pairing.

When it comes to the order of teaching the letters, most professionals who study alphabet issues have no objection to using alphabetical order to teach the letter names. That seems sensible because, if children know anything about the alphabet, they are likely to know how to recite it in order or in portions of order. (As discussed in Chapter 4, that is not the case for the letter sounds.) It is interesting that children's knowledge of both letter names and letter sounds is related to the order of the alphabet itself. It appears that teachers pay more attention to the letters at the beginning of the alphabet than those at the end. Actually, although it was a very long time ago, I (Isabel) am quite sure that I did that, too.

Learning the letter names does not seem to be a major obstacle for young children. We believe that letter names should be taught and established before letter sounds are introduced. Letter names need to be taught if for no other reason than the pragmatic use of letter names in classroom talk: "Your papers are in the *P* cubbyhole." And with letter–sound instruction: "The letter *s* stands for the /s/ sound"; "You said the sound for *d*, we are looking for the sound for *b*."

Teaching Letter–Sound Correspondences

Principles for Teaching Letter–Sound Correspondences

Three principles underlie the instructional strategies for teaching letter–sound correspondences. One that has already been established (Chapter 4) is that the sequence adapted for teaching letter–sound relationships enables several words to be read with a handful of correspondences. Toward that end, it is essential that teaching letter–sound correspondence incorporates blending, which we consider in Chapter 6. When a new correspondence has been introduced, that correspondence, in conjunction with previously learned correspondences, needs to be used in blending. That is, teaching letter–sound correspondences must be integrated with blending. In that way, the accumulation of learned correspondences enables new words.

The second principle is that attention needs to be brought to the target grapheme in all positions in which it is found in words. Simply put, children need to learn that a *t* is /t/ in *tan* as well as in *pat*, and they need to learn this from the very beginning of instruction. In fact, there is evidence that most children, even poor readers, are able to decode the first letter, or grapheme, in a word. But many young learners do not decode the last graphemes in words well, and they are especially poor at decoding the medial grapheme (McCandliss et al., 2003).

In the McCandliss and colleagues (2003) study, results of a pretest administered before children who were poor readers engaged in an intervention showed that they could correctly decode the first grapheme in words 70% of the time, the final grapheme 54%, and the medial, which was a vowel, 40% of the time. It is likely that it is both the within-word position of all the vowels in all the words in the study and the nature of vowels that caused the medial decoding problem. But whatever the cause, given the role of vowels in English, the results suggest that, at best, the children could accurately read merely 40% of the pretest words. Needless to say, this is enormously serious for children's progress as readers.

The notion that letter position plays a role in decoding problems is supported by the McCandliss and colleagues (2003) data. So it follows that position within a word is relevant to the application of letter-sound knowledge.

The third principle for the letter–sound instructional strategies is that pho neme awareness is folded into the specific letter–sound correspondence being taught. This contrasts with the kind of phonemic awareness instruction that deals with sounds in spoken words with no letters present (NRP, 2000). As noted in Chapter 3, phonemic awareness can be enhanced through the use of printed letter cards. In fact, the reader will notice some similarities between the activities of Chapter 3 related to phonemic awareness and the activities of this chapter related to letter–sound correspondences. Both sets of activities involve printed letter cards and require the student to segment phonemes. The similarity is intentional, and we believe that these types of activities can help students' phonemic awareness, as well as their letter-sound knowledge.

Strategies for Teaching Letter–Sound Relationships

Before presenting lessons introducing letter–sound relationships, we note that we have made use of a "script" format. Sometimes we provide the actual words or dialogue that a teacher might use in teaching the lessons. We did this, as we did in Chapter 3, because it is an economical way of presenting the information, not because we expect teachers to use the exact words that we have chosen. Our intention is not just to provide the steps in a procedure but also to share the reasons for the steps. As teachers become familiar with the procedures and principles underlying their use, they can then adapt the dialogue to meet the needs of their students and to reflect their own teaching style.

Materials

To teach the lessons for letter–sound relationships represented by consonants, you will need the following materials:

- Large letter cards that you can use for demonstration purposes.
- Pocket chart for displaying the large letter cards.

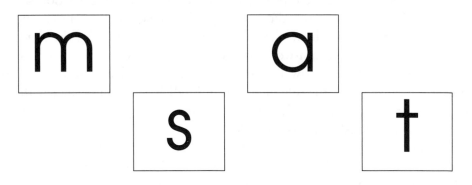

- A set of individual letter cards for each student.
- Individual Word Pockets for each student to use in sorting and displaying letters.

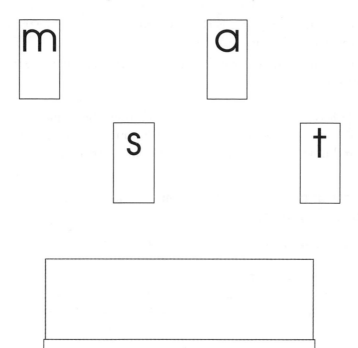

The letter cards and directions for making the Word Pocket can be found in Appendix 4.

Lesson Sequence for Teaching Consonant Letter–Sound Correspondence

The goal of the lessons that follow is for a child to be able to look at letters in words and say the speech sounds that those letters represent. The six steps in the lesson for teaching a consonant letter–sound correspondence are as follows:

1. Develop phonemic awareness by focusing children's attention on the sound represented by a particular letter in the initial position.
2. Connect the printed letter with the sound the letter represents.
3. Discriminate among words that have the letter sound in the initial position and those that do not.
4. Develop phonemic awareness by focusing children's attention on the sound represented by a particular letter in the final position.

5. Discriminate among words that have the letter sound in the final position and those that do not.

6. Discriminate among words that have the letter sound in the initial and final positions.

In the sample lesson that follows, you can see how the sequence is carried out. Many steps in the sequence are followed by a commentary explaining why the step is provided and how it might function in children's learning.

A Sample Lesson for Teaching the Letter–Sound Correspondence for *m* /m/

Focus of lesson sequence	Procedure
1. Develop phonemic awareness of the target sound in the initial position.	*I know a story with a character called* Mary Mouse *who drank lots of milk.* *Who drank the milk?* *The words* Mary *and* Mouse *begin with the same sound: the /m/ sound.* *Watch my mouth: /m/.* *You say /m/.*

Commentary: The purpose of this phonemic awareness step is to kind of "start the engine" by focusing attention on the target sound to be learned. It is a very easy step because the teacher tells the children what to do, but the children have the experience of producing the sound and noticing what that's like.

Note: For older students, it is important to use more appropriate words. For example: The words *machine* and *manager* begin with the same sound, the /m/ sound.

Focus of lesson sequence	Procedure
2. Connect the printed letter with the sound the letter represents.	Show children the large letter *m* card. *This is the letter* m. *The letter* m *stands for the /m/ sound in* Mary *and* Mouse. *You say /m/. Each time I touch the letter* m, *say /m/.* [Touch *m* several times.]

Commentary: This is the whole point of the lesson sequence: to look at the written *m* and say /m/, but to do so in more complicated letter environments— for example, when several letters are being shown successively. An even more important context is one in which the letter appears within a word, such as *man* or *ham*. Even though the point of the lesson is to connect a printed letter with its sound, and this is what Step 2 does, this is not enough work with the *m* to /m/ relationship to assume learning. Thus we go on to the next step.

Focus of lesson sequence	Procedure

3. Discriminate among words that begin with /m/ and those that do not.	At this point, students will need their own letter *m* cards.
	    If the word I say begins with the /m/ sound, hold up your m *card and say /m/. If it doesn't begin with the /m/ sound, shake your head back and forth for "No."*
	    Example words include *monkey, many, house, make, table,* and *money*.

Commentary: Step 3 provides another opportunity to identify the /m/ phoneme at the beginning of words and to say /m/ in the presence of the letter *m*.

Note: Here we'd like to remind teachers of young children to use their skills and knowledge of children to make the preceding step and the other steps fun. For example, in the preceding step sometimes you could ask the children to lock their lips if the word does not begin with /m/, or put the *m* card behind their backs if the word does not begin with *m*. The secret to keeping attention is to vary slightly how children respond but not to overwhelm the point of the step by adding too many variations.

Focus of lesson sequence	Procedure

4. Develop phonemic awareness of the target sound in the final position.	*I am used to sweep the floor. What am I?*
	    After *broom* is said and repeated several times, explain that *broom* ends with the letter *m*, the letter that stands for the /m/ sound. Say some more words that end with the letter *m*, and have students repeat them.
	    Example words include *jam, room, drum,* and *farm*.

Commentary: Notice how soon the sequence of steps moves to the target in the final position. The reason is that one of the important principles underlying the instructional procedures here is that children learn that a given letter represents the same sound in any position in words. Recall the McCandliss and colleagues (2003) data showing that children with inadequate decoding capability decode final graphemes correctly only 54% of the time.

Focus of lesson sequence	Procedure
5. Discriminate among words that end with /m/ and those that do not.	This step is just like Step 3, but the focus is on the final position. *I'll say some words. If the word ends with the /m/ sound, hold up your m card. If it doesn't end with the /m/ sound, put your m card behind your back.* Example words include *ham, tree, broom, dream, drink,* and *drum.*

Commentary: As noted, this step is the same as Step 3, with the focus changed to the /m/ in final position. As such, it provides another opportunity to identify the /m/ at the end of words and to say /m/ in the presence of the letter *m.*

Focus of lesson sequence	Procedure
6. Discriminate among words that have /m/ in the initial and final positions.	Students will need their Word Pockets. *I'll say some words that begin with /m/ and some that end with /m/. When a word begins with /m/, put your letter m at the beginning of the Word Pocket. When a word ends with /m/, put your letter m at the end of the Word Pocket.* Some example words include *mix, drum, him, money, swim, milk, mouse,* and *ham.*

Commentary: In addition to providing children with practice noticing whether a word begins or ends with /m/, the requirement that the students place their *m* letter at the beginning or end of their Word Pockets connects the phonemic position with the visual position.

If /m/ is in the initial position of the word:

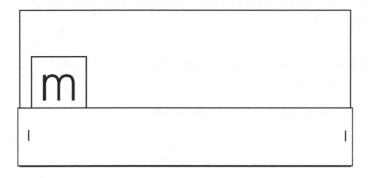

If /m/ is in the final position of the word:

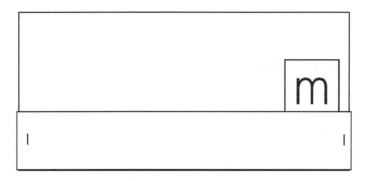

The six steps just discussed, and the many example words to which each step can be applied provide quite extensive instruction. For children who catch on easily, first reduce the number of example words in Steps 3 and 5. Subsequently, Steps 3 and 5 can be omitted. Finally, reduce the number of example words in the remaining steps. The preceding steps can be used for all single-letter graphemes.

The steps are also appropriate for the consonant digraphs *ch, sh,* and *th.* When teaching consonant digraphs, the letters should be on one card, and children should simply be told that the letters *ch,* for example, represent the /ch/ sound in words such as *chin* and *chair.*

Lesson Sequence for Teaching Short-Vowel Correspondences

The following six steps for introducing short vowels are the same as those for consonants; however, instead of moving from initial position to final position, the sequence for short vowels goes from initial position to medial position.

More attention is provided to the medial position. Commentaries are provided only if there is something different for vowels than for the corresponding consonant letter–sound step.

A Sample Lesson Sequence for Teaching the Letter–Sound Correspondence for *a* /a/

Focus of lesson sequence	Procedure
1. Develop phonemic awareness of the target sound in the initial position.	Provide several strong examples of words that begin with the target sound: *add, apple.* Have children repeat each word. Tell children the words begin with the /a/ sound. Ask children to say /a/ several times.

Focus of lesson sequence	Procedure

2. Connect the printed letter with the sound the letter represents.	Show children a large letter *a* card.
	    Say the letter name.
	    Tell children that the letter *a* stands for the /a/ sound in the target words: *add* and *apple.*
	    Tell children to say /a/ each time you touch the *a* letter.

Focus of lesson sequence	Procedure
3. Discriminate among words that begin with /a/ and those that do not.	Students will need their own *a* letter cards. Have children show their *a* letter cards and say /a/ when you say a word that begins with /a/ and put a finger over their lips when a word does not start with the /a/ sound. Some examples include *after, app, window, glass, add, dog, ask,* and *absolutely.*

Focus of lesson sequence	Procedure
4. Develop phonemic awareness of the target sound in the medial position.	Tell children there are a lot of words that have the /a/ sound in the middle. *I'll say some words that have the /a/ sound in the middle—like* baat *and* caan. *You say them after me and stretch out the /a/ as I do:* caat, jaam, maan, snaap, glaad. *This time when I say a word, I won't stretch out the /a/ sound, but listen for the /a/. First I'll say a word, and then you say it:* mat, flap, glad, hat.

Commentary: Identifying a vowel phoneme in the middle of a word is much more difficult than doing so at the beginning of a word. The reason is that in speech phonemes often overlap with the previous phoneme (i.e., we begin saying the /a/ sound in *bat* while a remnant of /b/ is present). Thus we recommend stretching out the vowel sound on the first encounter.

Focus of lesson sequence	Procedure
5. Discriminate among words that have a medial /a/ and those that do not.	*I'll say some words that have the /a/ sound in the middle and some words that do not have the /a/ in the middle. Hold up your a card and say /a/ if you hear a word that has /a/ in the middle. Close your eyes if the word does not have the /a/ sound.* Example words include *baath, buus, maap, taan, hiip, paast, choomp,* and *chaamp.* Do another round in which the words are said naturally.

Commentary: Notice the recommendation to stretch out the vowel phoneme during the first round. This may be especially important as the children will be discriminating among several medial vowel phonemes, which are articulated in close speech proximity to each other.

Focus of lesson sequence	Procedure
6. Discriminate among words that have /a/ in the initial and the medial positions.	*This time when you hear a word that begins with /a/, put your letter a card at the beginning of the Word Pocket. When you hear a word that has /a/ in the middle, put your letter a in the middle of your Word Pocket.* *Examples include apple, tap, ant, sad, band, ask, ran, ashes, fan, and fast.*
Note: Depending on how students respond, you may want to stretch out the /a/, especially in the medial position, and then do another round in which the words are said naturally.	

If *a* is in the initial position of the word:

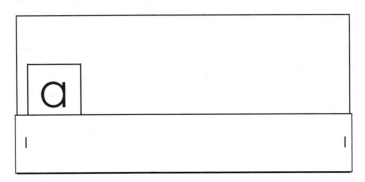

If *a* is in the medial position of the word:

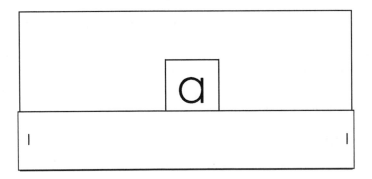

    The previous procedures are applicable to all the short vowels: *a, e, i, o, u.* Note that it is important that students practice discriminating among letter–sound correspondences.

After several letters have been introduced, do quick game-like activities in which you show each letter and ask for the sound. As students accumulate more letter–sound correspondences, continue the games with small sets of letters that include the newer letters and some earlier ones and both consonants and vowels.

Lesson Sequence for Teaching Two-Letter Graphemes and Their Phonemes

The goal of the sample lesson that follows is for a child to be able to look at two-letter graphemes and say the speech sound that the letters represent (e.g., vowel digraphs, diphthongs, and r-controlled vowels). The procedures are also appropriate for phonograms, as well as other pronounceable units that are represented by more than one letter. The steps in the lesson for teaching correspondences for phonemes represented by multiple letters are:

1. Connect a two-letter grapheme with the phoneme the letters represent.
2. Connect the printed letters with the phoneme the letters represent.
3. In cases in which two two-letter graphemes represent the same phoneme, connect both graphemes with the phoneme (e.g., both ea and ee can represent the long-e phoneme).
4. Discriminate among words that may be competitive with target graphemes.

A Sample Lesson for Teaching Two-Letter Graphemes and Their Phonemes

Using the ee as in seed and the ea as in meat as an example, the steps for teaching two two-letter graphemes that represent the same phoneme are provided next.

Focus of lesson sequence	Procedure
1. Connect ee to long e.	Make the word seed in the pocket chart with letter cards. Read the word and ask the children to read it. Explain that when there are two e's together in a word, they stand for the long-e sound, the sound they hear in the middle of seed. Remove the s and the d. Tell students to say /ee/ when you touch the letters ee. Return the s and d and read seed. Ask children to read the word or say the sound as you run your finger under the word or point to the two e's. Go back and forth between seed and ee.

Commentary: Notice that the new grapheme first appears in a word and then is pulled out of the word. One reason that we prefer to start with a word is that in typical letter–sound sequences, vowel digraphs are introduced after the short vowels. In order not to create confusion between, for instance, one *e* and two *ee*'s, we think it wise to provide the new letter sound in a strong visually presented word before dealing with it in isolation.

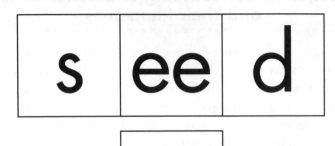

Focus of lesson sequence	Procedure
2. Connect *ea* to long *e*.	Make the word *meat* in the pocket chart with letter cards. Read the word, and ask the children to read it. Explain that when *e* and *a* are together in a word, they sometimes represent the long-*e* sound, the sound in the middle of *meat*. Remove the *m* and the *t*. Tell students to say /ee/ when you touch the letters *ea*. Return the *m* and *t* and read *meat*. Ask children to read the word or say the sound as you run your finger under the word or point to *ea*. Go back and forth between *meat* and *ea*.

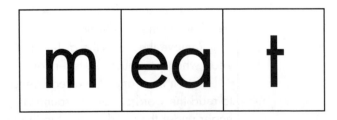

Focus of lesson sequence	Procedure
3. Connect *ea* and *ee* to long /e/.	Put *seed* and *meat* one under the other in a pocket chart. Have students practice reading both words, making the point that *ea* and *ee* both can stand for the long-*e* sound in words such as *seed* and *meat*.

Focus of lesson sequence	Procedure
4. Discriminate among words that may be competitive with *ea* and *ee* words.	Write the words *meat, eat, see, seat, set, sat, meat, met, mat, bee, bet,* and *flea*. Ask the children to read the words.

Commentary: Short-*a* and short-*e* words are included in the preceding list as a means of requiring students to deal with the vowels in the words. That is, if all the words were long-*e* words, students would be less likely to process the vowels. Note that in Appendix 1, Sequence E, there are 15 lists of words that contrast long-vowel digraphs with their potentially competitive short vowels.

Introducing Long Vowels of the CVCe Pattern

We and all the teachers we know introduce the CVCe pattern (consonant–vowel–consonant–*e*) by simply demonstrating what happens when an *e* is put at the end of particular CVC words (*hid* to *hide, mat* to *mate*). Our preference is to acknowledge the silent-*e* "rule" but to put the instructional emphasis on children engaging with the rule, that is, changing *can* to *cane, cane* to *can, tub* to *tube*, and the like. In Appendix 1, Sequence E, all the lists require discriminating CVC's and CVCe's. However, students should be reading text in which both the CVC and CVCe appear: *tub, tube*, and so forth.

Isabel's Favorite Letter–Sound Anecdote

I've used this anecdote in other publications, so you may know it. I love it because I can see those children shouting out their responses and the slight annoyance on the teacher's face.

Many years ago, while I was pursuing my PhD, I worked part time at the University of Pittsburgh's Learning Research and Development Center, where I was engaged in a project to develop a reading program that would allow children to proceed at their own rate. A colleague and I (Beck & Mitroff, 1972) went out to a kindergarten class in May, gave the teacher an *m* letter card, and asked her to teach the *m*- to -/m/ relationship. We audiotaped the lesson.

The teacher held up the *m* letter card and said: "This is an *m*. The name of the letter is *m*, but the sound is /m/ as in *mmmountain*. I want to hear everyone say it."

One child said *m*, two said /m/. Another said *mmmountain*. The teacher said, "No, I want you to say the sound. Listen: /m/ as in *mmmountain, mmmother, mmonkey*. Who can think of another *m* word?"

Hands went up. One child said, "*Mica*, like my name." A second child said, "We went to the mountains once. It was our vacation. We slept in a tent."

With so many concepts floating about, it seemed clear that not all the children would have understood that the letter *m* represents the /m/ sound in speech. So we developed a very simple instructional procedure: go from the letter name to the letter itself. We tried it out with another teacher.

The teacher held up the *m* card and said, "The name of this letter is *m*. You say the name. The *m* stands for the /m/ sound at the beginning of the word *make*. I'll point to the letter, and I'll say its sound."

She pointed and said /m/ several times and then put the card down in front of one child and said, "You point to the letter, and you say its sound." And the child replied, "Its sound."

The moral of this story is that all the best-laid plans can go awry, especially with children!

• • • • • • • • • • • •YOUR TURN • • • • • • • • •

Identify several students in your classroom or a colleague's classroom who do not know or are weak in their knowledge of consonant and short-vowel letter–sound correspondences. If you do not have a child like this in your class, perhaps you can ask a colleague if one of her or his students could help you. Do a very quick check to identify several correspondences that are unknown to the child. A check can be just a list, not in alphabetical order, of consonants and short vowels of which you ask children to say the sound. Depending on the time of the year and the grade, you may have this information from the results of formal tests. Choose three correspondences to teach the children. For younger children, it would be best to use two consonants and one vowel; for older students, one consonant and two vowels will probably give you better information. It is not wise to teach the short *e* and short *i* in the same lesson, as their articulations are too similar.

Make the letter cards and use the procedures discussed in this chapter to teach the letter–sound correspondences. After instruction, assess learning by showing the children each letter and asking them to produce the sound. Then ask yourself:

- Did the children learn all the correspondences? If not, why not? Do you need to go over all of them again? Do you need to go over one that seems to be getting mixed up?

- What did you observe about your ability to present the procedures? How did the students respond? Is there something you need to do more smoothly? Did your pace provide an active lesson?

- As a means of getting comfortable with teaching vowel phonemes that are represented by multiple spellings, it might be useful for you to develop an instructional sequence for teaching the *ay* in *day* and the *ai* in *rain*. The framework for teaching *ee* and *ea* is appropriate for teaching *ay, ai, oa, ow,* and other two-letter graphemes.

CHAPTER 6

Blending

This chapter builds on the concepts presented in Chapter 5 on letter-sound instruction. After children have learned a few letter–sound correspondences for consonants and at least one vowel, they are ready to read some simple words. Learning how to blend will allow them to do that. Blending is a crucial component of being able to decode written words into speech. The importance of blending was emphasized in the NRP's (2000) report, which stated that "programs that focus too much on the teaching of letter–sound relationships and not enough on putting them to use are unlikely to be very effective" (p. 10).

To start, we discuss two issues involved in blending. First, when children attempt to figure out a word by blending sounds, it is not necessary for them to produce a perfectly precise pronunciation. Rather, they need to be able to come up with an approximate pronunciation, which they can refine by matching their pronunciation to that of a word they already know from spoken language. Even as adults, we sometimes need to do that; I (Isabel) do it with medical and pharmaceutical terms, for example. That is, I know some pharmaceutical terms from having heard them said out loud in a physician's office or in drugstores, but upon first seeing such a term in print, I may pronounce it roughly. However, if I can match it to an oral term, I refine it. In particular, I am thinking of the time I asked a pharmacist what the ingredient in cold medicines that can cause some people to become jittery was. He told me that it was *pseudoephedrine*, and I repeated it. A few days later, I learned from the newspaper that pseudoephedrine was being abused by some. When I read *pseudoephedrine* in the newspaper (the first time I had ever seen it in print), my inner speech rendition of the word was wobbly until I recognized that I knew the oral version and was able to refine my approximation with the word in my spoken repertoire and pronounce it properly.

The second issue with blending is that it can be quite difficult for young readers to get the hang of. In this regard, I have long been interested in the lack of instruction that children receive about how to blend words. In the late 1970s, my conclusion about four programs that labeled themselves code-emphasis programs was that only two dealt with blending in any way whatsoever (Beck & McCaslin, 1978). Today, I would say that I gave too much credit to those two programs because I don't think that the approaches really taught children what to do when they needed to put phonemes together to pronounce a word. The problem in those older materials was not that the instructional strategies for blending were not working. The problem was that there was a virtual absence of any useful instructional strategy. The teacher's editions essentially told the teacher to say something like "Stretch out the sounds and blend them together." How to "blend them together" is the problematic link.

Short-Term Memory Issues

We have noticed, on a fairly regular basis, that short-term memory issues may impair students' decoding when they are just learning to decode CVC words. Imagine the following scenario (which is actually quite common). A teacher is trying to help a student, David, decode the word *pat*:

TEACHER: Look at this word. Go ahead: Sound it out.

DAVID: /p/ /a/ /t/.

TEACHER: Now, what is the word?

DAVID: *Tan.*

Some might suggest that David's changing of the phoneme /p/ to /t/ is the result of lack of letter–sound knowledge. We suspect that the reason the child struggled has more to do with short-term memory issues than with knowing his letters and sounds. Is the memory factor in blending really a big problem? After all, first-grade children normally have a memory span that can easily encompass three elements (as shown, e.g., by the Memory for Digits subscale of the Stanford–Binet, which expects memory of three digits at age 3 and of five at age 7). Tests such as digit memory, however, require only that the items that an examiner provides be held in memory. Items need not be generated, and no competing processing interferes with retention. This is not the case during decoding. A substantial amount of other processing (i.e., putting the sounds together) must occur simultaneously with the retention of the phoneme elements. This additional processing is likely to interfere with remembering the sounds, or rehearsal of the sounds may interfere with other processing. Even if our David's short-term memory capacity is larger than three, his ability to hold three independent phonemes in memory while performing all the other cognitive processes involved in reading is limited.

So here is what we think happened when David tried to read *pat*. He was retrieving letter sounds and attempting to hold the sounds in short-term memory and blend them into a recognizable word. While attempting to hold /p/, /a/, and /t/ in short-term memory, only /t/ survived because David had reached the limits of his short-term memory. Psychologists call this phenomenon the *recency effect*, that is, the likelihood of retaining the most recent item (in this case, the sound /t/) in short-term memory. For this reason, it is necessary to enable students to blend phonemes in a way that does not tax short-term memory.

Successive Blending

Is blending taught better now? Yes and no. Sometimes we see teachers asking children to imitate the teacher's rendition of stretching out the sounds. Imitation is a good first step, but instruction has to go further if children are to learn to apply blending independently. What we have seen more often is final blending, which is similar to being asked to stretch out the sounds. That is, teachers ask children to say each sound in a word, /c/ /a/ /t/, and then to blend the three sounds. The problem with final blending is that one has to keep three meaningless phonemes in short-term memory and then blend them.

In order to address short-term memory issues at the intial stages of the decoding process, we strongly recommend successive blending (which has sometimes been called *cumulative blending*). In successive blending, students say the first two sounds in a word and immediately blend those two sounds together. Then they say the third sound and immediately blend that sound with the first two blended sounds. If it is a four-phoneme word, then they say the fourth phoneme and immediately blend that sound with the first three blended sounds. The strong advantage of successive blending is that it is less taxing for short-term memory because blending occurs immediately after each new phoneme is pronounced. As such, at no time must more than two sounds be held in memory (the sound immediately produced and the one that directly precedes it), and at no time must more than two sound units be blended.

Consider what *crust* would be like if an individual were using successive blending:

/c/ /r/ /cr/ /u/ /cru/ /s/ /crus/ /t/ crust

The underlined portions show where blending occurs and illustrates that no more than two sounds need to be held in short-term memory.

Given these issues, I (Isabel) developed a very ritualized procedure for teaching blending, in which physical actions accompany the oral blending. The notion was that the physical action could provide a kind of external representation of what goes on during the blending process.

For example, a child who can demonstrate that he or she can perform the blending procedure independently would start with the letter cards *s*, *a*, and *t* separated from each other and proceed as follows:

1. Point to the *s* and say /s/.
2. Point to the *a* and say /a/.
3. Physically slide the *a* over to the *s*.
4. Slide his finger along the *sa* and say /sa/.
5. Point to the *t* and say /t/.
6. Move the *t* card next to the *sa* to create the word *sat*.
7. Slide his finger under *sat* and say *sat* slowly.
8. Read the word naturally, and indicate that the word is *sat*.

The point of teaching children to blend is so that they have a procedure in their repertoire that they can call on if they need to. Once a child can independently engage in the steps of blending a new word, there is no need for the child to continue to blend words overtly. Blending is a little like the saying "A little salt is good; too much is not healthy." Once children can demonstrate that they know the procedure, they do not need to engage in it routinely.

However, as a way of keeping blending available in children's repertoires, I have seen teachers occasionally fold blending into an activity to check decoding. Specifically I am thinking of the time I observed a small-group session that a first-grade teacher arranged for several children who seemed to be floundering in a particular whole-class lesson. That one child was having difficulty with words ending in *g* was clearly shown when he read *dot* for *dog* (earlier he had read *hot* for *hog*). In the small-group session, the teacher pointed to *dog* and asked the child to blend it. When he got to Step 5 and pointed to the *g*, he looked sideways at his teacher. She smiled, and he said /g/, and proceeded to read *dog*. This time, when he looked sideways, he smiled at the teacher. Then they both laughed.

Teaching Successive Blending

Materials

To teach the lesson for successive blending procedure, you will need the following materials:

- Large letter *s a t* cards for your use during instruction.
- Pocket chart for displaying large letter cards.
- A set of individual *s a t* letter cards for each student.

Procedures for Teaching Successive Blending

The intention of the following procedures is to introduce children to blending by first having children watch you as you do a step and then doing that step themselves.

Place your letters in a pocket chart with spaces between them.

(**s** . . . **a** . . . **t**)

Have students place their cards on their desks in the same way.

s a	Point to the letters one at a time and say, "/s/ . . . /a/." Then tell the students to point to their letters and say the sounds with you as you say them again.
sa	Slide the letter *a* over to the *s*. Run your finger under the *sa* and say, "/sa/ . . . /sa/."
s a	Then move the *a* back to where it was.
sa	Tell students to slide the letter *a* over to the *s* and to slide their fingers under the *sa* and say "/sa/" as you do the same with your cards.
sa t	Slide your finger under the *sa*. Say "/sa/," holding the sound until you point to the *t* and say "/t/." Have students do the same with their letters.
sat	Move the *t* over to the *sa*. Slide your finger under the *sat* and say, "/sat/. This word is *sat*." Move the *t* back to its original position. Have students move the *t* over to the *sa* and read "/sat/."

The techniques for teaching the successful blending procedure include a series of steps that lead the child from imitating the procedure to performing it independently. Essentially, the teacher repeats the linking and blending of sounds three times. At each repetition, the teacher systematically fades out two supports in the process (saying what to do and using her finger to show what to do) and gives greater responsibility to the child, as follows.

1. The teacher models the blending procedure. She models the sounds and the blends and uses finger-pointing procedures and intermittent verbal directions.

2. The children imitate the model while the teacher repeats both the verbal cues and the finger cues to assist them.

3. The teacher repeats the procedure, but this time does not model the sounds or the blends. She gives only the verbal cues and the finger cues to assist.

4. The procedure is repeated. This time, the teacher drops the verbal cues. She gives only finger cues.

5. The child performs the pointing, sounding, and blending steps.

As noted, the detailed procedures given here are provided to introduce children to successive blending. Based on our own observations and, conservatively, hundreds and hundreds of teachers' comments, most children have been able to learn the chain and, even more important, have been able to use the steps to figure out new words. Also very important is their eventual ability to collapse several steps (e.g., /m/ /ast/ or /ma/ /st/). There are individual differences when children are chunking sounds. It matters not, as long as some form of blending preceded the naming of the word.

A strong advantage of the successive blending chain is the precise information available to the teacher in terms of locating an error. If a child makes an error while performing the chain, the teacher knows where the error is—that is, which link in the chain is incorrect. With this kind of precise information, the teacher can give the child a direct prompt. For example, if a child's inability to develop a correct candidate pronunciation of a word was caused by a substituted or omitted phoneme, the teacher could point to the letter and ask the child to say the phoneme. If the child does not provide the phoneme, the teacher could prompt the sound with a silent mouthing cue (showing what the mouth looks like when the phoneme is uttered). For example, when blending the phonemes in *black*, if the child said /b/ /a/, the teacher could point to the *l*, ask for the sound, and if needed provide a silent mouthing cue (show the student what her mouth looks like when she says the /l/ sound); or, if all else fails, she can provide the sound.

As another example, if a child made an error in the blending of the first two letters in *set* and said /sa/, the teacher could run her finger under the *se* and ask the child to say the sound of the two letters together. The availability of precise error information enables the teacher to go right into where the problem is and deal with it. This is in contrast to simply knowing that a child didn't read *black* or *set* correctly.

Successive Blending with Initial Consonant Blends

Successive blending is a strategy that can be taught as soon as a student knows the correspondences for a few consonants and a vowel. As such, students will have had a fair amount of repetition decoding CVC words. The expectation is that students will eventually recognize the words as units and find successive blending wholly unnecessary. However, we encourage use of the strategy at a later juncture, that is, when students are being called on to decode words with initial consonant blends, such as *slip, bring,* and *spot.* Initial consonant blends present a number of interesting issues, two of which we discuss here.

Challenges Reading Initial Consonant Blends

We have observed that when students are first learning letter–sound relationships, particularly after successive blending, they become particularly comfortable pronouncing the CV portion of the CVC word (e.g., /ma/ within /mat/). Some time later, when students are called on to decode words with initial consonant blends, they often slip a vowel sound in between the two initial consonant sounds. Following this theory, for instance, *slip* might become *sulip, prop* might become *perop, flip* might become *fulip,* or similar sounding nonsense words. Perhaps this occurs because of the large exposure they have already had with CVC words.

Additionally, in the study by McCandliss and colleagues (2003), there was a related pattern regarding which consonant within a blend students had difficulty with. In a pretest administered to students before they participated in an intervention, the researchers asked students to read a list of pseudowords. The results were analyzed by position within a word. Some of the relevant findings for this chapter showed that students' decoding was relatively accurate for the first consonant in a word, whether a consonant occurred singularly (*t* as in *top*) or as the first consonant within a consonant blend (*t* as in *train*). Accuracy for consonants in the second position of a beginning consonant blend (such as the *l* in *slip*) was significantly less accurate than decoding accuracy for consonants that appeared in the first position of a consonant blend (such as the *s* in *slip*) at the beginning of a word.

Unlike the pattern of position effects that appeared in the beginning of a consonant blend, position effects within the final region of a word showed that the final consonant of a word was superior to the first consonant in an end-of-word consonant blend. It seems that the problem is in the interior of a word (the *p* and the *n* in *spend*). The reasoning that we suggested is that students often ignore the second consonant of a consonant blend at the beginning of a word because they are looking for a vowel in the second position. It may be that students ignore the first consonant in a final blend because they are looking for a single consonant that ends a word. It might be that they are trying to make a CVC word out of a CCVCC word.

Successive Blending with Initial Consonant Blends

Recall the earlier strategy for successive blending of a word such as *sat.* Ultimately, the student will learn to decode: /s/ /a/ /sa/ /t/ /sat/. Essentially the same procedure can be adapted to a word such as *slip*: /s/ /l/ /sl/ /i/ /sli/ /p/ /slip/. The advantage is that the student is required to pronounce both sounds in the blend, /s/ and /l/, separately and then put them together: /sl/. When students make errors reading such words on the printed page, it can be useful to call attention to each letter in the blend and encourage the student to say the two phonemes together quickly. The primary goal is for the student to become used to pronouncing consonant blends without a vowel or a schwa in between the consonants. Our experience has been that when students are able to pronounce initial consonant sounds in a blended fashion, decoding the rest of the word falls into place. That is, once a student is able to pronounce /st/, he will find it relatively easy to pronounce *step*.

Isabel's Favorite Anecdote

At the beginning phase of learning to blend, children tend to have a heavy hand when they slide a letter card. That is, as they slide letter cards, their fingers press on the cards quite firmly. From that tendency arose one of my (Isabel's) very favorite anecdotes, which I relate next.

When working out the blending procedure and the chain of prompts, I tried the steps out with first-grade children early in the school year. I observed one child who the teacher had told me had just caught on to the procedures and was independently pointing and engaging in the steps. I had noticed that in the course of pointing the child was pressing his finger quite hard. The child was slow and deliberate and seemed to be giving birth to the word, as a colleague who saw him suggested. He completed the steps perfectly and then raised his hand, shook it up and down (the way you might when you've been writing for a long time), and said, "Whew!" My colleague asked, "What's the matter? Are you tired?" The child replied, "No, my finger is hot."

• • • • • • • • • • • YOUR TURN • • • • • • • • •

Try to find a situation in which you can teach a student to blend. The only prerequisite is that the child know the letter–sound correspondences for three consonants and a vowel that can be combined into at least two words. For example, *m, a, n,* and *t* would allow *man, mat, tan,* and *tam*; *m, a, s,* and *d* would allow *mad, sad, dam,* and *Sam.* It is a good idea to practice the procedures with an adult before trying it with a child.

Word Building

This chapter deals with Word Building, an activity that supports decoding and word recognition by giving students opportunities to consistently experience and discriminate the effects on a word of changing one letter. As such, the procedures require students to focus attention on every letter in the sequences of letters that make up words. This attention to letter sequences helps students develop an understanding of English orthography, or spelling patterns.

Developing a sense of predictable English spellings is an important component of reading acquisition. Good readers have a well-developed sense of English orthography, which may be explicit or implicit. For example, if you saw a word that started with *btrz*, you would not identify it as an English word. Or when you see a simple word such as *train*, you know instantly that without the *t*, the word is *rain*. You also know that if the letters *s* and *p* were put in front of *rain*, the word would be *sprain*. These examples are simply instances of your understanding of written English. And because you have such a sense about English, when you read you are able to concentrate on the ideas you are reading about, not the individual words. Word Building helps students develop this sense of how written English works, as well as the details of many spelling patterns.

Word Building lessons are sequences of words in which there is progressive minimal contrast from word to word. That is, given a first word, each subsequent word is different from the previous word usually by one letter (e.g., *man, can, cat, hat, hit, hid, had*). Within each Word Building sequence, children are given a small set of letter cards and directed by the teacher to form a word (*hit*) and read it. Then the teacher instructs children to exchange a letter, delete a letter, or insert a letter, which transforms the current word into the next word in a lesson sequence (*him*). To be successful, children need to pay attention to all the letters in a word.

Being able to attend to all the letters in a word represents full alphabetic decoding, which contrasts with partial alphabetic decoding (Ehri, 1999). In the latter, children might apply their letter-sound knowledge to some of the letters in a new word but not to each of the letters in it. How many of us have heard children read *hat* for *hit, ran* for *rain, back* for *black*, and the like?

The advantage of full alphabetic knowledge goes beyond correctly reading *hit, rain*, and *black*. Several theorists have suggested that full alphabetic decoding plays a role in a self-teaching process (Ehri, 1999; Perfetti, 1985; Share & Stanovich, 1995). The self-teaching process suggests that engaging in a correct but perhaps belabored process may support more sophisticated performance. With this in mind, Share and Stanovich (1995) made the point that engagement in alphabetic decoding may serve as a bootstrapping or self-help mechanism that helps readers progress from early attempts to pronounce new words toward accurate identification of familiar words in ways that capture the important orthographic content that is necessary for accurate and fluent word recognition.

Empirical results from the use of Word Building are quite positive. In McCandliss and colleagues' (2003) intervention mentioned earlier, children who had inadequate reading skills after 1–3 years of schooling engaged in Word Building for 20 sessions. Compared with a matched control group, children in the Word Building group made significantly greater progress on standardized tests of decoding, comprehension, and phonological awareness.

The Word Building Sequences

Word Building sequences are divided into eight categories (see Appendix 1, Sequences A–H).

Category	Contents
A	Individual consonants and short vowels *a, i*, and *o*
B	Short vowels *e* and *u*
C	Consonant blends
D	Consonant digraphs
E	Long vowels of the CVCe pattern
F	Long vowels of the CVVC pattern (digraphs)
G	*R*-controlled vowels
H	Diphthongs

In most cases, a grapheme is introduced in one sequence, and then the next several sequences require the reader to discriminate between the new grapheme and another grapheme, which had been taught previously. For example, lists A4–A6 are set out as follows:

A4: short *i* *p, i, t, s, r, m, d, d, k*	**A5:** short *i*; short *a* *s, i, t, f, a, p*	**A6:** short *i*; short *a* *b, i, t, d, r, p, s, a*
pit	sit	bit
sit	fit	bid
sip	sit	rid
rip	sat	rip
rim	fat	sip
dim	fit	sit
did	sit	sat
kid	sip	bat
rid	sap	bit
rip	tap	pit
sip	sap	pat

A4 introduces the *i* grapheme, standing for the /i/ phoneme, for the first time, and then A5 and A6 require students to discriminate between /i/ and /a/.

The content of the sequences is discussed in the appendices. Here we turn to the procedures for presenting Word Building.

Procedures for Building Words

First, it is important that students are able to recognize the letters and know the letter–sound correspondences for the words they are about to build. We have structured the lists, particularly A and B, so that the early lists use letters that are usually taught early in kindergarten. We have also introduced the five vowels in the same order that they tend to be taught in kindergarten (*a, i, o, e, u*). As such, the A and B Word Building lists are approximately aligned with what is usually taught in kindergarten and then reviewed at the beginning of first grade.

The words in list A5 are used to illustrate the procedures.

Materials

- Large letter cards for the letters in A5, *s, i, t, f, a, p*, for teacher demonstration.
- Pocket chart for displaying large letter cards.

- A set of individual letter cards for each student. Appendix 4 provides all letters and letter combinations, which can be duplicated and laminated for each child.
- Individual Word Pockets for each student for sorting and displaying letters, the directions for which are provided in Appendix 4 (optional).

Student Letter Cards

Before the lesson begins, students should place their letter cards on top of their desks.

Teacher Demonstration

The teacher starts a lesson by using her large cards to make the first word, *sit*, in the pocket chart. The teacher reads the word, asks the children to read it, and tells them that she is going to change one letter in *sit* to make a new word.

> "I am changing the *s* to the letter *f*. The new word is *fit*. Read the word with me [*fit*]. Now, I'm going to change one letter in *fit* to make a new word."

Change the *f* in *fit* to *s* and have students read the word (*sit*).

Words Students Build

Tell students that it's their turn to build words and that you will tell them which letters to use.

> "Now you can build words. I'll tell you what letters to use. Remove the *i* from the middle and put in its place the letter *a*. What is that new word?" (*sat*)

Continue by having students change letters and having each word read aloud.

1. "Take away the *s* card from the beginning and put in its place an *f* card at the beginning. What word did you make?" (*fat*)
2. "Change the *a* to *i*. What's the word?" (*fit*)
3. "Change the *f* to *s*. What's the word?" (*sit*)
4. "Change the *t* to *p*. What's the word?" (*sip*)
5. "Change the *i* to *a*. What's the word?" (*sap*)
6. "Change the *s* to *t*. What's the word?" (*tap*)
7. "Change the *t* to *s*. What's the word?" (*sap*)

As each word is made, write it in a column on the board, and when the sequence is complete, have the column of words read. These same procedures can be applied with occasional minor differences to all the Word Building sequences. It is useful for students to manipulate their own cards at their desks. This helps students to stay more engaged and supports the development of a sense of control over the letters and words. At the same time, it is important that the teacher is also adding, removing, and substituting cards to make words at the large pocket chart.

What's So Different about Word Building?

Full Alphabetic Decoding

Teachers have been engaging in letter substitution for decades, in the forms of word wheels and flip books. It has been my (Isabel's) experience, however, that some teachers develop phonics word wheels or flip books that tend not to put attention where it is needed (i.e., on what is a new or difficult phonic element). Think about a word wheel that a teacher developed to bring attention to the newly introduced short *i* vowel sound. In the word wheel, the *i* remains constant and the initial consonant changes (e.g., *hit, pit, sit*). Then the final consonant is changed (*him, hit, hid*). This was done because the teacher's belief was that by continually showing the *i* and asking that words with the short *i* vowel sound be read, the short *i* would be reinforced. Certainly this is not all wrong. The caveat, however, is that if the vowel sound is always the short *i*, then students' attention needs to be focused on the consonants more than on the *i* because, if all the words have the *i* vowel, there is little need to process the *i*.

If the content goal of a lesson is to know, for instance, the *i* to /i/ relationship, then the new vowel should be contrasted with at least one other vowel. Again, the reason is that we want children to process the *i* to /i/ relationship, and without discriminating it from another vowel, it is not clear that much learning will take place. For this reason, most Word Building lists involve discrimination of this type.

Relatedly, if the content goal is to reinforce a new consonant letter–sound relationship, then the consonants should change so that the child needs to discriminate among newly introduced and previously introduced consonants. Thus, as noted, the idea of substituting letters to form words has been around for some time. But traditionally such activities are not done consistently, and it is not clear that attention is focused on what is important.

Attention to All Letters in a Word

As noted earlier, children who have difficulty with decoding tend not to pay attention to all the letters in a word, as required by full alphabetic decoding. The progressive minimal-contrast activity—one letter changes and a new word results—inherent in Word Building requires students to do this. The lists have been carefully developed to include frequent changes to letters in the initial, medial, and final position whenever possible. This scaffolds the process of decoding each letter position within a word, especially the positions that children may ignore: the medial and final positions.

More Attention to Vowels

There is a lot of evidence that the vowels in English are difficult. Therefore, in the Word Building sequences, vowels are given a lot of attention. In many sequences, there are words that are different from one another only in the vowel. Thus, as children engage in the Word Building sequences, they will need to pay attention to the vowels. I (Mark) have conducted Word Building on a regular basis with struggling or borderline students. At the end of each year, I administer a series of pseudoword assessments. My expectation is that there will still be some confusion with short vowels. Surprisingly, those assessments have shown very little confusion with short vowels, which suggests that Word Building is accomplishing one of its primary goals: solidifying letter–sound correspondences.

Discrimination

The Word Building lists (Appendix 1) were deliberately designed, in most cases, to ask the student to discriminate between the target grapheme and another grapheme that has already been taught and that tends to be confused with the target grapheme. For example, lists E1–E3 involve discrimination between the CVC (short *a*) pattern and the CVC*e* (long *a*) pattern. Similarly, list G12 asks students to discriminate between the /ur/ grapheme and the /ar/ grapheme. As much as is practical, the alternative grapheme has been chosen based on our collective experiences of where students tend to make the most frequent errors.

Where Should Word Building Begin?

The answer to this question depends largely on the target population. In a whole-class environment in which a basal program is being followed, Word Building can easily be included in regular weekly lessons based on the letter–sound patterns being taught. For example, if the basal lesson of the week focused on the letter *i* standing for the short /i/ sound, then Word Building with sequences A4–A9 would make sense. It is, of course, not necessary to use all six sequences if a student appears to be proficient after fewer lists.

Word Building is also useful when trying to get a handle on what's going on with a particular student who sometimes gets it and sometimes doesn't. Here the Specific Phonics Assessments (SPA) can be administered as diagnostic assessments.[1] Additionally, SPAs can serve as a placement instrument to determine the appropriate Word Building sequence in which to place students who transfer into a class later in the year. The SPAs can also be helpful for struggling intermediate students.

Word Building is also strongly recommended for struggling students, usually in smaller groups, as well as in one-to-one situations. With struggling students, Word Building is useful as a primary intervention.

What Do I Do When Students Make Mistakes?

An important teaching opportunity exists when a child misreads a word. The major teaching strategy is to show the child the difference between what she read and what she should have read. As an example, suppose your directions said to put *h* at the beginning, *o* in the middle, and *t* at the end, and, instead of reading *hot*, a child reads *hat*. Immediately show the child the difference. That is, write the two words vertically:

hot
hat

and ask the child to tell you what is different about the two words. There are other ways of correcting and prompting, but a major rule of thumb is to let the child immediately compare her response with the correct response.

Connecting Word Building to Text

It is important that students have opportunities to make connections between the words that they have built and written text in the form of sentences, paragraphs, and stories. There are several sources for such texts. We discuss two: decodable texts and Silly Questions.

But first a word about comprehension. The primary purpose of decodable texts and Silly Questions is to reinforce decoding in actual text. But we must never lose sight of the fact that comprehension is the ultimate goal of reading. Both the decodable text and Silly Questions will give students a chance to grapple with

---

[1] Appendix 2 lays out eight SPAs, which are aligned with the Word Building lists. After students have been taught all of the words in a particular sequence (say D, consonant digraphs), the end of the Word Building sequence directs attention to the appropriate SPA (in this case SPA-D). For convenience, both Word Building sequences and SPAs follow the same A–H organizational structure. The assessments are presented in greater detail in Chapter 8.

some ideas and work through them to make sense of text and construct meaning. While keeping a close eye on phonics—grapheme–phoneme correspondence and errors—teachers should also ask open-ended and meaningful comprehension questions about the text that is in front of the students.

Decodable Texts

Decodable texts are stories in which a target grapheme is repeated in a number of words throughout the story. The passages have characters, plots, and other elements of a story. Providing opportunities for students to read decodable text, preferably aloud with an adult, reinforces the decoding of words with letter–sound patterns from Word Building and supports the development of automaticity. When I (Mark) engage in Word Building, I approach the reading of decodable text as an important part of the process and usually have students spend about one-third of their time reading. Of the available decodable texts, some come as supplementary materials with commercial basal series. Others are freestanding products, some of which are available on the Internet and at bookstores.

As already discussed, it is important that students have opportunities to read connected text in which words with target graphemes are repeated. Following are Examples 1 and 2, which are excerpted from two different commercially available texts that the developers describe as decodable texts. Each purports to focus on the CVC*e* long-*a* pattern. Below each excerpt, the number of times the passage includes a CVC*e* long-*a* word is noted.

Example 1:
In the forest, there lived a **snake** and an **ape**.

The **snake's name** was **Jake**.

The **ape's name** was **Kate.**
- 7 unique CVC*e* long-*a* words (*snake, ape, snake's, name, Jake, ape's, Kate*)

Example 2:
Jane's frog got away!

Where did **Wade** end up?

He jumped in the fish tank.

What a way to have fun!
- 2 unique CVC*e* long-*a* words (*Jane's, Wade*)

With the primary criteria for good decodable text being repetition of target grapheme(s), Example 1 is clearly preferable. And the obvious reason is that it contains seven unique long CVCe long-*a* words, compared with two in Example 2.[2] But examination should not stop here.

Better decodable text with repetition is available if one looks hard enough. However, in an ideal world, decodable text would contain many more words with the target grapheme and several words with another grapheme, already learned, that tends to be confused with the target grapheme. This affords opportunities to elicit discrimination, just as we have provided in the Word Building lists. So let's look at Example 3, in which we made a few small changes to Example 1, so that both long-*a* and short-*a* words were included. Both CVCe and CVC words are bolded and an underline is added for CVC, as well as VC, words.

Example 3:

In the forest, there lived a **snake, <u>an</u> ape, <u>and</u> a <u>bat</u>**.

The snake's name was **<u>Mac</u>**.

The **ape's name** was **<u>Pat</u>**.

The **<u>bat's</u> name** was **Dale**.

- 6 unique long-*a* CVCe words (*snake, ape, snake's, name, ape's, Dale*)
- 6 unique short-*a* CVC or VC words (*an, and, bat, Mac, Pat, bat's*)

Better

The hypothetical Example 3 is preferable to Example 1 because students are required to discriminate between CVCe words (just learning) and CVC words (already learned). The goal is for students to flexibly and nimbly decode CVC and CVCe words when they encounter both in text.

We are unaware of examples of decodable text available that include consistent and substantial discrimination. However, we suggest that Example 3 illustrates how those who work with beginning readers—teachers, reading specialists, coaches—might adapt some texts to make them more useful for decoding practice. Also, as a reminder to teachers and parents: no matter what a label says, we suggest checking to see whether a text contains consistent and frequent examples of target pattern(s) so they can be used as effective decodable text.

Silly Questions

Toward providing some decodable material, we have developed Silly Questions. They are called Silly Questions because, in most cases, they are ridiculous (e.g., "Can a cat rap?"). The children read and answer the questions. Our experiences indicate that the children find them funny, and when asked to explain why they

---

[2]Example 2 also falls short because it includes many other words with the letter *a*, representing many different phonemes, such as in *away, tank, what, a, way, have.*

answered as they did, they often come up with some creative answers, such as the time I (Mark) asked a student, "Can you hide a pig in a hut?" and she answered, "Why would you want to?" Another time a Silly Question asked, "Could a vet's leg get red?" One child said "no" and another said, "Yes, if a cat bit it." We have included two Silly Questions at the bottom of every Word Building list. A glance at some Silly Questions shows that they are not difficult to write. We know teachers who truly enjoy writing them. I (Isabel) know of a group of primary teachers who got together and wrote some. I was told that they had a hilarious time. The two questions that we provided for use at the end of each list can serve as examples. Teachers can write those questions on the board, or put them on sentence strips for repeated use.

Why do the Silly Questions at all? One reason is that they provide a connection to text that enables students to read complete thoughts and practice decoding words with particular patterns in those sentences. Furthermore, the Silly Questions require students to comprehend and discuss the ideas presented in the questions. And finally, we have found that students enjoy grappling with the questions and are usually quite engaged.

Additional Activities

In addition to customary Word Building, there are other activities that can reinforce the content of Word Building lists.

Decoding to Encoding

As indicated in the Word Building procedures, the directions tell the child which letters to put in what place and which to change and then to read the resultant word. This decoding approach is viewed as the primary approach.

A second way to go through the words in a list is for the teacher to say a word and ask the students to move the letter cards to spell the new word. For example, "Change one letter to make *tent* say *sent*." The child's job then is to remove the *t* card and replace it with the *s* card so it spells the word *sent*. We know that decoding and encoding can reinforce each other, and so we recommend using this encoding strategy some of the time following a decoding session.

Dictation (Words)

Students can keep Word Building journals in which they can write some of the words that they have built. The teacher can say a word (e.g., *pat*) and have the student write it. It is most helpful for students to write the words in vertical columns so they can see how the changes in letters result in new words.

Dictation (Sentences)

Teachers can provide sentences that include several words from the lists and have students write them. For example, from Word Building list A5, "I can sip as I sit."

Student-Directed Sequences

Pairs of children can conduct their own Word Building sequences. Individual magnetic letter boards and letters are useful here.

Born Teachers

Many years ago, when I (Isabel) was trying out Word Building, I visited some first-grade classrooms in April that were using Word Building. The first visit was to a first grade at the beginning of the day. When I entered the room I saw that the principal was there monitoring the class until a substitute teacher arrived. The children were engaged in several activities. The principal explained that she had told the class that they could read books at their desks or that several children could get together and play some available board games, of course with the mantra, "If you can be quiet." There were three groups of children, two of whom were engaged with board games and a third group of three students who were in front of the pocket chart. One student, let's call her April, was standing by the pocket chart, and the two others had positioned their desks in front of the pocket chart.

April began by singing, "Are you reeaady?" The two students answered, "Yes, we're reeaady." April immediately proceeded to teach Word Building. She did so with clarity, appropriate pacing, and humor. "Put your *m, e, t* letter cards together on your desk. [No word pocket] Read the word. Change the *t* to *n*, read the word," and on and on. It was virtually perfect. I complimented the "teacher" on the excellent teaching and the "students" on their attention and following directions.

The two students at their desks wanted to show me that they could teach Word Building, too. But time was getting short, and somehow it was determined that they would show me how they could teach blending. The problem that there were two girls who wanted to teach blending was resolved when I suggested that one teach the first step and the other teach the remaining steps. April then became the student. The two teachers were astonishingly good. If some teachers are born, here were three of them.

The girls and I began to chat, and the principal motioned to the door so she and I could chat in the hall. I learned that the girls were teaching the procedures to their Sunday school classes, their younger siblings, and their siblings' friends. When I returned to the classroom, I asked the three girls why they did so much teaching, and one of the girls, who talked like a 50-year-old, said, "These kids have got to learn to read." I asked what was so good about blending and Word

Building. One answered something like, "If you don't know what to do, you really do know what to do." I interpreted that as "if you can't decode a word, you have some procedures you can use."

I asked why they used blending and Word Building, since there were other ways to teach reading. They couldn't imagine other ways. "How can you read without knowing the sounds?" "How can you read without knowing how to put the sounds together?" So I suggested that there were ways that kids were shown words and memorized the whole word. The girl who spoke like a 50-year-old shook her head and said, "It will never work!"

• • • • • • • • • • • YOUR TURN • • • • • • • • • •

A number of teachers who were first implementing Word Building told me that although they felt comfortable with the strategies, they found that when they were presenting Word Building with their classes they had to spend so much "thinking time" getting the steps straight that they had difficulty paying attention to what the children were doing. The theoretical explanation is that they were not yet automatic and had to spend too much of their mental resources on presentation. (We discuss automaticity in the last chapter of this book.) The teachers indicated that they took some advice from a Word Building workshop that they had attended and got a partner—another teacher sometimes, but more often an adult who lived in their home.

One of my happiest memories is of the time the husband of one of the teachers was her partner. His first response was "This is so simple," but after some go-throughs, he humbly indicated, "This is not easy!" The teacher who reported the incident told it to a group of teachers while I was present. There was loud applause from the teacher audience, with comments something to the effect that they could give him much harder things to try.

It is important to emphasize that there is nothing hard about presenting the strategies, but no one can become smooth and fluent without some practice. The teachers that I have observed most recently were all taught by Mark, and they are were quite marvelous. They changed pace, they watched what the children were doing, they went back several steps if they saw that it seemed necessary, they kept a light tone, they said funny things, and so on. My recommendation is that it will be to your advantage to do what I suggest—get some adults, either other teachers or any adult, and practice. Better still, if you have some children who are struggling, try Word Building with them. Or borrow some children from another class. Once you get comfortable with the procedures, it works very well.

CHAPTER 8

Assessment

As we were talking about this chapter in preparation for writing it, we got onto the subject of the large number of types of tests, and for no reason at all we began naming them: standardized, objective, multiple-choice, teacher-developed, achievement, norm-referenced, criterion-referenced, summative, diagnostic. We stopped at diagnostic because what we are going to discuss in this chapter is in the realm of diagnostic, and it was no longer fun to name types of tests.

The current educational context has been called the assessment and accountability era. We're sure some of our readers think children are being overtested and that the nature of the standardized tests that they are given precludes gaining an adequate picture of what children know and can do. Such assessments, norm-referenced assessments, tell you where a student is in relation to other students who take the test. A criterion-referenced assessment gives information about how a student performed in relation to established criteria.

The assessment that we discuss in this chapter, the SPA, provides information about a student's competence with specific content. In the case at hand, the content is the ability to decode words, which are composed of predictable phonics patterns. That is, it will tell you exactly with which phonics elements students are proficient, and likewise exactly with which phonics elements students are having difficulty. As such, the SPA can more finely tune intervention and direct a teacher or reading specialist to the phonics elements with which a student needs to engage. After intervention, a follow-up administration of the SPA will help assess the effectiveness of interventions and provide some ideas about where to go next. To accomplish all of these goals, the assessment uses the decoding of pseudowords as its primary focus.

The Specific Phonics Assessment

There are eight SPAs that are aligned closely with the eight Word Building sequences. The Word Building sequences are found in Appendix 1 and the SPAs in Appendix 2. The first two pages of Appendix 2 provide Administration and Scoring Guidelines, which apply to all eight SPAs. Each SPA consists of two pages, the Teacher Page and the Student Page. The Student Page contains both real and nonsense words that the student is asked to read. Students can read from the Student Pages in Appendix 2 or online from our book's website: *www.guilford.com/p/ beck10*. The procedures are simple. The student reads the words, and the teacher marks errors on the Teacher Page.

When to Administer

Once the phonics patterns for a specific sequence have been taught and a student has had some opportunity for practice, the SPA for that section can be administered. At the end of every Word Building sequence in Appendix 1, a prompt is provided that directs you to the appropriate SPA in Appendix 2. For example, a student who has completed Word Building Sequence D (lists D1–D12) can then take SPA-D.

Sample SPA

Here we provide a sample Teacher Page, which we use to point out the features of an SPA. Following the Teacher Page is the corresponding Student Page. In the case at hand, SPA-E (Appendix 2) focuses on long vowels of the CVCe pattern and covers the content in Word Building lists E1–E15 (Appendix 1). As you can see on the left of the sample SPA, there are two categories of words: Long Vowels—Real and Long Vowels—Nonsense.

Teacher Page
Specific Phonics Assessment E
CVCe Long Vowels

	# long vowels correct	% long vowels correct
1. Long Vowels/CVCe Real		
make bike cute ride	_____/8	_____%
code tape tune bone		
2. Long Vowels/CVCe Nonsense		
rike dobe gake dute mape	_____/16	_____%
zide roke lipe fune jate		
fane bome tupe bige zove vube		

Nonsense Long Vowel/CVCe Recap

C*a*Ce (gake, mape, jate, fane)	_____/4	_____%
C*i*Ce (rike, zide, lipe, bige)	_____/4	_____%
C*o*Ce (dobe, roke, bome, zove)	_____/4	_____%
C*u*Ce (dute, fune, tupe, vube)	_____/4	_____%

Student Page
Specific Phonics Assessment E
CVCe/Long Vowels

Real Words	Nonsense Words	
make	rike	fune
bike	dobe	jate
cute	gake	fane
ride	dute	bome
code	mape	tupe
tape	zide	bige
tune	roke	zove
bone	lipe	vube

Scoring Word Mispronunciations

Traditional scoring practices are encouraged. Generally, errors are indicated by crossing off an incorrectly pronounced letter and writing what the student said above the incorrectly pronounced letter. Words correctly read as units are designated by a solid underline: pad. Words read phoneme by phoneme, /p/ /a/ /d/, are designated by short lines under each letter: p a d.

Fractions and Percentages

On the preceding Teacher Page, across from "1. Long Vowels/CVCe Real," the teacher enters the number of target phonemes in real words correctly read, which, when entered over the denominator, in this case 8, is a fraction. Let's assume that the student read the target phoneme correctly in 7 of the 8 real words. You would enter the numerator 7 over the provided denominator, 8, and arrive at the fraction 7/8. You are then asked to convert the fraction into a percentage, so $7 \div 8 = 87.5\%$. The percentage 87.5% is then entered in the second column.

Moving to "2. Long Vowels/CVCe Nonsense," the teacher enters the number of words in which a target phoneme was correctly pronounced over the denominator, in this case 16, and the resulting fraction. Assuming the student decoded the target grapheme correctly in 5 words, the administrator would enter the fraction 5/16 in the first column, which converts to the percentage 31.3%.

Why bother to convert the fractions to percentages? Comparisons of fractions are not useful when the fractions have different denominators. It is only through use of percentages that we can make a useful apples-to-apples comparison of how well a student decoded real words compared with nonsense words. By comparing the total percentage of real words with the total percentage of nonsense words, one can get an idea of whether the student is memorizing whole words without appreciation of the alphabetic principle. Remember Theresa from Chapter 2? Had she taken such an assessment, all indications are that she would have scored high on the percentage of real words and quite low on the percentage of nonsense words. Recall that it wasn't until Lisa, the teacher, brought Theresa's response to class, where we analyzed them, that Lisa was able to get the full picture about Theresa. An SPA would have alerted Lisa a lot earlier to Theresa's problem.

Recap Section: Nonsense Words Only

In every SPA, a recap section is included. Among all of the nonsense words assessed, there will always be four that include a specific grapheme. For example, in our previous sample Teacher Page, for long vowels of the CaCe pattern, the student was asked to decode four nonsense words: *gake, mape, jate, fane*. The administrator of the test enters in both fractional terms (___/4) and percentage terms (0, 25%, 50%, 75%, or 100%), how many times the student pronounced the long *a* sound and left the *e* silent. Because we are not testing consonants in this SPA, those errors (e.g., *gade* for *gake*) are not included as errors for our purposes. Thus a student would get credit for having read *gake* correctly.

Observations/Recommendations

Probably the most useful information on the Teacher Page is the notes the teacher writes. "Observations/Recommendations" will include specific information about which graphemes a student has difficulty with and any recommended course of action. For example, they may be as simple as noting patterns a student is having difficulty with, such as *ea* or */u/* for *y*. More general observations can also be noted. Possibilities might include: "accurate, but slow," "fails to read as units," "inconsistent."

Unitization

Although the primary goal of the SPA is to determine whether students are accurately decoding predictable phonics patterns, in our experience, there is another use for the same information; that is, to determine whether students are reading phoneme by phoneme or as units. Often, at early stages, many students begin to recognize CVC words as units. More struggling students, however, continue to sound out such words phoneme by phoneme. As noted earlier, one student might read the word *dig* as a unit, and another might sound out each phoneme. The second student is reading just as accurately as the first, but she is not recognizing the word as a unit. Phonics instruction with short *i* is not the called-for intervention because she is accurate. Repetition reading of CVC words would be of benefit.

Case Studies

What follows are three examples of students who took the SPAs at the beginning of second grade. All three students had been considered struggling readers based on classroom performance and formal tests in first grade and early second grade. I (Mark) decided to administer several SPAs for specific sequences, looking at patterns that had been taught in first grade. These students are included as examples of how the data from the SPAs guided my instruction and interventions going forward. The following analysis is derived from the students' performances specifically on the CVC*e* portion of the assessment in early second grade.

London

London did quite well on the CVC*e* portion of the SPA in September of second grade. A truncated version of her results follows:

London (September)	# long vowels correct	% long vowels correct
1. Long Vowels/CVCe Real	8/8	100%
2. Long Vowels/CVCe Nonsense	14/16	88%
Nonsense Long Vowel/CVCe Recap		
long *a*	/4	%
long *i*	/4	%
long *o*	/4	%
long *u*	/4	%

Given London's scores, it was not necessary to identify how well she did on each of the four CVC*e* graphemes. Phonics was not her challenge. She had been identified as a struggling reader based on fluency and classroom performance in first and second grade. It was therefore necessary to examine fluency and comprehension and decide on the next step.

Billy

Now let's look at another second-grade struggler, Billy. In contrast to London, as shown here Billy performed poorly on the first CVC*e* SPA of second grade.

Billy (September)	# long vowels correct	% long vowels correct
1. Long Vowels/CVCe Real	7/8	88%
2. Long Vowels/CVCe Nonsense	3/16	19%
Nonsense Long Vowel/CVCe Recap		
long *a*	1/4	25%
long *i*	1/4	25%
long *o*	1/4	25%
long *u*	0/4	0%

In almost every case, when Billy decoded a nonsense word, he pronounced the short version of the vowel (e.g., *gak* for *gake*). This large discrepancy between real words (88%) and nonsense words (19%) helps us to conclude that Billy is able to memorize words but is not yet able to sound out words he's never seen. If this doesn't change, we predict that over time Billy's memory load will become too heavy to carry.

Another useful piece of information that can be gleaned from the results is that Billy performed approximately the same on all four of the long vowels. He did not, for example, read most long *a* words correctly and most long *i* words incorrectly. With an exception or two, he simply read all of the real words correctly and all of the nonsense words incorrectly. The conclusion is easy here: Billy has difficulty with the rule as it applies to all long vowels, not just one or two specific long vowels.

The goal is for Billy to generalize a correspondence and then apply it to all appropriate words. Clearly, the called-for interventions for Billy are activities geared toward understanding and discriminating between CVC and CVCe words such as *tap* and *tape*, Word Building, reading of decodable texts that are composed of CVC and CVCe words, and sentence dictation. That is exactly what I (Mark) did for each of the four common CVCe patterns for approximately 4–6 weeks, three times per week, for 20–25 minutes per session. The results from the follow-up SPA show that these approaches were successful.

Billy (November)	# long vowels correct	% long vowels correct
1. Long Vowels/CVCe Real	8/8	100%
2. Long Vowels/CVCe Nonsense	14/16	88%
Nonsense Long Vowel/CVCe Recap		
long *a*	4/4	100%
long *i*	3/4	75%
long *o*	4/4	100%
long *u*	3/4	75%

Billy clearly responded to intervention and made great strides in understanding the long vowel/silent *e* rule as demonstrated by his 88% overall score on the nonsense words, an increase from 19% a few months earlier. He was able to apply it to nonsense words, and, perhaps best of all, he was able to apply it to all long vowels. Because the rule is very consistent, Billy learned to appreciate the consistency and used it when reading text. None of this would have been possible if I did not have the information from the September assessment to guide me.

Carol

Carol also took the CVCe portion of the assessment in September. As can be seen, her results were mixed.

Carol (September)	# long vowels correct	% long vowels correct
1. Long Vowels/CVCe Real	7/8	88%
2. Long Vowels/CVCe Nonsense	11/16	69%
Nonsense Long Vowel/CVCe Recap		
long *a*	4/4	100%
long *i*	4/4	100%
long *o*	3/4	75%
long *u*	0/4	0%

Carol also did much better with real words than nonsense words. And, as her score indicates, she had a specific problem with long *u*. Unlike Billy, who had had difficulty applying the rule in general, a closer look at the percentages indicates that Carol had difficulty with one long vowel. For interventions, we focused on the long-*u*-silent-*e* pattern (e.g., t*u*n*e*). I kept in mind that long *u* silent *e* is often taught at the end of first grade without much opportunity for review.

Carol (November)	# long vowels correct	% long vowels correct
1. Long Vowels/CVCe Real	7/8	100%
2. Long Vowels/CVCe Nonsense	14/16	88%
Nonsense Long Vowel/CVCe Recap		
long *a*	4/4	100%
long *i*	4/4	100%
long *o*	4/4	100%
long *u*	2/4	50%

After interventions, Carol did improve. As you can see, there was progress, but the long *u* grapheme remained problematic for her.

The Specific Phonics Assessment Is and Is Not . . .

As illustrated, the SPA gives precise information about students' accuracy with specific phonics patterns. But the SPA does not assess automaticity nor irregular high-frequency words. The SPA does not assess every conceivable phonics pattern or even every single one taught between grades K and 2. <u>It focuses on most of them, particularly the most consistent and the patterns used in more words</u>.

I (Mark) have used the SPAs regularly for K–2 students, both for individuals and for a total classroom population. I have also used them for the occasional student in the intermediate grades. Although they do not always provide all of the information needed, I have found them to be an efficient, effective way of gathering information about students' proficiency with phonics patterns and whether progress is being made.

You Got Any More of Those Crazy Words? I Love Them

Using nonsense words for assessment can cause certain difficulties with some students, particularly the first time they encounter them. I recall giving SPA-B to a student, apparently the first time he ever was asked to decode nonsense words. He was bright and talkative. As he decoded the 20 words from SPA-B, the dialogue went something like the following.

> DEANDE: /t/ /i/ /g/ *tig, nup, lon.* . . . What kind of words are these?
>
> MARK: Remember, they are nonsense words, not real words. They don't make any sense.
>
> DEANDE: *pab, hef, geb, duk.* Hey, *duck* is a real word.
>
> MARK: Yes, but it's spelled differently.
>
> DEANDE: *rak, rop, hib, jad, laz, mik.* This is the craziest thing I ever had to do in school.
>
> MARK: Keep going.
>
> DEANDE: *Tuv, toz, gub.* Are you sure I'm supposed to do this, Mr. Beck?
>
> MARK: Yes.
>
> DEANDE: *sov, lek, rez.* Who came up with this?
>
> MARK: Not important. Finish up.
>
> DEANDE: *nif.* There, I'm finished. Wow! Wait 'til I tell my mom what I did in school today. She'll never believe it.

For a long time after that encounter, every time DeAnde saw me in the hall, he asked, "Hey, Mr. Beck! You got any more of those crazy words for me? I love them."

••••••••••••••YOUR TURN••••••••••••

Consider Julie, who, at the end of kindergarten, is given SPA-B. Based on the truncated version of her results in the following box, what kinds of conclusions can you draw? What would you do to help Julie going forward?

Specific Phonics Assessment B
CVC /VC/ Short Vowels (*a, i, o, e, u*)

	# long vowels correct	% long vowels correct
1. Short Vowels Real	6/10	60%
2. Short Vowels Nonsense	12/20	60%

Nonsense Short Vowel Recap

short *a*	4/4	100%
short *i*	3/4	75%
short *o*	4/4	100%
short *e*	1/4	25%
short *u*	0/4	0%

Observations/Recommendations

The student regularly pronounces /y/ for *u*.

CHAPTER 9

Multisyllabic Words

Sooner or later, most students learn to decode single-syllable words. They may do so slowly, and that is a problem, but most students can get through single-syllable words. This is not the case for multisyllabic words. Once a second syllable, and, more so, a third or fourth syllable, is introduced, several issues arise. One of the most prominent is that some students find the length of multisyllabic words intimidating. Relatedly, they do not know where syllables begin and end, so they don't know which chunks to work with. That is, they are unfamiliar with what sequence of letters in a word constitutes a unit that they can decode separately from other subword units. Thus this chapter focuses on the decoding of multisyllabic words.

In the first part of this chapter, we discuss three overarching skills related to decoding multisyllabic words: analysis, pronunciation, and synthesis. But first we want to share one of the most interesting misreadings of multisyllabic words either of us had seen, which was brought to my (Isabel's) attention by one of my master's program students, whom we'll call Martha.

What in the World Is Andrew Doing?

As part of a class assignment, I asked my students to have a struggling reader read some multisyllabic words aloud and to write the student's responses next to the target word. Martha brought to my attention the misreadings of one of her students, whom we'll call Andrew. I had also asked my students to tell me a little about their students. Martha wrote that, despite being a poor reader, Andrew was intelligent. She added that he was exceptionally friendly, impulsive, talked a lot, never sat still, and was very sweet. Following are some examples of Andrew's responses to the assessment of decoding multisyllabic words that my student administered:

Word	Andrew's response
nauseous	nearsiseous
bountiful	beautiful
expected	exited
logical	local
machetes	matches
experiences	expects
culprit	culpit
persist	present
untenable	unable

What Can We Conclude from Andrew's Misreadings?

As can be seen, Andrew appeared to use the beginning and ending portions of target words, but virtually ignored medial syllables. He either made up a medial syllable (as in *nearsiseous* for *nauseous*), changed a medial syllable (as in *exited* for *expected*), omitted medial syllables (*local* for *logical, expects* for *experiences, unable* for *untenable*), or changed the target word to a likely known word that had the correct beginning and ending (*beautiful* for *bountiful, present* for *persist*). It appears that Andrew's primary problem was his inability to identify syllables or pronounceable chunks.[1] I suspected that he had no clue about where words divide into syllables. If he were given direct instruction on syllable division, I suggest he would make progress.

That the medial syllables were the most difficult for Andrew is consistent with the findings in a study by McCandliss and colleagues (2003) that showed that medial graphemes in one-syllable words are the most difficult for students to decode. Interestingly, Andrew showed the same effects of position for decoding multisyllabic words as was found for single-syllable words. I wish I could tell you more about Andrew, but it was at the end of the semester.

What to Do?

I presented Andrew's misreadings in the first edition of *Making Sense of Phonics* and have always been dissatisfied that I did not offer a more thoughtful suggestion

---

[1]There can be disagreement about the precise divisions between syllables. What students need to be able to do is to divide a word into pronounceable chunks, which are often syllables, but not always. For example, dividing the word *basket* into chunks such as *bask-et*, although not the standard syllabication of *basket*, would still allow a reasonable pronunciation.

about what might be done for Andrew beyond providing direct instruction about syllable division. So, while writing this second edition, I thought carefully about what kind of intervention might help Andrew beyond direct instruction. Upon reflection, I remembered that my student Martha had indicated that Andrew was "impulsive." And I had an idea. "Uh-huh," I thought, "maybe I am barking up the wrong tree." Maybe lack of understanding of syllables is not the primary problem. He appeared not to be trying to figure out syllables but just diving into reading the words. Was impulsivity operating here?

Impulsivity can be a problem in any or all aspects of reading, but it seems that it shows its stripes more strongly when multisyllabic difficult words come into play. So to pursue that thought, I would determine whether Andrew had any understanding at all about the separation of words into syllables. Toward that end, I would ask him to read a list of words similar to what his teacher had given him, but this time I would tell Andrew that he had to look at each word for three seconds before he read it, and I would put my finger on the paper after three seconds as a signal so he'd know when he should read each word. The purpose of the delay was to see whether Andrew's potential impulsiveness was reduced and he took the time to look at the words. As another test of my hypothesis—that impulsiveness might be the feature that gets in Andrew's way—I would include several of the words from the assessment Martha gave him that we showed at the beginning of this chapter. That would allow me to consider any differences in what he said.

Upon reflection, my suspicion is that both issues play into Andrew's difficulties.

They Don't Know What They Know

We have observed that, when decoding multisyllabic words, students have more knowledge than they might be aware of. For example, students usually can decode CVC words (*cat, men*) by the end of kindergarten or soon after and become fairly proficient with many CVC words, both real and pseudowords. Decoding two CVC words into a multisyllabic word, such as *bas* and *ket* into *basket*, is the next logical step and not challenging for most when limited to only two syllables.

Many of the tools provided in Chapters 4–7 help to support the decoding of CVC pseudowords and can be assessed through SPAs, which we discussed in Chapter 8. Most important, students need to be encouraged to recognize that they are able read words such as *pencil, happen, basket*, and *invent*, drawing on previous knowledge and skills. This notion applies equally, but perhaps less consistently, to other multisyllabic words that have single-syllable patterns, such as CVC*e*, *mistake*; CVVC, *contain*; and *r*-controlled, *portal*, as well as other orthographic letter strings. We look further into other single-syllable patterns that are found in multisyllabic words later in this chapter.

Eric's Story

The decoding of multisyllabic words poses difficulties beyond decoding of single-syllable words. I (Isabel) asked my friend (let's call him Eric) to read some multisyllabic pseudowords and to do so slowly so he could tell me what he was doing.

I showed him the pseudoword *obbodious* and asked him to divide the word into pronounceable subunits. Following is a reconstruction of my conversation with Eric about why he had made his choices.

- Eric identified *ob* as the first syllable because he thought he "knew" that within multisyllabic words, syllables often fall between two adjacent consonants. He also said, rather assuredly, something like, "I can't think of a word that starts with *obb*." (Subsequently we checked the *American Heritage Dictionary* [Pickett et al., 2000] for *obb* and found only *obbligato*, "used as a direction in music.")

Notice that Eric used two sources to identify *ob*: vague knowledge and experience. The notion that one "knows" something does not necessarily mean that one can provide a rule or rationale.

- Eric identified *bod* as the second syllable. He indicated that it could be *bo* (the long-vowel sound of *o*), but that *bod* (the short-vowel sound of *o*) "went better with the first syllable, *ob*." That is, he liked *ob-bod*.

Our guess is that Eric saw *bod* and preferred that CVC to the long vowel in the open syllable *bo*. Perhaps, given his experience as a reader, Eric unconsciously considered probabilities between *bod* and *bo*. In the English corpus of words, are there more CVC second syllables than CV second syllables? We don't know, and we don't know that anyone knows.

- Given Eric's decision to identify the second syllable as *bod*, he had to choose *i* as the third syllable; otherwise, the third syllable would have to be *ious*, which he thought was not very frequent. Interestingly, when he chose *i*, he remarked correctly that there are a lot of words in which a single vowel is a syllable.

In that comment Eric demonstrated his knowledge of a major requirement for a syllable: it has to have a vowel.

- Given Eric's decisions to this point, he had to identify *ous* as the final syllable and indicated that there are a lot of words that end in *ous*.

So what can be said about what Eric knew and did to divide the word into subunits? He knew that a syllable consists of a letter or several letters that must include a vowel. He knew that syllables are usually divided between adjacent consonants. He thought that there were two possibilities for the second syllable, either *bod* or *bo*, and he chose *bod*. Actually, the second syllable should be *bo* because, if it were a real word, the second and third syllables would usually be divided between the second *o* and the *d*. As such, *bo* would be an open syllable, and the *o* would be pronounced long. The final decision is where to divide *ious*, and Eric did so based on a previous statement that a single vowel can be a syllable. Thus the word was divided as *ob bod i ous*. If nothing else, that is a reasonable syllabication, and it can be pronounced. If it were a real word, Eric could have matched his rendition to the actual word and altered his rendition as necessary.

Such knowledge goes beyond what is needed for decoding single-syllable words because for single-syllable words the vowel environment is given rather than needing to be derived by the reader, and stress is not an issue. Next, we discuss other considerations that enter into the multisyllabic domain.

The Three Skills Needed for Reading Multiple-Syllable Words

From our experiences of hearing students stumble over multisyllabic words, especially Mark's substantial experience with struggling readers, Andrew's unusual responses at the beginning of this chapter, Eric's responses to *obbodious*, and our own analyses of decoding long pseudowords, we have concluded that supporting students' reading of multisyllabic words requires three skills.

1. *Analysis*—where to divide a written word into syllables.
2. *Pronunciation*—how to pronounce the individual syllables.
3. *Synthesis*—how to combine the syllables into a spoken word.

Next, we discuss each of the three skills separately, although most of the time they are interwoven. We deal with interweaving after we discuss each skill individually.

Analysis

Initially, in order to chunk a word, an individual needs to know where the first syllable ends. A student who is unable to separate the first syllable in a word may read too far into a word or stop too soon, both of which can make it difficult to pronounce the resultant chunks. For example, try to read the first two words that follow (nos. 1 and 2), which have been divided into chunks incorrectly. As an adult, you might be able to tell at a glance what the word is. Nevertheless, still try to read the words using the incorrect syllables, as that is what a student who divides a multisyllabic word incorrectly could encounter.

1. inv-is-ib-i-li-ty
2. ext-em-por-i-zat-ion

You may or may not have pronounced the words correctly. Now, read the next two words (nos. 3 and 4), which provide correct syllable divisions, and remind yourself how easily you can pronounce the word.

3. ses-qui-cen-te-na-ry
4. ma-neu-ver-a-bil-i-ty

In most cases, adults indicate that the correctly syllabicated words were easier to pronounce.

In order to assist teachers and students to divide words into syllables, we provide some of the more important guidelines:

1. When a word includes two adjacent consonants, the syllables are divided between the two consonants.
   - Examples: *bas-ket, hap-pen*
2. When a word has a single consonant (or a two-letter consonant digraph) with a vowel before and another vowel after the consonant or digraph (VCV words), the consonant usually belongs with the second syllable.
   - Examples: *ba-ker, ma-chine, pi-lot*
3. At the end of a word, when a consonant comes right before the letters *le*, the consonant usually belongs in the same syllable with the *le*.
   - Examples: *gig-gle, un-cle, sim-ple*
4. Single vowels can often stand for one syllable.
   - Examples: *pres-i-dent, el-e-phant, cell-o-phane*

It is suggested that teachers use these guidelines to help students understand where to divide syllables, which will help them to know how far into a word to decode before going on to the next syllable.

Pronunciation

Once a student has analyzed a word and separated it into syllables, he needs to be able to pronounce the chunks. The type of syllable has a lot of influence on pronunciation. In almost all cases, the pronunciation of the vowel is the critical issue. What follows is a very brief look at six common types of syllables, each of which influences the pronunciation of a vowel. The first four categories include spelling patterns generally taught by the end of first grade.

1. *CVC/closed syllables*. Many syllables follows the CVC patterns in which the vowel is short. Such syllables are often called *closed syllables* because the vowel is closed in by the consonants on each side (*hap-pen, pen-cil*).

2. *CVCe*. Some syllables follow the silent-*e* pattern in which the vowel is pronounced long (*pan-cake, in-vite*).

3. *CVVC*. Some syllables include adjacent vowels in which the first is long and the second is silent (*ex-plain*).

4. *r-controlled*. In many syllables when a vowel is followed by the letter *r*, a somewhat altered vowel sound is pronounced. Examples include *ar* (*carpet*) and *or* (*chorus*), as well as the phonemes that *ir* (*thirsty*), *ur* (*curtain*), and *er* (*perfect*) represent.

5. *-le*. When there is a consonant in front of the letters *le* at the end of a word, the /l/ phoneme is pronounced after the consonant sound (*mum-ble*).

6. *Open syllables*. When a single consonant falls between two vowels, the first vowel is pronounced long and the consonant becomes part of the next syllable. It is called an *open syllable* because the vowel is not closed in by a consonant at the ends of the syllable (*pa-per*).

Synthesis

As mentioned earlier, a fair amount of the time students should be able to recognize syllables from their knowledge and experience with known patterns in single-syllable words (e.g., CVC, *jen*; CVCe, *tate*; CCCVC, *sprot*). But sometimes there can be an obstacle to immediately reading a word by syllables. A reader will encounter a string of letters that she does not recognize as a pronounceable chunk. In such an instance, the reader will need to decode the syllable phoneme by phoneme and synthesize the phonemes into a pronounceable chunk. If there are more than three phonemes, we suggest that Chapter 6 be revisited and the cumulative blending routine be retrieved. The cumulative blending routine was developed to help children to learn to blend phonemes into words during the earliest phases of learning to read and to do so without overtaxing short-term memory. In the case of words of more than two syllables, our recommendation is to use the cumulative blending routine but at the syllable instead of the phoneme level.

I (Mark) recently had an interesting experience with five students while reading *Ms. Beard Is Weird* from the popular Weirder School series by Dan Gutman (2012). In the excerpt, Andrea, a bit of a sycophant, is trying to impress her third-grade teacher with her knowledge of the Civil War and says:

> "Is it true that the Civil War started in 1861 when eleven Southern states decided to leave the United States and form their own country called the *Confederate States of America*?"

When my students arrived at the word *confederate* they all hesitated, so I told them to use their fingers to find the syllables. With a little guidance, most of them were able to say *con-fed-er-et* (sometimes *ate*). However, when I asked them to read the word, I heard *confedet, conferet, confret, confident, confederate* (long *a*). Interestingly, the students had read the syllables accurately but could not synthesize them correctly.

So the children and I worked out synthesizing the word using the cumulative blending routine. Following is what I led the students to do. The places where syllables are synthesized are bolded.

/con/ /fed/ **/confed/** /er/ **/confeder/** /ate/ **/confederate**

The goal is for *confed* to take up one position in short-term memory and then hook the *er* on to *confed* for *confeder*. Now we have three syllables in one position in short-term memory, and finally *ate* is hooked on to *confeder* and the word *confederate* has been decoded. As we discussed in Chapter 6, 7-year-old children have memory spans of about seven items, so why worry about three or four syllables? Remembering seven items that an examiner provides does not involve identifying the chunks in a multisyllabic word, pronouncing those chunks, and then synthesizing them into a word. Thus we assert that the load on short-term memory is a feature that can make decoding multisyllabic words an issue.

One more thing about *confederate*. When children decode single-syllable words, the majority of those words are words already known from oral language. Indeed, teaching children to read the words they already know from oral language is what the early phases of reading instruction are about. We made the point in Chapter 6 that when children attempt to figure out a word by blending sounds, it is not necessary for them to produce a perfectly precise pronunciation. Rather, they need to be able to come up with an approximate pronunciation, which they can refine by matching their pronunciation with that of a word they already know from spoken language.

The third-grade students working with *confederate* did not have the advantage of working out a pronunciation that they could refine because it is likely that they did not have an oral representation of *confederate* in memory. Both of us (I. L. B. & M. E. B.) enjoyed the student's pronunciation of *confederate* with the long *a*. She had followed the regular VC*e* orthographic pattern, loudly pronouncing the last syllable *ate*, but had no idea that the pronunciation might need to be refined because she did not have the word in memory. And therein lies a somewhat serious wrinkle with unfamiliar multisyllabic words. When an unfamiliar multisyllabic word is not known, the reader cannot match her pronunciation with the correct one. Relatedly, the meaning would be unknown. Of course, such a situation offers opportunities for authentic teaching moments.

Interweaving

There are probably three or four ways one might go from an unfamiliar written word to a pronunciation of the word. The least integrated approach is to engage in each of three skills one at a time: first divide, then go back and pronounce each syllable, then go back and synthesize. Notice that in this way the reader decodes every syllable before even beginning to synthesize. Thus the reader needs to hold all the syllables in short-term memory before combining them.

In contrast, the most integrated way is to separate off the first syllable and pronounce it (*con*), identify the second syllable and pronounce it (*fed*), hook the second syllable on to the first (*confed*), and so on. The synthesis happens along the way each time a new syllable is pronounced. There is, however, research that shows that skilled readers divide long words into syllables in the course of their initial visual encounter (Mewhort & Campbell, 1981).

We asked some adults to decode some fairly long multisyllabic pseudowords, and they seemed to interweave the three skills. But there was no way we could know whether they had already determined the syllable boundaries before pronouncing the first syllable. Several adults did not at first hook each syllable onto the previous syllable(s), but with about three syllables on the burner, some went back to the beginning and put together the three syllables they had already pronounced separately before going on to the next chunk.

No research has looked at that issue. Our hunch is that there is advantage to the most interwoven approach to decoding. We think that there would also be value in providing students who struggle with a step-by-step approach to decoding multisyllabic words, similar to steps we provided for blending phonemes into words in the early stages of learning to read.

An Example of a Student's Analysis of a Word

Let's use the word *cellophane* and a student, Jake, who has had instruction in dividing and pronouncing multisyllabic words. Jake's working through the word provides an example of some problems that arose and potential solutions Jake used to decode *cellophane*.

1. Jake decoded *cell*, but when going to the next syllable, he, like many students, was resistant to identifying a single vowel, in this case *o*, as a syllable. So Jake looked for other possibilities to identify the second syllable.

2. He recalled something about syllable junctures being between two consonants, so he tried *op hane* and read *cell-op-hane*. It didn't sound like any word he knew, so he was again left with *ophane*.

3. He recognized the long *a* in the VCe in *ane*, hooked the *h* onto the front and got *hane*, which hadn't helped him in Step 2.

4. Perhaps his recognition of the problem in Step 2 prompted him to recall that *ph* is a two-letter grapheme that represents /f/ and that words should not be divided between them.

5. He decoded *phane*.

6. Now he was left with the single *o* syllable and was prompted with weak but available knowledge that a single vowel can be a syllable.

7. Jake read *cellophane*!

Notice how Jake was able to decode the word through a combination of understanding patterns, reasoning, and use of trial and error.

Learned Helplessness

One of the primary challenges in decoding a multisyllabic word is not to get overwhelmed by the length of a word. When students see a word that is "too long," they often fail to read every syllable in the word, and the result is a spoken word that doesn't completely resemble the printed word. Remember *confret*? Remember Andrew's misreadings at the beginning of this chapter?

Psychologists have described a phenomenon known as "learned helplessness." It is a condition of believing that one is unable to take the necessary steps to accomplish a desired goal. Learned helplessness has been tied to psychological conditions such as depression, as well as difficulty in school. We have witnessed students who, upon encountering a multisyllabic word, appear to give up when they see the length. When urged, some students usually start and often get a reasonable rendition of the first syllable and maybe even the second syllable. They may stop there, or some may skip to the final syllable as if any internal syllables did not exist.

A student, when reading an unfamiliar multisyllabic word, is grappling with overlapping issues (related to analysis, pronunciation, and synthesis). If he doesn't have a pathway to follow to accomplish the task, he can easily become overwhelmed, attempting to juggle the various cognitive processes.

A primary goal of reading instruction is to help students find a process to achieve a goal. The antidote to helplessness is competence, which requires two kinds of teacher support. First is the more affective kind, providing supportive suggestions that might persuade a student to attempt a task, such as "It's a long word, but we can work on it in pieces"; "Take your time"; "It will help if you use your fingers." Second, there is the cognitive kind of support, direct teaching of how to divide words into chunks, how to pronounce the chunks, and how to synthesize the chunks. The good news is that we have encountered some struggling readers who, with a little coaching, were actually able to read multisyllabic words to a greater extent than they thought possible.

In the next chapter, we present Syllasearch, an activity that engages students in the three skills needed—analysis, pronunciation, and synthesis—to pronounce a multisyllable word.

The Possibility of Falling into a Hole

As we have discussed, when some students have difficulty decoding a multisyllable word, it is not too uncommon for them to skip a syllable. A teacher friend—we'll call her Sara—told me (Isabel) about an incident with her student, Roger, who had a tendency to skip syllables.

She had asked Roger to read the word *dangerous*. He stumbled, hesitated, and then pronounced the word *daggers*. Sara showed him where his mistake was and how to decode the word accurately, and she pronounced *dangerous*. Sara then asked Roger what it was that made him skip syllables, and he said something about it being easier that way. Sara said that it might be easier but that, when he skipped syllables, the word he came up with was not the word on the page.

"So?" said Roger, trying to minimize the importance of reading it correctly. "Then, think about this," retorted Sara. "If you were walking in a construction zone and you saw a sign that said 'dangerous,' but you read it incorrectly, you might end up falling into a hole." Roger giggled and then said aloud so the whole class could hear, "She's saying I'm going to fall into a hole."

• • • • • • • • • • •YOUR TURN • • • • • • • • •

For each of these words, answer the following questions: *Ethiopia, persuadable, octogenarian, posthumous, remarkable, cooperation, Azerbaijan, communist, mitochondria, numerator.*

- As adults, much of our knowledge is tacit, and it is sometimes difficult to recall the explicit rule or purpose for engaging in a behavior. As such, you may find it useful to consider the syllable division guidelines from page 105. Where are the syllables divided in the preceding words? In which cases are the rules not followed (if any)? Or you might want to first determine the syllable boundaries without looking at the guidelines on page 105. And then look back to see how your version squares with the guidelines.

- Which of the pronunciation patterns from page 106 are included and in which syllables? Are there any syllables that are irregular—that is, that do not follow any of the guidelines?

Syllasearch

Syllasearch is a teacher-directed large- or small-group activity that focuses students' attention on syllables in multisyllabic words. Students examine how to divide a word into syllables and how to pronounce those syllables, and then they synthesize the syllables into meaningful words. They identify syllables within words and combine syllables to produce words.

The procedures, materials, and actual lessons are provided in this chapter. In Appendix 3, we provide 35 word and syllable lists organized into four sequences. Sequence A involves two-syllable words with phonics patterns that are prevalent in single-syllable words usually covered in the first grade. Sequence A can be introduced as early as mid- or late first grade or the beginning of second grade. Sequences B through D are generally appropriate for use throughout second grade and, as needed, in third grade. We have also seen value in using Syllasearch in intermediate grades as an intervention for those struggling students who have difficulty with multisyllabic words.

As an example, we have provided list C5 (Sequence C, Lesson 5) here. We use this matrix in a later section when we describe how the matrices develop during a lesson. For now we mention how the matrices are formatted. As you can see, the first column lists words, and the next two or three columns are syllables that make up those words. All the syllables from a particular word are never next to each other in a row. All 35 matrices are provided in Appendix 3.

C5

person	per	tle	ous
perfect	gen	son	man
travel	tra	per	
shovel	sho	er	
gentle	pros	fect	
gentleman		vel	
generous			
prosperous			

Next, we provide a description of a Syllasearch lesson as it would be taught using words and syllables from List C5.

Materials

1. Word cards and syllable cards. The materials for each matrix consist of 7 or 8 word cards and from 12 to 18 syllable cards. We have made enlarged versions of all of the words and syllables used in Syllasearch available on our book's website: *www.guilford.com/p/beck10*. A subsequent section discusses how to access them.

2. Pocket chart. A pocket chart on which all the word and syllable cards in a matrix can be placed and moved about as needed. Instead of a pocket chart, some teachers prefer sticky tack or tape on the back of the cards so they can be placed on a whiteboard or chalkboard and moved around.

3. Syllasearch stories. For each Syllasearch lesson, we have provided a story on our book's website (*www.guilford.com/p/beck10*) that includes all or most of the words in each matrix. Some teachers may choose to create packets of all the stories within one sequence.

Parts of a Syllasearch Lesson

The following chart summarizes the four parts of a Syllasearch lesson.

1	**Syllables and Words** *Part to Whole or Whole to Part*
2	**Collect the Words**
3	**Create Nonsense Words**
4	**Read the Story**

In the first part, *Syllables and Words*, the teacher has students identify, decode and combine syllables into words or identify syllables within words. In the second part, *Collect the Words*, students come to the board and make words from the individual syllables. In the third part, *Create Nonsense Words*, several students come to the board and create a nonsense word of up to five syllables. In the fourth part, *Read the Story*, the students read a brief story containing all or most of the words.

Syllables and Words

There are two versions of Syllables and Words, which we describe as *part to whole* and *whole to part*. In part to whole, students are asked to decode individual syllables and then read the syllables together as a word. Part to whole encourages decoding, recognition of phonics patterns, and combining syllables into recognizable words. In whole to part, the teacher reads the complete word to the students and has them decode and encode the pieces. Whole to part encourages students' understanding of where syllables separate and reinforces some decoding (reading) and encoding (spelling).

In both cases, it is anticipated that (1) as the teacher works through the words and syllables, a matrix of mixed-up syllables will develop in the middle of the board, and (2) a separate word list will develop of completed words. For every lesson, the words and syllables for words in a matrix are provided in Appendix 3.

Here we present the procedures for engaging in each of the two versions of Syllables and Words. As you and your students engage in either of the procedures, a matrix will gradually develop. It matters not which version you use; the matrix that develops will be exactly the same for both procedures. Although the strategies of word first or syllable first are different, the location of the cards on the matrix will be exactly the same.

Procedures for the Two Versions of Syllables and Words

Part to Whole	Whole to Part
1. Teacher holds up one syllable card, for example, the *gen* from *gentleman*.	1. Teacher holds up word card, for example, *gentleman*.
2. Teacher asks, "What does this [indicates the *gen* card] say?"	2. Teacher says, "This word is *gentleman*."

3. Student says, "gen."
4. For *tle* and *man*, teacher and students repeat (1), (2), and (3).
5. Teacher holds up *gentleman* word card.
6. Teacher asks class to read the word.

3. Teacher asks, "In the word *gentleman*, what do the letters g e n say?" (decoding approach)
4. Student says, "gen."
5. Teacher repeats (3) for *t l e* and *m a n*.

(*An alternative to the decoding approach above is to ask students to encode the syllable.*)

Encoding Alternative
• Teacher repeats (1) and (2) above.
• Teacher then asks, "What are the letters that spell *gen*? . . . that spell *tle*? . . . that spell *man*?"

The Lesson/Matrix

Each syllable goes up on the matrix as it is read or spelled.[1] For example, using the matrix for C5, the syllable card *per* should appear at the first column, first row, in the matrix that will be developing. The syllable card for *son* should appear in the second column, second row. Then in a column to the right or left of the matrix, the completed card for *person* is placed.

Here is what the matrix will look like when you have completed the first word:

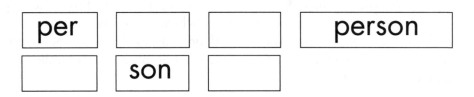

---

[1] All the syllable cards from any one word should not be in the same row.

Here is what the matrix will look like after you have done the first three words:

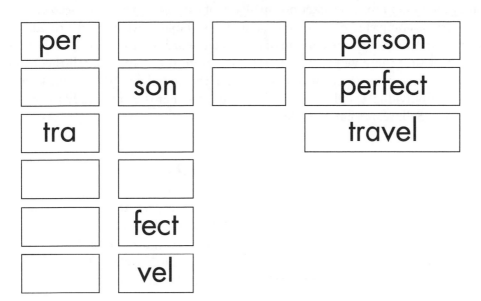

Here is what the matrix will look like after completion of Syllables and Words:

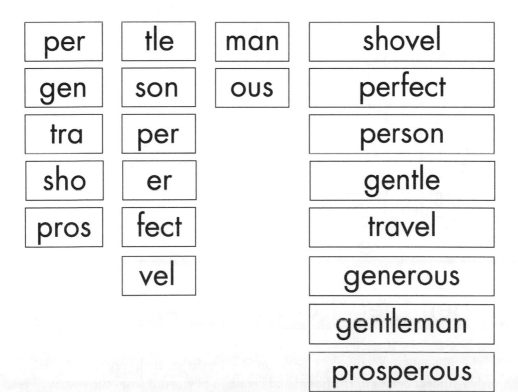

It is not important that the matrix be replicated exactly. What is important is that syllables next to each other not spell any of the words from that lesson. When the matrix is complete, tell students that all the syllables have been identified. Then direct their attention to the column of completed words on the right and alert them to the fact that those words will disappear. Before that happens, tell them to try to commit several words to memory. Remove the completed words, but keep the matrix of individual syllables up. Tell the students that they are ready to go on to the part of Syllasearch called Collect the Words.

Collect the Words

Collect the Words proceeds in the same fashion, whether after part to whole or whole to part. Students collect words by combining syllables from the matrix columns. One by one (but quickly), students are instructed to come to the matrix, place syllable cards together, build a word, and read it to the class. Then the teacher quickly places a complete word card on the board or pocket chart. The matrix will look like the following at this point:

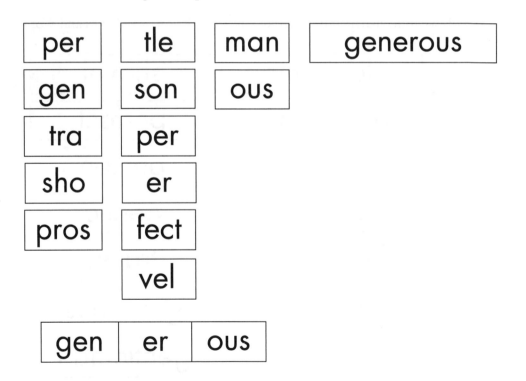

The individual syllables go back on the board in their previous location. Another student comes to the board and creates a new word from the matrix. The teacher places that complete word card in a column. Students can write the word as the teacher places the completed word card in the column.

Continue in this same way until all the words have been built, pronounced, and written. At the completion of this version of Collect the Words, the final display should look as follows, with the exception that the list of words can be in any order:

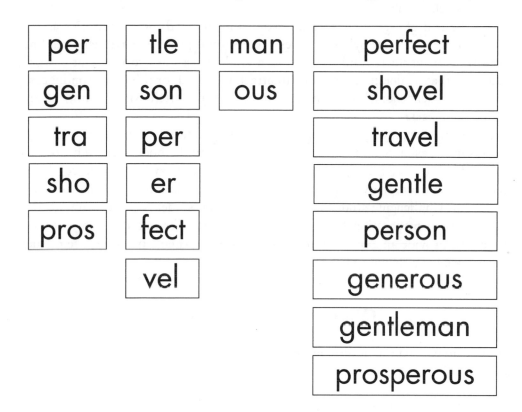

per	tle	man	perfect
gen	son	ous	shovel
tra	per		travel
sho	er		gentle
pros	fect		person
	vel		generous
			gentleman
			prosperous

Create Nonsense Words

Students are very fond of making nonsense words. One or two students come to the board to put syllables together that do *not* make a real word and pronounce the made-up word. Most teachers call these *nonsense words* (e.g., *chapmalade*). Some teachers and students have developed other names for such words (e.g., alien words, silly words, wacky words). Sometimes teachers ask students what a given word might mean in nonsense-word language. Students enjoy making up such words, and it provides an opportunity for the teacher to observe how accurately the students are decoding individual nonsense syllables. Again, it is important to move quickly.

Read the Story

Just as we described in Chapter 7, it is important that students have an opportunity to connect most of the words from a lesson to a text. We have written little stories of between approximately 50 and 200 words for all 35 lessons. They are available online at *www.guilford.com/p/beck10*. See Appendix 5 for information about how to access the story files. Because of space limitations, the Syllasearch stories are not included in the book.

At the end of every Syllasearch lesson, students read the little stories associated with the particular Syllasearch lesson in several possible ways: echo reading, chorally, with partners, and the like. If a student hesitates too long at a word, indicating that he doesn't know how to attack the word, or if he mispronounces a word, the student should be encouraged to break it up (often using his fingers) and decode the pieces.

Reading text provides good opportunities to practice dividing a word into syllables. On occasion one can ask a student to come to the board and indicate how she divided the word into syllables, decoded the separate syllables, and combined them into the word. If a young student can actually explain the steps, she is highly competent. Challenging students to explain to other students can be quite useful. Sometimes, in preparation for reading a story, a teacher might coach a student on how to provide an explanation of the steps. Over time, consistent use of such means have been shown to be effective.

Other Ways of Practicing

We recommend several additional activities for use from time to time. Some suggestions:

1. Have students make their own sets of syllable and word cards and follow along in a lesson.

2. Ask students to work in pairs to make some words with the syllables, both real and nonsense words, and ask their partners to pronounce them. Partners alternate between making words and pronouncing words.

3. There are a variety of game-like overlays that can be applied to Syllasearch, in particular, timing—for instance, keeping track of how fast a student or a pair of students can build some of the words in a matrix. Similarly, organize teams and time how long it takes all members in a team to build several words.

4. Start a story using one of the target words in the first sentence, then ask another student to continue the story by thinking of another sentence that includes a target word. Award points for doing this. This can be difficult, so teachers might tell students that if they feel stuck they can pass their turn to you, but they won't get any points. This is a good activity after the class has read a story for a lesson because the story may provide some ideas.

Management Issues with Syllasearch

Our experience with Syllasearch has been that the challenges are far more related to organizational and management issues than to students' decoding and encoding of words. One of the most difficult aspects is developing the cards and a storing system so the cards can be retrieved easily. A copy of all the words and separate syllables for each lesson is found in Appendix 3. Electronic versions are also available on our book's website. Teachers only need go to *www.guilford.com/p/beck10* to download and print the file for any lesson. There is one file for each matrix, 35 in all, on our website.

Every word and syllable on our website is presented in very large type, so they are appropriate for classroom use and easily readable from a distance. All the cards will need to be printed and cut from 8½" × 11" pages. Printing on card stock and laminating will make the cards more permanent and usable the following year. We like to use different-colored card stock (say, blue for A1–A7, yellow for B1–B9, etc.) to make organization and storage easier.

A way to keep track of where the syllable cards go in a matrix is to put a small code in the corner of each card—for example, on the *per* card (column 1, row 1) and on the *son* card (column 2, row 2). When you get to a repeated syllable (e.g., *tion* will already be on the matrix when the syllables for *motion* are requested), point out to the students that the syllable is already on the matrix. The use of one syllable in several words is particularly beneficial.

A typical Syllasearch session from start to finish in a whole-class setting should take 20–25 minutes, but first you'll need some experience with refining procedures and learning to move things along quickly. Some suggestions:

1. Move quickly and keep your eye on the clock. Syllasearch involves four activities and can take some time. Keeping the entire lesson to less than 25 minutes should be everyone's goal. Collect the Words is the step during which students are most likely not to be at full attention because only one student is at the board. As suggested earlier, having the other students write the words in a journal is useful. However, the younger students' writing may be too slow to require that they write the words. If the four steps and the seven or eight words run the risk of taking too long, teachers should be flexible, occasionally skipping a word or short-circuiting a procedure.

2. Have students participate in the management of the lesson. Choose assistants. As cards are being placed, rearranged, removed, and then put back together, there are opportunities for distraction and wasted time. Students can be trained to be helpful with the many cards. For every lesson, I (Mark) nominate a few students, often as many as five, and have them sit near the matrix to hold onto word and syllable cards and make them available to me quickly so things move speedily. I also have several students in charge of pulling off pieces of tape available to me at a moment's notice. After a

few weeks, students know what to do and are eager to help and make the lesson go more smoothly. The more students feel invested in the process, the less likely they are to feel disengaged.

3. Mix it up. Occasionally vary lessons (perhaps every five lessons) to involve different activities. Some of the suggestions in the previous section can help in this regard. Moreover, teachers are the best source we know who can vary lessons and add twists that engage their students. If you develop an idea that works well, we will be grateful to hear from you.

4. Stay organized. Having cards ready to go prior to class will minimize wasted time and distractions and help the lesson go more smoothly.

Final Thoughts

Our experiences with Syllasearch and multisyllabic words have led us to think about the decoding of syllables as requiring a classroom-wide effort. Awareness of syllables is beneficial to students when it is used in the classroom opportunistically, not just in the planned 20- to 25-minute lessons; during group reading, for example, when a student hesitates at a word and indicates he doesn't know how to proceed. After some training, I (Mark) found that all I had to say was, "Use your fingers," which really means to break it down to decodable subunits and then pronounce it. In a majority of cases, students, when doing so, will learn that they can read the word accurately.

It is important for everyone who works with children, including teachers, assistants, aides, and reading specialists, to recognize and take advantage of opportunities to read multisyllabic words in text when those opportunities arise during a school day. I have seen a number of students who gradually begin to overcome their earlier sense of helplessness. There are few things that are better to see than a student who has hesitated at a word wave off another student who wanted to tell him the word.

Our Favorite Syllasearch Anecdotes

Over the years, teachers have told me (Isabel) about some of the meanings students create for a given nonsense word. We repeat some of my favorite responses that were in the first edition of *Making Sense of Phonics*, as well as a new one that a teacher friend, Shelley, shared with us. Isabel's favorites include *mabrisous* is a thing that could make you sick; *chapmalade* is something that you smear on your skin so your skin feels nice; *brister* is an alien planet. When a fifth grader indicated that *pronoy* meant that you are annoying someone, the teacher suggested that maybe he had seen a similarity between *annoy* and *pronoy*. The student quickly responded that they were similar, but that *pronoy* was annoying someone more than just annoying!

Perhaps my all-time favorite is the student who synthesized five syllables from a matrix and slowly read *procelerable*. When the teacher asked what it might mean, the student responded, "I haven't a clue. I'm lucky to just be able to say it!"

Shelley's Favorite

As we write this, Shelley, who was teaching Syllasearch with third graders, told us about a student's response to what the meaning of the nonsense word *eviduedent* might be. Below is the discussion that ensued.

JANINE: As Janine points to the syllables and says, *eviduedent*.

SHELLEY: What might *eviduedent* mean?

JANINE: **It's a word in a song.**

LUCIEN: That would never be in a song.

JANINE: [Sings.] Eviduedent, eviduedent, do you know what eviduedent is?

LUCIEN: So what is it?

JANINE: I'm not going to tell you because you don't think it could be part of a song.

SHIRLEY: [whispering to Janine] What does it mean?

JANINE: I don't know.

• • • • • • • • • • • •YOUR TURN • • • • • • • • • •

Locate a second- through fourth-grade book and write down the first 50 or so multisyllabic words you see. Then make a list of all of the syllables and count how many and what percentage fall into the following categories: CVC, *-le*, CVVC, CVC*e, r*-controlled, open, irregular. How can you use your findings when teaching decoding of multisyllabic words?

● Select a Syllasearch matrix from Appendix 3. Make the syllable and word cards and use the procedures described in this chapter to teach a lesson. Then ask yourself: Do I think the students learned anything? If yes, what? If not, why not? Was the Syllasearch set at an appropriate level for the students? Was the set too easy? Too hard? Would it be useful to repeat the lesson?

● Reflect on your ability to present the procedures. Are there steps you need to do more smoothly? Have you developed a code for the syllable cards that allows you to keep track of them? Did your pace provide an active lesson? How did the students respond?

CHAPTER 11

Orthography
A "Sticking Point in Word Recognition"[1]

Written English has four major components: (1) phonology, the sounds in speech; (2) orthography, the spelling system; (3) semantics, word meanings; and (4) syntax, how words fit together in sentences. Some writers include morphology as a major component, others view it as part of semantics. Instead of syntax, some writers refer to the ways words fit together as grammar. Nevertheless, no matter the label, the four components of written English are sound, spelling, word meaning, and sentence organization. These components are not independent; rather, they interact in the course of an individual engaging in reading and writing.

Much of what we dealt with in this book is the phonological system, the correspondence between graphemes and phonemes and how to blend the phonemes into words. Knowledge of the phonology of English is critical. In fact, Ehri (2005) has called the phonological component the glue that holds the whole language system together. Nevertheless, if the phonological component is all that is available to a reader, there is little chance that that individual will be able to recognize words quickly enough to have adequate word recognition skills. Figuring out a pronunciation of a word phoneme by phoneme is very resource costly.

In Chapter 9, through our discussion of multisyllabic words, and Chapter 10, with our presentation of Syllasearch, we moved our focus from the grapheme–phoneme level to the decoding of larger letter strings, in particular syllables. At that point, the orthographic system came into play. Given that it turns out that

---

[1] Cunningham, Nathan, and Rahec (2011, p. 275).

lack of knowledge of and use of the orthographic system has been found to be a "sticking point in word recognition" (Cunningham et al., 2011, p. 275), we provide a discussion of role of orthography.

Orthography

Orthography is a language's spelling system. It is the system by which writers encode oral language through the use of specified ordered letter sequences. Knowledge of orthographic English includes knowledge—mostly tacit—of whether a letter sequence could be a word (*fulsimanette* could, *rftloma* could not) and the probability of whether certain letters could legally appear in certain positions. For example, English words do not start with *nd*. The idea of recognizing orthographic constraints, tacitly or explicitly, is a part of orthographic knowledge that influences word recognition. As examples of orthographic constraints, consider Massaro and Taylor's (1980) discussion of consonants and vowels:

> One of the most noticeable constraints in English orthography is the difference between where consonants and vowels occur in words. Vowel sounds are relatively infrequent in initial or final position in English words. Therefore, the reader can expect words to begin and end with consonants, except for final *e*, which is not pronounced. For example, when the letters *a, e, i, o, u* and *y* occur in a five-letter word, they occur in first position only 9% of the time and in final position only on 1% of their occurrences . . . therefore vowel letters can be expected more often in the medial position than in the initial and final positions. (pp. 749–780)

An example of a reader who had knowledge of and used the orthographic system is found in Chapter 9, where we reported Eric's decoding of *obbodious*. He said, "I can't think of a word that starts with *obbl*." He was virtually right, as the only word that started with *obb* in an abridged dictionary was *obbligato*, a musical direction. In Chapter 9, when decoding *cellophane*, Jake showed his knowledge of an orthographic constraint when he realized that he couldn't have a syllable boundary between *ph* because together they were a grapheme.

Orthography and Reading

More than 50 years ago Eleanor Gibson and her colleagues (Gibson, Pick, Osser, & Hammond, 1962) asserted that children's lack of knowledge of and ability to use the orthographic system is implicated in slow reading and that slow reading is implicated in inadequate reading. Moreover, Gibson and her colleagues targeted the problem not as difficulty decoding whole words or letters but as decoding at the spelling pattern level. Support for the theory that lack of knowledge of English orthography is an impediment to reading is provided by research that shows time and time again that poor readers have difficulty reading pseudowords, which are legal letter strings that can be pronounced but that do not spell a real word (e.g., *sher*). Such pseudowords are, however, part of pronounceable multisyllabic words (e.g., *gusher*).

In the 1990s and 2000s, many research studies considered the role of orthography in reading and identified lack of the use of orthography as a limiting factor in reading competence. Now there is evidence that "orthographic processing has been found to be a unique and separable construct and . . . accounts for a significant amount of variance among individuals in word recognition" (Cunningham et al., 2011, p. 264). There are two parts of Cunningham's statement that bear commenting on.

Let's start with the second part, "[orthographic processing] accounts for a significant amount of variance among individuals in word recognition." This is a researcher's way of saying that certain statistical analyses have provided evidence that good word recognizers have adequate orthographic knowledge and that poor word recognizers' orthographic skills are inadequate. The first part of the statement, that "orthographic processing has been found to be a unique and separable construct" means that in addition to competencies that we already know influence word recognition, such as phonological skills, a reader's use of orthography is an *additional* ability that is characteristic of good word recognizers. Thus there is empirical evidence that phonological skills *plus* orthographic skills are required for competent word recognition.

How Do Children Gain Orthographic Competence?

Those who study orthography generally agree that children learn about orthography from extensive reading. Share (2008) has hypothesized about how reading enables learning about orthography through his proposed self-teaching mechanism. In the course of reading, a child uses her phonological skills to decode an unfamiliar word, and that action makes the orthographic features evident. For instance, in the course of reading, a child gets to a word, say *splurged*, that she does not recognize; the child uses her letter–sound correspondence knowledge and pronounces it and matches it with a word known from oral language. In the course of the detailed analyses of the graphemes to get to the phonemes in *splurged*, she encounters specific letter patterns. For example, maybe she already recognizes *ur* as a pattern but notices *urge* and uses her phonological skills to relate *urge* to its pronunciation. Subsequently, it is likely that she would recognize *surgeon* and *urgent* more quickly than she noticed the details of *splurge*. And the theory would predict that when she studies the American Revolution in fifth grade, she will have little hesitation pronouncing the new word *insurgency*.

We do not know anyone in the field who would disagree that lots of reading is the premier way to learn about English orthography. Unfortunately, even with encouragement and inducements, many students do not read much (see, e.g.,

Anderson, Wilson, & Fielding, 1988). Thus we look to some direct approaches targeted to developing orthographic knowledge.

Beyond Encouragement to Read, What Can Be Done?

The first thing that needs to happen is that the educational practicing world—teachers and those who influence teachers and publishers who develop curricula for schools—become informed about the role of orthography in reading. From our vantage points, this important component of reading is not very frequently separated out in instructional materials, except in association with spelling. Orthography certainly belongs with spelling, but it also belongs with reading. Indeed, reading and spelling should go hand in glove. Children need be asked to spell and write the words that they are learning to read. Spelling is an excellent way to focus attention on orthography because spelling requires learning the details of sequences of letter strings.

In contrast to the instructional world, there is a lot about orthography in the research literature, and more and more interesting and useful understandings are being developed. The instructional worlds and the research worlds need to come together over orthography as they have in other areas, with phonology a prime example. Quite a while ago, researchers Massaro and Taylor (1980) put a toe into the instructional world when they asserted "children should be able to learn some of the constraints in English orthography at about the same time that they usually learn phonics" (p. 740). We agree and considered how we might help students learn about English orthography. The direction toward an answer comes from, among others, Berends and Reitsma (2007), who make the point that "focusing children on specific orthographic elements of a word leads to more detailed word-specific orthographic representations in the mental lexicon" (p. 136). In the next section we look at some activities that hold potential for focusing students on specific orthographic representations.

But first a reminder. Accuracy at the word or grapheme–phoneme level needs to precede attention to orthography. This does not mean that children need to be accurate with all of the 42–44 correspondences needed to decode most words before dealing directly with orthography. Rather, we think that with accuracy for a subset of correspondences, orthographic attention to spelling patterns and words that include known correspondences can be undertaken in parallel with the introduction of new grapheme–phoneme correspondences. For example, if a child can decode words, say with one vowel and several consonants (e.g., *a, p, t, n*), albeit phoneme by phoneme, attention to orthographic segments with those letters can be engaged.

Before we provide examples of some activities, we stress that there is an over-arching requirement for their implementation: attitude. The requirement is that the attitude toward the sheets be light and that game-like features—speed, races, points, and so forth—be incorporated.

Practice Sheets[2]

There is enough in the literature that indicates that single word oral practice drills are useful, but we steer clear of whole-class flash-card drills, if for no other reason than that there is no way for a teacher to know whether all children in a class are attending to and responding to the words or whatever is on the cards. We prefer that children orally read words from practice sheets. Practice sheets are rows and columns of empty cells. On a standard 11″ × 8½″ paper, a practice sheet can accommodate up to about six columns and 22 rows for a total of 132 empty cells, which the teacher can use to write any lexical segment—letters, words, spelling pattern. Of course, various adaptations for different activities can be made. With individual practice sheets, because children have their own sheets on their desks, the teacher can scan the room and identify, fairly accurately, those children who may not be attending. Additionally, requiring children to point to each word is a positive practice because it may help the student focus on the word at hand, as well as providing teachers with another clue about those who may need to be encouraged to attend. Another advantage of practice sheets is that they are very easy to make.

Choral Reading of Words or Subword Units

The activity is to read the words aloud, with the teacher leading the pace and increasing the pace as appears appropriate. This kind of repeated practice has been shown to increase rate (Levy, 2001). Given that single words are appropriate for oral reading with practice sheets, the content can range from reading simple CVC words (e.g., *an* words) to reading words with advanced spelling patterns (e.g., *ound, ought*) and multisyllable words that contain orthographic sublexical items (e.g., *unforgiven*). But repetition can get tedious, so maintaining students' attention on the task is a very important consideration.

Maintaining Attention

There are several ways to keep attention on the content when children have been asked to reread lists. For example, after the first choral reading, boys and girls can alternate reading the words: boys read the first word, girls read the second word; the group reads the first half of the column quietly and the second half of the column loudly. Each student reads a word in a predetermined order—for example, up and down rows of desks, clockwise in a circle. But earlier the teacher has identified some secret confederates—that is, accomplices who have been told that when it's their turn to read a word, they should make a mistake. The class knows that this will happen, but they don't know who the accomplices are, and they don't know

---

[2]Computer programs seem best for game-like drills. However, the constraints in schools—especially in expertise and funds—lead us to offer suggestions that do not require technology.

how many times it will happen. What they do know is that when they hear a mistake, they should say something appropriate, such as *ooops!* or *nope!* or *no way!*. When this activity is running smoothly, it is a favorite, and children seem to pay particularly close attention.

How Should Words Be Grouped?

The nature and the order of the words in a column are important features. How should words be grouped? The words can be grouped by word family (e.g., the *an* family words follow one another, then the *ap* family words are grouped, and so on), or words from several families are mixed (*can, cap, map, man, pan,* etc.).

Which is better? Levy (2001) provides findings that bear on that question. With poor second-grade readers, grouping words results in more rapid learning than presenting words in mixed order. But when retention was assessed, students who had worked with families of words did significantly worse than students who were trained with mixed-word sets. This suggests that if students are not very competent with reading *an, at, ap* words—that is, if they still resort to some phoneme decoding—then the family approach is the way to go. But if they appear to be decoding those family words as wholes, albeit slowly, then the mixed approach seems most appropriate.

Speed Drills

Practice sheets are ideal for speed drills. Independently, children read down columns of words, and when the teacher calls time (e.g., 30 seconds, 60 seconds), children mark the word where they stopped. Children then try to beat their time. Another way to practice is to establish a criterion—a specific number of words in a specific time. Students practice until they reach the criterion. Several authors point to the importance of keeping strict time limits, which Tan and Nicholson (1997) defined as 1 or 2 seconds per word. With young children speed drills might consist of a limited number of words—maybe five—randomly repeated several times across the rows.

The question of whether children should read across the rows or down the columns has come up in the literature. Felton and Meyers (1999) imply that they should read across the rows when time is constrained to a specified amount, such as 1 minute. Massaro and Taylor (1980) specify down the column. But they were discussing a different activity, a visual search activity that has promise.

Visual Search

Visual search has been used in a number of experiments. It involves an individual visually scanning a specified area for something—an object, a letter, a word. Among the reasons that visual search is used in experiments is that it requires attention. Massaro and Taylor (1980) suggested that the task be used in association with supporting the development of orthographic subword items for children learning to read. We provide their directions:

> Students could be asked to search for letter clusters in common English words. It is not necessary (and, in fact, not desirable) that all of the words be in the child's written vocabulary. Students could be given a vertical list of words and asked to search the list from the top down, check each word that contains a particular letter cluster. A stopwatch could be used to measure the search time, and some score could be given in terms of the number of [specified items] found and the time it takes them to identify the specified item. Following the game the children can discuss where they have found letters and clusters and what general rule of thumb might be helpful. (p 740)

We see extensive possibilities for visual searches and developed some ideas. Note that we do not think that the practice sheet with cells is appropriate for the search task. We envision one kind of visual search presentation, as shown. Notice that we did not make the number of targets consistent.

→Check All the Words That . . .

contain *br*	contain *an*	contain *lant*	contain *plant*
brown	plan	slant	plantable
green	piano	lantern	supplant
string	reader	talent	recount
brilliant	similar	predict	mention
sabre	animal	gallant	rescues
chapter	storage	planter	replant
cluster	letters	matches	plantings
rubric	ankle	jubilant	servant
rustle	initial	relation	traveler
hybrid	position	antelope	salient
bring	brand	insulant	medium
being	remark	response	repaired

Visual searches can be done with and without speed. As mentioned earlier, Massaro and Taylor (1980) suggest that after a search the teacher and children discuss in what positions in words they found the target letter string. The authors' intent seems clear; they want children to become cognizant as to where specific letter strings are likely located. In the case of *br*, the generalization is that the *br* cluster can be found at the beginning and middle of words, not at the end. *An* and *ant* may be found in all three locations, beginning, middle, and end, and *lant* at beginning and end. Such discussion may result in knowledge of actual locations of a letter string in a specific word. But perhaps more important, such discussions may alert children that a given subword string is found in certain positions and not in others. Although they may not learn specific locations for a certain string, they at least may develop an understanding that position is a consideration that matters.

Word Games

Hangman/Wheel of Fortune

The original game is played around the world. The TV show *Wheel of Fortune* is an adaptation. The game can be played by two players or a group of players, each of whom takes a turn at being Player A, with the remaining players on the guessing side. The object of the game is to determine a secret word from knowledge of the category to which the word belongs and the number of letters in the word. The number of letters is represented by written dashes with spaces between the dashes. A player on the guessing side offers a letter. If the letter belongs in the word, Player A fills in the letter on the appropriate dash everywhere it appears. In the original hangman game, if an incorrect letter is offered, that individual moves toward the "gallows." If the word is identified before arriving at the gallows, the player who identified the word wins; if not, the player is "hanged." Of course, other rewards and consequences can be developed. Among the things that might be learned are, first, choose a vowel if it's a long word; also, choose a second consonant if there's a consonant at the beginning of a word that can start a consonant cluster. For example, if the first letter is *b*, try an *r* or an *l*; and so forth. The idea is not necessarily that children are told to follow some probabilities, but rather that they get a sense of such matters. As attempts to spell a target word materialize, sequences of letters and their positions are shown.

Find Little Words in Big Words

The examples in the following chart show from one to three little words.

open pen	vegetable get, table, able
apartment part, art, me, men	microwave crow, row, wave
personal per, son	environment iron, on, men, me
opportunity port, or, it, unity	whisker whisk, his, is
origin or, rig, in	forget for, or, get, forge

Many additional examples can be found on the Internet. An example to work out with a class is *information* (*inform, in, for, or, form, mat, at, on*).

Anagrams

An anagram is a word made by using letters of another word in a different order. Often the words are provided by category. With animals as a category, the first word is the target word and the second column is another word that uses all the letters of the target words.

act	cat
pea	ape
tab	bat
bare	bear
flow	wolf
loin	lion
looped	poodle

An Instructional Invention That Focused on Subword Units

The assumed relationship between orthographic knowledge and fast word recognition guided the design of two computer programs. The aim was to increase orthographic knowledge by arranging conditions that encouraged extensive identification and manipulation of subword units. My talented and creative late colleague, Steve Roth, and I (Isabel) developed two computer programs, Construct a Word (CAW) and Hint and Hunt (HH; Roth & Beck, 1987) to enhance the accuracy and speed of word recognition processes for students whose reading performances were substantially below average by the time they reached the intermediate grades.

The participants for the study were the 108 children from all fourth-grade classes in two schools in a large city. Children in both schools were from low-socioeconomic-status (SES) backgrounds, and all were African American. The schools were several blocks apart and were selected because of their similar histories of low reading achievement and the similar low-SES background of students. In the school in which the computer instruction was given, there were 59 students in three classrooms. There were 49 students in three classrooms in the control school, with similar SES backgrounds. Students in the experimental classroom participated across 20 weeks for three 20-minute computer sessions per week.

This provided each student with 20–24 hours of computer use over the course of the study.

The principal activity of both programs was composing words of orthographic letter strings. For CAW, we developed 20 levels of materials sequenced according to the length and complexity of the words that they form. We created a pool of some 250 word parts that, when combined across all 20 levels of materials, would produce several thousand words. The principal activity of HH, like that of CAW, involved attending to subword letter strings. However, in HH the specific goal was to increase the efficiency with which vowels and vowel combinations are used to identify words.

The goal was to achieve accurate and automatic processing not for a set of words but rather for a large set of multilayer subword units that are present in thousands of other words. In this sense the program was designed to develop decoding skills and orthographic knowledge that are generalizable.

Another aspect of the programs' design was rapid response rates. The programs encouraged fast responses in order to create a game-like activity that would maintain students' interest over long time periods. It is important to point out that the emphasis on rapid response rates in the programs' design did not assume that speeded activities cause efficiency. Rather, the role of speed was motivational, that is, to create a game-like atmosphere that would encourage extensive practice.

The instruction led to substantial increases in the accuracy and efficiency of students' decoding and word recognition processes. Moreover, the improvements were also general in the following ways. First, decoding improvements were found in tasks that were different in form from the activities of the instruction. Second, the effects were not limited to a specific set of words contained in the instruction, nor to words per se (i.e., pseudoword decoding was enhanced as well). Third, the decoding improvements led to advances in speed as well as accuracy. It is important to note that only students who were low in ability on all tasks achieved decoding improvements. Students who were more adequate decoders at pretest did not show changes in either speed or accuracy. The magnitude of the changes for the low groups was substantial when considered in terms of standardized norms.

The computer programs that provided CAW and HH are far out of date. But the ideas and the evidence that manipulation of onsets and rimes with students' control of how fast they want to attempt engaging in the activity and the number of times they want to attempt any set suggest that current development of the approach for the computer is worthwhile. Furthermore, a paper-and-pencil version could be developed that uses the approach. (Details of how both programs function are provided in the published article; Roth & Beck, 1987.)

Poor readers do not notice larger orthographic units. For example, in Levy's (2001) work they did not "see" the same orthographic segments when their occurrences were not made obvious. But when the same orthographic unit was in some way made visible in a useful way (e.g., by grouping words in their families), learning was facilitated. Color as a way to bring attention to orthographic units was not helpful. But attention can be brought in additional ways, including teacher comments. The goal of orthographic activities—to focus attention on word and subword units—might be thought about as the mantra for orthographic instruction. The point is to move knowledge of grapheme–phoneme correspondences to knowledge of the pronunciation of larger orthographic units, (e.g., *tice* to /tice/, *cog* to /cog/, *then* to /then/, *come* to /come/, *phob* to /phob/, *sys* to /sys/). Ehri (2005) makes the critical point clearly: children must acquire basic connections between orthographic patterns and their phonological equivalents. This supports automaticity, which is the topic of our next and last chapter.

Isabel's Anecdote

I had given an assignment to a methods class to develop the content for several of the word games. The next week one of the students, a third-grade teacher, reported that one of her children gave her a slip of paper with *prestidigitation* written on it and suggested that it would be a good word for finding little words in. The teacher asked where he got the word, and he said his dad remembered finding little words in it when he was in school. His dad had told him that it had to do with what magicians do.

The next week another student in my class told us that one of the children's parents had told the child that she could find lists of long words on the Internet and to search for words of six or more syllables. The word got around, and the teacher was inundated with long words. She then made a rule that she wouldn't accept a word unless whoever offered the word knew something about what it meant. That reduced the deluge, especially of medical terms, the meanings of which were easy to find but still out of reach.

The teacher wanted to put an end to it, so she made the rule that bringing in words would depend on the students' language arts report card grades. An A allowed two words and a B one word. The response from a child was, "Why are you trying to slow down our education?"

• • • • • • • • • • YOUR TURN • • • • • • • • • •

We have received positive feedback from teachers about each of the word activities we offered. Generally the comments are that all age groups like the search for subword units. The younger children like finding the little words in big words, and the older children like the hangman game. Try the activities out with your classes. How did they go? How might you adapt them? Ask the children which units they think should be the object of searches, which big words to use, and the like.

CHAPTER 12

Automaticity

Presently there seems to be a lot of talk about fluency, but not so much about automaticity. Perhaps this is the case because automaticity came into the current instructional world under fluency with the NRP's (2000) position that fluency was one of the five major components of reading skill. NRP defined fluency as "the ability to read text quickly, accurately and with proper expression [prosody]" (p. 3–5). Of those three components, the first one, "read text quickly," is closely associated with automaticity. In fact, doing something at a fast rate is a hallmark of automaticity: "speed is an important criterion for automaticity because an increase in speed . . . is characteristic of the development of automaticity. For every task that can be automatized, performance gets faster with practice" (Logan, 1997, pp. 123–124).

We view automatic word recognition as the core of fluency. A student who reads words automatically is likely a fluent reader. Other writers also stress prosody (smoothness, tone, expression; Allington, 1983), but we see word recognition automaticity as the linchpin to fluency and suggest that rapid, efficient word recognition at least supports prosody, if it doesn't produce it.

In the first 11 chapters of this book, we kept an eye on the relationship between speech and written language at the word and subword units. Our goal was to provide our readers with strategies and mechanisms that they can use to teach students to accurately decode and recognize words. However, decoding and recognizing words accurately is only the beginning—an essential beginning, but not sufficient for becoming a competent reader. In order to explore this issue, we first present two teaching experiences that describe children in the early grades who are not on trajectories to successful reading; one from Isabel, another from Mark.

Isabel's Story

My initial teaching experiences were in first grade, 1 year in southern California and the other on the East Coast in an urban school district. That there were 40 children in each of those classes may tell you how long ago it was. At the end of the 2 years, my assessment of the status of their reading was that, of the 80 children, about 60 appeared to be on their way to becoming good readers; of the remaining 20 children, less than half, say about seven or so, were at the top of my worry list, as they were in serious trouble. The remaining 13 or so children were shaky. What I meant by shaky is that they were hesitant readers. They read correctly, but they didn't seem to have confidence.

I observed this even more clearly when I taught third grade. I would tell these shaky third-grade students, "You're right. You're doing fine. Have more confidence." It didn't help; they just were not as confident as the good readers. Although I had some misgivings about how those 12 or so children would fare, my general conclusion was optimistic; that is, if they didn't get discouraged, they'd be all right. It would just take them longer.

Circumstances during my first 3 years of teaching did not allow me to stay in the same place, so I could not check on how my shaky students were doing in second grade. In contrast, Mark, in his position as a reading specialist, is able to follow some students, and he will tell you about Alex.

Mark's Story: The Case of Alex

I had known Alex since he was in kindergarten, although I didn't work closely with him until he was in second grade. In kindergarten and first grade, Alex was considered a good student. He could figure out the pronunciation of words that could be sounded out, and he knew the required irregular high-frequency sight words. Moreover, he rarely made mistakes.

At the beginning of second grade, his teacher informally rated his reading as at the lower end of the middle group, but by the second semester of second grade, she thought his reading had dropped to the struggling group because he seemed to be working very hard—too hard—to get through a sentence. Although she knew Alex was a slow reader, he was not making any progress. On top of all that, his scores on the comprehension sections of weekly reading tests were falling. And his motivation to read had stalled. None of this made much sense because he was a very accurate decoder. His decoding was so good that he could decode words that included graphemes that had not yet been covered in the phonics sequence his teacher followed.

When his second-grade teacher asked me to "look at Alex," I suggested that first she and I look at his fluency scores. Alex's folder included his first-grade fluency scores. Across the 1½-year record, Alex's fluency scores were always below benchmarks in terms of correct words per minute (CWPM), but his accuracy scores were high. At the beginning of second grade his fluency scores were further below benchmarks.

What was going on with Alex? Had it been back in my early years of teaching, when I (Isabel) described those 13 first graders, at the beginning of this chapter, as being shaky, I would have said the same about Alex. I would have identified the reason as I had decades earlier: Alex lacked confidence. Moreover, my solution would be the same as it had been for my 13 shaky first-grade readers: it would just take Alex longer. And I would have been wrong. Fortunately, I learned better.

Sometime in the 1970s, I attended a colloquium at the University of Pittsburgh that was presented by Charles Perfetti, a very prominent psycholinguist who has studied reading for many years, and I became acquainted with the role of automaticity of lower level processes in reading. What I had mistaken for lack of confidence was likely lack of automaticity. Alex was the quintessential example of an accurate, but not automatic, reader.

Accuracy is, of course, a necessary, but not sufficient, condition to becoming a competent reader. Being able to recognize and decode words correctly is half of a full cup, perhaps even the easier half to achieve. To a large extent, the first 11 chapters were about accuracy. In this chapter we visit the other half of the cup: automaticity.

Properties of Automaticity

A while back, in their attempts toward understanding automaticity deeply, researchers identified properties in addition to speed that were involved in automaticity. Let's look at several properties that appeared in one way or another on most lists: effortlessness, autonomy, and absence of consciousness.

Effortlessness

Recently, I (Isabel) was enrolled in a gym class. On one occasion the instructor began to teach us to walk on a straight line the way police are purported to ask a possibly inebriated individual to walk—heel of one foot virtually touching the toe of the other foot. Our instructor, Beth, walked the line almost continually, talking all the while. "Cheryl, focus on a spot farther out than where your feet are." To a student who sneezed, "God bless you. Do you want a Kleenex?" Then she noticed a student who told us that she would be leaving early to get to the airport. In the middle of the class, as that classmate went to the door, Beth said, "Have a great trip." One of the characteristics of effortlessness is being able to do two things at the same time. Beth could walk the straight line and talk at the same time. To do so, one of the activities has to be automated, and since Beth made novel comments to specific students, walking the line was the automatized activity. As for those of us in the class, our attempts to walk the straight line might be compared to a young child who is attempting to blend her first CVC word.

Like my instructor walking a line, students who read automatically are doing so without much effort at all. They recognize the words and make their way through the text without attention being paid to components of the word. And students who do so can devote their attention to comprehension, which is what they need to do to become proficient readers.

Autonomy

You do something that you don't intend to do. A task is considered autonomous if an individual seems compelled to do it. The example is the well-known Stroop effect. There are various versions of the Stroop task, but the easiest to explain, without showing colored drawings, is the stimulus that is used in the task. An individual is presented with the printed names of colors in ink that is not the actual color of the printed word. For example, the word *blue* is printed in orange ink, the word *green* is printed in red ink, and so on. The instruction to an individual who is engaging in the task is to report the *color of the ink*. For example, she is supposed to say "orange" even though the printed word is *blue*. Most adults cannot do that easily. Although the reader is trying to report the color of the ink and trying not to deal with the meaning of the word, the reader cannot help but process the meaning of the print. The Stroop effect demonstrates the interference caused by reading a word even when the task calls for naming a color. Look for images of the Stroop test on the Internet. There appear to be a number of them, and you can actually take the test on some sites. Even though you know the "trick," it doesn't seem to help very much.

Absence of Consciousness

We knew an individual who virtually could not prevent himself from reading if print was in sight. When chatting at the breakfast table, should a cereal box be placed near enough to read, the individual stopped participating in table conversation and read the box cover. Should someone suggest that reading while others are at the table was inappropriate, the individual's response would be something like, "Sorry. I wasn't aware I was doing that."

The Importance of Automaticity

Psychologists have studied automaticity for over 100 years. In the early years the interest was on perceptual–motor skills, but it shifted to cognitive skill in the 1970s.

The cognitive orientation focused on reading, with the publication of LaBerge and Samuels's (1974) highly influential theoretical paper on the role of automatic processing in all human beings' limited capacity. LaBerge and Samuels concluded that word-level automaticity in reading develops over time through the reader's making associations and connections among features, lines, graphemes, and the like until words are ultimately recognized as units and recognized automatically. Let's look at the role of automaticity in reading in the context of the goal of reading—comprehension of text.

A start to understanding the process is an appreciation of the fact that reading is a very complex skill. Developing that appreciation is hindered by the fact that reading appears to be such a mundane endeavor. In this regard, Just and Carpenter (1987) captured the complexity of reading when they made the point that

> an expert can make a complex skill look easy. But the apparent effortlessness of a chess master or concert pianist does not deceive us. What we sometimes fail to appreciate is that skilled reading is an intellectual feat no less complex than chess playing. Readers of this book are, in many ways, as expert at reading as chess masters are expert at chess. But because of the deceptively effortless look and feel of reading . . . reading skill is not given as much credit for complexity as other forms of expertise. (p. 3)

The mental operations involved in reading include recognizing words and associating them with concepts stored in memory; developing meaningful ideas from groups of words (phrases, clauses, sentences); drawing inferences; relating what is already known to what is being read; and more. For a reader to comprehend a text, all these mental operations must take place, many of them concurrently or in functional parallelism.

That a reader has to do so much produces a conflict with the fact that human information-processing capacity is limited. People simply cannot pay active attention to many things at once. Hence the conflict between the fact that reading requires the reader to coordinate a number of mental operations and the fact that human information processing is limited.

The negative impact of engaging in a complex process in which lower-level subprocesses have not been developed to automaticity is easily recognized in the psychomotor domain. Borrowing from an example offered by Samuels, compare a competent basketball player and a novice basketball player as each dribbles during a game. The competent individual dribbles efficiently, giving no conscious attention to dribbling. That individual can direct attention to the higher-level components of the game, such as avoiding a steal, getting into position to pass, or maneuvering to a place where the ball can be dunked.

Now think of a youngster who knows how to dribble but needs to pay a certain amount of conscious attention to dribbling to do it well. In a game, if that child devotes too much attention to dribbling, the higher-level components, such as passing and shooting, may not be performed successfully. But if the novice diverts too much attention to the higher-level components, dribbling ability could break down, and he might lose the ball. Similarly, if a reader needs to spend too much mental energy in getting through the words, it is highly unlikely that the meaning of the material that is being read will be well understood.

Consequences of Nonfluent Reading

Many children develop automatic word recognition as they proceed through formal reading instruction with no special attention given to its development. Other children going through the same formal reading instruction come away lacking automatic word recognition skills. It is more than likely that a vicious cycle begins here. Those children who develop effective word processing skills early in the learning-to-read process are the ones more likely to read, especially out of school. This extra practice in reading exacerbates word-recognition-skill differences between those who read often and those who don't. For those who do not read often and are likely destined to have inadequate word recognition skills, early instructional intervention aimed directly at building automatic word processing proficiency is essential. We discuss this issue toward the end of this chapter.

The Acquisition of Automaticity

Earlier we considered other properties besides speed—effortlessness, autonomy, absence of consciousness—that are characteristic of automaticity. Now we consider another question: What is it that practice and repetition, which are the bywords of developing automaticity, do?

Theories of Acquisition

To answer the preceding question, let's consider three theories that are particularly relevant to reading: strength theory, instance theory, and chunking theory.

Strength Theory

This theory asserts that practice strengthens the bonds between a stimulus and a response. For example, the link between grapheme *s* with its phoneme /s/ or the syllable *per* with its pronunciation and a written word with its speech representation gets stronger. Those connections may start out weak, but practice makes them stronger. The analogy might be that the connection is first a flimsy thread, then packing string, then clothesline rope, and eventually rigging used on boats.

Instance Theory

Logan (1997) suggested that every instance of a stimulus "lays down a separate memory trace or an instance representation that can be retrieved when the [stimulus] repeats itself" (p. 130). In terms of reading, the instance theory is represented in long-term memory. The theory postulates that with many memory traces, retrieval from memory can be thought about as a race among instances, and "the more likely it is that one trace will be retrieved exceptionally quickly" (p. 132).

Chunking Theories (Unitization)

Chunking refers to reducing a response from several pieces to larger pieces and then one piece. It could be by chunking /c/ /a/ /t/ to the onset *c* and the rime *at* and, best of all, to the whole word *cat* or chunking the syllables *ad van tage* to *advantage*. The fewer the chunks the reader needs to deal with, the less use of limited resources. Logan (1997) suggests that theories of chunking underlie unitization. According to LaBerge and Samuels (1974), once a student can, with repetition, recognize a word as a unit, the need to pay attention to the letters singularly or in strings disappears, and the whole word is recognized. Thus the reader's mental resources can be focused on higher level components of reading—such as word meaning and inferencing, which are essential to comprehension.

Let's take a look at unitization and how it plays out in the course of learning to read. Initially, a student usually learns to read words by associating graphemes with phonemes and then sounding them out one step at a time. Early on, a student may read the word *dig* as /d/ /i/ /g/ . . . *dig*. Proper phonics instruction enabled the student to do so, and we initially applaud his accuracy. However, the student is still processing at the grapheme level and not yet at the completed-word level. In order to develop into an automatic reader over time, he needs to recognize and process the word as a unit: *dig*.

Evidence of Unitization in Common Words

Drewnowski and Healy (1977) conducted a letter detection study with adults who were asked to read a passage and cross off the letter *a* every time it appeared. They found that adult readers were more likely to err when the target letter was found in very common words, such as in *and*. They did, however, notice the individual letter *a* more often in less familiar words, such as *ant*. It seems likely that the reader is reading familiar words as units and never processing the individual letters. This provides some evidence that familiar words, those that readers have encountered with a great degree of repetition, are more likely to be read as units. This finding has been replicated a number of times (see, e.g., Marino & Ferraro, 2008). Given that the populations in these studies were competent adult readers who had a lot of exposure to such words, the conclusion is that repetition enhances one's ability to read words as unitized packages, rather than processing them letter by letter.

Unitization and Fluency

Harn, Stoolmiller, and Chard's (2008) work sheds some light on the relationship between unitization and fluency in young children. To explore unitization, the authors added a dimension to the Dynamic Indicators of Basic Early Literacy Skills (DIBELS) called Nonsense Word Fluency (NWF). In the NWF, first-grade students were asked to decode two- and three-letter nonsense words, such as *ap, lon*, and *bep*, and, as specified in the scoring directions, they were given credit for each phoneme they pronounced correctly independent of whether they produced the word as a unit.

As part of the administration of the NWF, the authors also kept track of whether students demonstrated unitization when they read *lon* instead of /l/ /o/ /n/. With that data in hand, students were then assessed for oral reading fluency, the CWPM. Results showed that students who had read the words as units demonstrated significantly higher fluency scores than students who read phoneme by phoneme. Harn and her colleagues' work provides some evidence about what may have been going on with Alex. Although we can't know for certain, we suspect that Alex's performance on a pseudoword assessment may have looked like *g e b*, the standard marking for phoneme by phoneme reading, and not *geb*, the marking for unitization. Alex's potential continued lack of unitization suggests that his fluency may suffer. And real-world experience tells us that that is exactly what happened. As such, we are left with the notion that encouraging unitization, even for children as young as in first grade, may be an important property of developing reading fluency.

Having considered properties of and some theories about the acquisition of automaticity, we devote the remainder of this chapter to some practical implications for improving automaticity.

Practice and Repetition

The clear implication of the three theories of acquisition of automaticity that we have mentioned is that practice and repetition enhance automaticity. In addition to the influence on developing automaticity, the critical role that volume of reading makes to vocabulary development and comprehension is well established (Stanovich & West, 1989). Those who read a lot will encounter many repetitions of common words, as well as encounters with new words. And then more reading will allow encounters with new words, and on it goes.

Of course, we know that those who read more become better readers. We know this, but all too often we do not fully appreciate the amount of repetition, the actual volume of reading, necessary to become automatic and therefore fluent. And if we do not deeply appreciate the scope and cause of the problem, we are in less of a position to fix it.

Along these lines, let's look at Anderson and colleagues' (1988) study with fifth-grade students who were required to keep track of the number of minutes that they read at home. Based on certain assumptions and mathematical probabilities, the total number of minutes was then correlated with total number of words likely read by the students during the school year.

In the following table we summarize and highlight some data from that study. The left column reports the average number of minutes students read each day across the school year. The percentiles are the ranks into which those numbers of minutes fall. For example, 21.1 minutes per day ranked in the 90th percentile for number of minutes that that group of students read. And the last column is the number of words a student in each percentile rank would cover in one school year.

Number of minutes read at home per day	Percentiles	Number of words read at home per school year
65.0	98th	4,358,000
21.1	90th	1,823,000
9.6	70th	622,000
4.6	50th	282,000
1.3	30th	106,000
0.7	20th	21,000

Let's examine the numbers from the point of view of a struggling, less-than-fluent reader. A reader in the lowest 20th percentile may be reading as few as 20,000 words at home in fifth grade, which is not much. In order to be raised to the 50th percentile level, he may need to read about 280,000 words, which is a fourteenfold increase from 20,000.

What are the practical implications of those numbers? Before we offer a few, we would like to suggest that developing a certain mindset is a critical first step. I (Mark) spend at least 75% of my time with struggling readers between kindergarten and fifth grade. Most of them are not automatic or fluent readers. I believe that increasing the amount of appropriate and meaningful reading that they do in school has to be among my primary goals (at least from about mid-first grade on). Every minute that I read with them in groups, working on decoding or engaged in other reading processes, I always carry in the back of my mind the idea that the number of words they read, the number of minutes they are reading over the course of the school year, is very important. Many of my decisions along the way flow directly from this mindset.

We are very dedicated to encouraging at-home reading through motivation and rewards. The problem, however, is that those who need to read at home the most are the students least likely to do so. In one current pilot attempt to increase out-of-school reading, we have seen increases in amount of reading for about 80% of the children. The 20% who are not engaging are the less skilled readers. Of course, a large part of the reason that those children do not participate is that reading is too hard. Therefore, although it will not close the gap between those who read at home and those who don't, increasing reading in school can go part of the way.

Refining Instructional Practice

We think about two sides to the idea of refining instructional practice. One side is that practices that are not helpful for automaticity should be closely examined or eliminated. Such a candidate is the practice of moving children through their reading materials at a constant pace, proceeding on to harder and harder selections, regardless of a child's ease in reading. A word pool that is constantly increasing in size and difficulty may allow little opportunity for automatic word recognition to develop.

The other side of refining is to examine promising practices and consider how they might be enhanced, as well as considering potential practices that are at best underused. Because promising practices all fall under repeated reading, let's start with a very brief description of repeated reading.

Repeated Reading

Repeated reading is the most recommended instructional strategy for improving automaticity. To the best of our knowledge, repeated reading as a pedagogical approach was brought to the modern reading instructional world by Samuels (1979). Samuels was coauthor with LaBerge (1974) of the widely read and highly influential theoretical paper about the role of automaticity in reading. Samuels's interest in the creation of instructional strategies for developing automaticity was based on his observation of typical classroom reading instruction. When students read aloud, Samuels became concerned with the lack of fluency that they exhibited. He placed the blame on the rapid pace with which lessons proceeded. He noticed that students were getting new texts, which included new words, at least several days a week, if not daily. And they read each text once.

In Samuels's version of repeated readings, students read aloud a short passage to an individual (e.g., teacher, cross-age tutor, highly skilled students, parent volunteers). In between reading the passage to the other individual, students practiced reading the passage on their own, generally four times. When a satisfactory level of fluency as measured by CWPM was reached, the procedure was repeated on a new passage.[1] In a synthesis of research on the effects of instruction targeted to increasing reading rate, the repeated-readings approach, more than any other, demonstrated increased reading rate (Chard, Vaughn, & Tyler, 2002).

The Nature of Texts Used for Repeated Reading

One of the recurrent themes in fluency research is that the materials students read for fluency practice should not be too difficult. For instance, Pikulski and Chard (2005) make the point that "controlling the difficulty of text . . . seem[s] to be associated with improved rate and accuracy for those students developing fluent reading" (p. 516). It seems sensible that repeated readings should be chosen in which students can recognize virtually all or almost all of the words. Otherwise, increasing rate is beyond what children should do. That is, accuracy is an essential prerequisite to fluency training. If children cannot read most of the words in a passage correctly, there is little point in encouraging them to read faster.

Generally, text difficulty is determined through application of readability formulas and other quantitative approaches, such as lexiles, that then provide numerical information. Readability formulas and lexile scores are content free. Each can be applied to any passage and result in a numerical score. Readability formulas will provide grade levels (e.g., 2.4 means that the text is appropriate for second graders in their fourth month of school), or a basal company's coding system will use 2.1 for the first half of second grade and 2.2 for the second half of second grade. The lexile scale runs from below 0 to above 1,100. Specific lexile scores do not have a one-to-one correspondence with a grade level; rather, lexiles provide a range of scores for a grade (e.g., the range for fourth grade is from 445L to 810L). To the best of my knowledge, the most widely used basal programs use both readability formulas and lexiles. The content-free nature of the variables used to establish readability does not tell us about the nature of the words within, say, a 1.7 readability grade level. One could have a 1.7 text with 90% of the words decodable or a 1.7 readability grade with 90% of the words not decodable.

WHAT WORDS COMPOSE TEXTS FOR YOUNG READERS?

The two categories of words that are of particular interest in repeated-reading practice are decodable words and high-frequency sight words. Decodable words can be sounded out, and high-frequency sight words that may have irregular spellings are taught as whole words.

---

[1]There are various versions of the general sequence of (a) assess CWPM, (b) read, and (c) assess CWPM. Sometimes CWPM is determined after each reading; sometimes a CWPM criterion is established and rereading occurs until it is reached. Sometimes the teacher reads the passage first. If the passage is being read to another individual, that person provides error correction and feedback. The details of the various versions are available in many sources, as are adaptations for group rereading.

Decodable Words. We focus on decodable words for the early grades because with minimal phonics instruction young children can decode such words. Moreover, most decodable, one-syllable words are made up of an onset and a rime and include subword units (*m an*) found in other single-syllable words (*plan*), as well as in many multisyllable words (*animal*). There has been some disagreement about what constitutes a decodable word for children just learning to read. A word can be categorized as decodable if students have been taught all the grapheme–phoneme correspondences needed to decode it.

Sight Words. Sight words is the label given to some high-frequency words that are taught as whole words to be memorized, purportedly because they cannot be sounded out. Additionally, high-frequency words, including function words (e.g., *a, my, the, to, like, he, come, get, let, this*),[2] are included because they are necessary to develop stories. Sight words and the way to teach them became institutionalized by Edward Dolch (1948) who published a list of the 220 most frequently used words in children's books. For those of our readers who are not primary-grade teachers, we think it could be hard for you to imagine the extent to which the Dolch words and the way to teach them have become institutionalized.

Presently, the "sight word" label has begun to appear in the cognitive psychology research literature. But the use of it in such literature has nothing to do with methods of teaching beginning word recognition or with how certain high-frequency irregular words are taught. Rather, the present use of the term *sight word* in the research literature describes a major property of competent reading. It refers to how competent readers read words. They do so by sight; they recognize them instantly, automatically.

Texts or Lists?

Connected text is the format that was used in the earliest repeated-reading endeavors and remains the norm. Some recent studies, however, in which students practice reading lists of words that they would encounter in connected texts, resulted in increased fluency for texts that included those words (Levy, Abello, & Lysynchuk, 1997). The findings about which is best—practice with connected texts or words in isolation—indicate that they both improve rate.

Another aspect of fluency practice is the extent to which words from one cycle of fluency practice are repeated in the next cycle. Rashette and Torgesen (1985) looked at this issue directly in a study with fourth-grade students. Students were divided into three groups. One group of students read text in which there was high overlap of words among the different passages read. In the second group, there was

---

[2]Some sight words can be sounded out and thus could be taught through phonics instruction, but they may have been included as sight words because they were needed to construct connected text before their graphemes were taught.

low overlap of words. A third group read independently. There were significantly greater increases in rate for the group in which there was high overlap. In contrast, when there was not high overlap, that group's increases were no greater than those of the third group, who read independently across the duration of the study. Common sense would not find it surprising that repetition has a positive effect. Theory, too, would predict positive results, but theory goes further and suggests how the effects might occur. For example, strength theory would point to repetition as a mechanism for strengthening bonds between written and spoken words.

Increasing Reading Volume in School

So the goal is practice and repetition. What activities, in addition to straight repeated reading, might help students in this regard? Here we offer two suggestions, but first we pause to consider one important issue. When reading in class, whole group or small group, who should do the reading?

Let's look at reading in a small group. In a group of six, there are only so many possibilities. Students can read a portion by themselves. Groups of two or three can read a passage. All six can read together. At times, the teacher may even read some. There is no one-size-fits-all method, but we suggest moving more and more to having all students read together much of the time. Mini-choral reading, one might call it. More reading is taking place, and there are fewer chances for off-task behavior. And more reading means more chance for practice and repetition. Less fluent readers are less self-conscious because they are not singled out. Faster readers can be coached to stay with the group. My (Mark's) experience has been that it is all quite doable and likely to yield better results. The difficult part is that students, particularly as they move into higher grades, do not like to repeat the same passage. Cleverness and creativity are called for. Next, we offer two possible ways to read with students and have them repeat.

Group Reading of Short Stories

A typical leveled or decodable reader at certain points in second grade may include about 14 pages, containing 350–600 words altogether. Imagine a group of five or six students engaged in reading such material. Typically, the students make their way through the text, reading it through only one time. Instead, I have often had them read as follows:

- Student A reads page 1. All six students repeat page 1.
- Student B reads page 2. All six students repeat page 2.
- And so on until the entire 14-page story is read.
- The group reads the entire story one more time with an eye on the clock, gradually realizing how much more easily and fluently they read when it's the second or third time through.

In the preceding example, one can make a case that the students, if following along at all times, actually read the words three times. And so they read 1,050 words, not 350. If they do so four times per week, 30 weeks per year, they will have read 126,000 words, a fair amount, instead of 42,000 words, which amounts to a threefold increase. Of course, assumptions and calculations can be challenged, but the overall point stands.

Readers' Theater

As students graduate to chapter books, it becomes even harder to encourage them to repeat passages. When the book contains substantial dialogue, I have taken the time to retype it in a reader's theater format. Certain parts, such as a character's thoughts or narration, are read as a group and denoted in italics. Students read the entire book the traditional way and then again, from the beginning, as a play. They are being tricked to repeat much of the book but are not likely to object.

Final Comment

We decided to include this last chapter on automaticity to reinforce the notion that although accurate word recognition is necessary, the goal needs to be accurate and automatic word recognition. All too often, we've heard adults describing a struggling student with the phrase "But I know he *can* do it." And our response is usually the same: "He *can* do it, but can he do it *automatically*?" Accurate word recognition is a half-full glass. Our collective goal must be to fill the glass to the top.

Mark's Anecdote

Imagine a second-grade student reading a passage for 1 minute. When he finishes, I'll say something like "Wow! You just read 64 words in a minute! You should be proud of yourself." Almost inevitably, the student reacts positively with some sense of accomplishment. With another student, who is a struggling reader, the same routine takes place. I might exclaim, "You just read 31 words in a minute! Did you realize that?" This student reacts positively.

On occasion, I've said, "Are you sure you're not in third grade?" When students look puzzled, I tell them that I am going to bring them to the third-grade classroom because they are doing so well. Once, my attempt at humor backfired, and a student said, "No, thank you. My brother is in third grade. I get enough of him at home."

• • • • • • • • • • • •YOUR TURN • • • • • • • • • •

If you think that your class needs to spend more time reading, try Mark's suggestion with a small group.

- Student A reads page 1. All six students repeat page 1.
- Student B reads page 2. All six students repeat page 2.
- And so on until the complete story is read.
- The group reads the entire story, one more time.

Do you think the students' reading was more fluent? Do the children think their reading was more fluent? How did the children feel about reading in this format? Are there ways to streamline the procedures and adapt them more for your students?

Word Building Lists

There are eight sequences in Appendix 1. Each comprises a group of spelling patterns, as shown in the following table.

Sequence	Content of sequence	Number of lists	SPA
A	CVC/Short Vowels *a, i, o*	15	SPA-A, to be given after List A15
B	CVC/Short Vowels *e, u*	15	SPA-B, to be given after List B15
C	Consonant Blends	6	SPA-C, to be given after List C6
D	Consonant Digraphs	12	SPA-D, to be given after List D12
E	CVCe Long Vowels	15	SPA-E, to be given after List E12
F	CVVC Long Vowels	12	SPA-F, to be given after List F12
G	*R*-Controlled Vowels	13	SPA-G, to be given after List G13
H	Diphthongs	6	SPA-H, to be given after List H6

Sequence A
CVC/Short Vowels (*a, i, o*)
Lists A1–A3

Sequence A, Lists A1–A3, introduces the short vowel *a* in the medial position. Consonants change frequently in both initial and final positions. The only vowel is the letter *a*, so this is one of the few times that there is not an opportunity for meaningful discrimination with another phonic element. Consonants are usually those encountered early in kindergarten. Note that the *-am* and *-an* rimes in A3 can be challenging for beginning readers.

A1: short *a*	A2: short *a*	A3: short *a*; *-am*; *-an*
m, a, d, s, t, p	c, a, p, t, s, m, r	r, a, n, m, p, c, t
mad	cap	ran
sad	cat	ram
sat	sat	pam
pat	sap	pan
mat	map	man
mad	mat	can
map	rat	cat
sap	rap	pat
tap	map	pan
map	mat	pam
Can a rat tap on a map?	Can a rat have a cap?	Can a cat and a rat rap?
Can a rat pat a cat?	Can a rat rap?	Can a man pat a cat?

Quick Check			
Can student read?	mat	→	If no, repeat A1.
	sap	→	If no, repeat A2.
	pan	→	If no, repeat A3.

Lists A4–A6

In List A4 the grapheme *i* is used for the first time. Two *d* letter cards are required in A4. Lists A5–A6 involve discrimination between short *a* and short *i*.

A4: short *i*	A5: short *i*; short *a*	A6: short *i*; short *a*
p, i, t, s, r, m, d, d, k	s, i, t, f, a, p	b, i, t, d, r, p, s, a
pit	sit	bit
sit	sat	bid
sip	fat	rid
rip	fit	rip
rim	sit	sip
dim	sip	sit
did	sap	sat
kid	tap	bat
rid	sap	bit
rip		pit
sip		pat
Can a kid rip his pants?	Can a bat fit on a cap?	Can a bat sit on a cap?
Can a kid rip a rag?	Can a man sit on the lap of a kid?	Can a cat fit in a pit?

Quick Check			
Can student read?	pit	→	If no, repeat A4.
	sip	→	If no, repeat A5.
	rid	→	If no, repeat A6.

Lists A7–A9

Lists A7–A9 require the student to discriminate between the short *a* sound and the short *i* sound. The introduction of the grapheme *h* can be difficult for students to pronounce initially because of its unvoiced nature.

A7: short *a*; short *i*	A8: short *a*; short *i*	A9: short *a*; short *i*
h, i, t, d, a, s	h, i, t, k, d, m, a	h, i, m, t, a, p, r
hit	hit	him
hid	kit	hit
had	kid	pit
sad	hid	pat
sat	mid	pit
sit	mad	hit
it	mat	hat
at	hat	rat
hat	ham	rap
hit	him	rip
hid	dim	rim
Can you fit in a hat? Can a man sit on the lap of a cat?	Can a mad cat hit a rat? Can a kid fit on a map?	Can a rat rap? Can a rat rip a hat?

Quick Check			
Can student read?	hid	→	If no, repeat A7.
	dim	→	If no, repeat A8.
	pit	→	If no, repeat A9.

Lists A10–A12

List A10 introduces the short vowel, *o*. Lists A11 and A12 require the student to discriminate between short *o* and short *a*.

A10: short *o*	A11: short *o*; short *a*	A12: short *o*; short *a*
h, o, p, t, m, g, d	p, a, t, r, o, l, h, g, m	p, o, t, h, a, d, r, g
hop	pat	pot
top	rat	hot
mop	rot	hop
hop	lot	hot
hog	log	pot
dog	hog	pat
dot	hop	pot
got	mop	dot
hot	map	rot
hop	mop	dot
mop	map	dog
top		hog
Could a hog sit on top of a pot? Could a hog hop on top of a mop?	Could you put a log on a map? Could a pig hop on a pot?	Could a dog pat a pig? Could a pig and a cat hop to a pit?

Quick Check			
Can student read?	hop	→	If no, repeat A10.
	lot	→	If no, repeat A11.
	dog	→	If no, repeat A12.

Lists A13–A15

List A13 requires discrimination between the short *a* and the short *o*. Lists A14 and A15 require the student to discriminate among three short vowels: *a*, *i*, and *o*. These lists ask students to discriminate, for the first time, among three different vowels.

A13: short *o*; short *a*	A14: short *o*; short *i*, short *a*	A15: short *o*; short *i*; short *a*
h, a, t, o c, n	d, o, t, h, a, i, l, c	d, o, t, g, i, r, a, p, h
hat	dot	dot
hot	hot	dog
not	hat	dig
cot	had	rig
cat	hid	rag
at	lid	rat
cat	lit	rot
cot	lot	hot
not	hot	hop
hot	hat	hot
hat	cat	hat
	cot	hit
Could you fit on a cot? Can the Cat in the Hat hop on a dog?	Could a cat sit on the lid of a pot? Could you hop on a cot?	Can you dig for a rag? Could a dog dig for a rag?

Quick Check			
Can student read?	cot	→	If no, repeat A13.
	dot	→	If no, repeat A14.
	hop	→	If no, repeat A15.

⇨ Administer Specific Phonics Assessment (SPA-A) (short *a*, short *i*, short *o*)

If students have difficulty with one or more of the three short vowels, review appropriate Word Building lists. Consider supplementary phonics activities, additional dictation, and additional reading of decodable text.

Sequence B
CVC/Short Vowels (*e, u*)
Lists B1–B6

List B1 introduces the grapheme *e* for the first time. The short *e* phoneme is often the most difficult of the five short vowel sounds. List B2 requires the reader to discriminate between short *e* and short *a*. List B3 requires the reader to discriminate between short *e* and short *o*.

B1: short *e*	B2: short *e*; short *a*	B3: short *e*; short *o*
m, e, n, t, p, g, l, v	m, e, n, t, l, a, s, g, b, f, d	l, e, t, j, v, g, o, b
men	men	let
ten	met	jet
pen	mat	vet
ten	met	get
pen	set	got
pet	let	jot
vet	leg	lot
let	beg	let
get	bag	leg
vet	beg	log
pet	bed	leg
pen	fed	beg
ten	fad	bet
Would a dog let ten men in his pen? Would a vet let a pig beg?	Can ten men sit on a bed? Can a kid get fed in a bed?	Would a man pat a pet's leg? Would a vet let a dog's leg get red?

Quick Check			
Can student read?	men	→	If no, repeat B1.
	set	→	If no, repeat B2.
	let	→	If no, repeat B3.

Lists B4–B6

Lists B4–B6 require the reader to discriminate between short *e* and another short vowel. B4 requires discrimination between short *e* and short *o*. B5 requires discrimination between short *e* and short *a*. B6 asks the reader to discriminate among three vowels: short *e*, short *a*, and short *o*.

B4: short *e*; short *o*	B5: short *e*; short *a*	B6: short *e*; short *a*; short *o*
t, e, n, p, o, l, g	t, e, n, p, w, a, g, b	p, e, t, o, y, a, g, c
ten	ten	pet
pen	pen	pot
ten	pet	pet
pen	wet	yet
pet	pet	pet
pot	pat	pat
not	pet	get
net	peg	got
let	beg	cot
get	bag	cat
got	wag	cap
lot	tag	yap
Would a pet get in a pot? Can ten men get a net on a pig?	Can a cap fit on a wet pet? Can a kid beg a dog to get in a pen?	Can a pet get a cap? Could you put ten cats in a pen?

Quick Check			
Can student read?	get	→	If no, repeat B4.
	peg	→	If no, repeat B5.
	pet	→	If no, repeat B6.

Lists B7–B9

List B7 introduces the grapheme *u*, the fifth and final short vowel. Students will often pronounce the grapheme *u* as /y/, a response that needs to be corrected. List B8 requires discrimination between short *u* and short *a*. List B9 requires discrimination between short *u* and short *o*.

B7: short *u*	B8: short *u*; short *a*	B9: short *u*; short *o*
b, u, g, r, t, n, d	f, a, n, u, r, b, t	c, u, b, o, r, t, n, f, j
bug	fan	cob
rug	fun	rob
rub	run	rub
tub	ran	tub
nub	run	rub
nut	rub	run
rut	tub	fun
rug	tab	run
bug	tub	rut
bud	rub	rot
bun	rut	jot
	nut	jut
Is it fun to pat and rub a pet? Can a bug run?	Would a cub cut a nut? Can you have fun in the tub?	Would you run with a dog for fun? Could you have fun with a dog in the tub?

Quick Check			
Can student read?	bug	→	If no, repeat B7.
	run	→	If no, repeat B8.
	jut	→	If no, repeat B9.

Lists B10–B12

Lists B10–B12 require discrimination between short *u* and one or two other short vowels. List B10 requires the student to discriminate between the short *u* and the short *a*. List B11 contrasts the short *u* and the short *e*. List B12 requires discrimination among three short vowels: short *u*, short *o*, and short *a*.

B10: short *u*; short *a*	B11: short *u*; short *e*	B12: short *u*; short *o*; short *a*
b, a, t, u, n, f	b, u, t, g, e, j	d, u, g, o, r, t, a, c
bat	bug	dug
but	beg	dog
bun	bet	dug
fun	but	rug
fan	bug	rut
ban	beg	rot
bat	bet	rat
but	jet	rot
tub	jut	dot
tab	jet	cot
bat	bet	cat
but	but	cut
nut		
Can a bat eat a nut? Can you eat a bun in the tub?	Can a bug have fun on a rug? Can a bug eat a nut and a bun?	Would a cat and a rat have fun on a rug? Can a cat cut a bun for a dog?

Quick Check			
Can student read?	nut	→	If no, repeat B10.
	bug	→	If no, repeat B11.
	rut	→	If no, repeat B12.

Lists B13–B15

Lists B13–B15 are lengthy and complex lists that require substantial discrimination among all five short vowels. They include an unusually large number of letter cards and should be saved for the very end of the B sequence.

B13: short a/i/o/e/u	B14: short a/i/o/e/u	B15: short a/i/o/e/u
p, a, t, i, o, g, e, r u, b	c, a, n, t, u, o, b, r, i, d, e	h, i, m, a, r, p, l, d, t, o, e, g, u
pat	can	him
pit	cat	ham
pot	cut	ram
got	cot	rap
get	rot	rip
got	cot	hip
pot	cob	lip
pet	cub	lid
pat	rub	lad
rat	rib	had
rut	rid	hid
rub	red	hit
rib	bed	hot
rip	ben	pot
tip	bed	pet
rip	red	get
rap	rod	gut
tap	cod	hut
Would a pet rat rub a cat? Can a rat rip a rag?	Can a big bed be red? Can a hog eat ten cobs and ten ribs?	Can a kid rap in a hut? Would a hot dog get in a tub?

⮕ ## Administer Specific Phonics Assessment (SPA-B)
(short *a*, short *i*, short *o*, short *e*, short *u*)

If students have difficulty with one or more of the five short vowels, review appropriate Word Building lists. Consider supplementary phonics activities, additional dictation, and additional reading of decodable text.

Sequence C
Consonant Blends
Lists C1–C3

The C sequence involves consonant blends. There are many possible two-letter blends, so these lists are not exhaustive. The blends included are among the more common ones.

Lists C1–C3 focus on a number of blends in the initial position. List C1 introduces *st, sl,* and *sp*; C2 introduces *sn* and *sl*; C3 introduces *br* and *tr*. Use of successive blending techniques, as discussed in Chapter 6, can be helpful at this point as students often find it difficult to blend two consonant sounds at the beginning of a word.

C1: *st*; *sl*; *sp*	**C2**: *sn*; *sl*	**C3**: *br*; *tr*
t, o, p, s, l, i	l, a, p, n, s, i, o, t	b, a, g, r, i, p, t
top	lap	bag
stop	nap	brag
top	snap	rag
stop	nap	brag
slop	slap	rag
slot	slip	rig
spot	lip	rip
spit	slip	trip
pit	sip	rip
pot	tip	rap
spot	top	rat
	stop	brat
Can you stop a top? Can you spot a dot on a top?	Could you slip when you stop? Can a pig slip on a nut?	Would you brag if you ran a lot? Could you trip if you had a bad leg?

Quick Check			
Can student read?	stop	→	If no, repeat C1.
	slip	→	If no, repeat C2.
	brag	→	If no, repeat C3.

Lists C4–C6

Lists C4–C6 focus on a number of consonant blends in the final position. List C4 introduces -*st*. C5 involves -*nd*, -*lt*, and -*st*. C6 includes *st, sp,* and *sl,* all in the initial position, as well as -*st* in the final position. The primary purpose of C6 is to familiarize students with the idea that the same blend can be found at the beginning and end of a word.

C4: -*st*		C5: -*nd*; -*lt*; -*st*		C6: *st*; *sp*; *sl*; -*st*	
b, e, s, t, p, a, g, u, r		m, e, n, d, s, t, l, b, f, r		s, t, o p, i, f, l	
bet	rust	men	bet	stop	slot
best	bust	mend	best	spot	slit
pest		send	rest	spit	lit
past		mend		pit	list
pest		men		spit	
pet		met		sit	
peg		melt		fit	
beg		belt		fist	
bet		felt		list	
best		melt		lost	
rest		met		lot	
Can a pet be a pest?		Can ten men rest on a cot?		Can a list get lost?	
Would a pig rest on a bed?		Can ten men send a pet to bed?		Would a pet stop if it got lost?	

Quick Check			
Can student read?	best	→	If no, repeat C4.
	belt	→	If no, repeat C5.
	lost	→	If no, repeat C6.

 Administer Specific Phonics Assessment (SPA-C) (initial and final blends)

If students have difficulty with one or more of the consonant blends, review appropriate Word Building lists. Consider supplementary phonics activities, additional dictation, and additional reading of decodable text.

Sequence D
Consonant Digraphs
Lists D1–D3

Lists D1–D3 introduce two consonant digraphs, -*ck* (always at the end of a word) and *th*, which can be in the initial or in the final position. List D1 introduces the -*ck* grapheme. List D2 introduces the *th* grapheme in the initial and final positions. List D3 involves -*ck* in the final position and *th* in both the initial and final positions.

    Note: It is important to place two-letter digraphs (*ck, th, sh,* and *ch*) on one letter card together.

D1: -*ck*	**D2**: *th*	**D3**: -*ck*; *th*
r, o, ck, t, s, d, m, p, h	th, a, t, h, m, p, b	s, a, ck, i, th, p, t, r, b
rock	that	sack
rot	hat	sick
rock	mat	thick
sock	hat	pick
dock	that	pack
dot	pat	path
rot	path	pat
rock	math	that
mock	bath	rat
mop	bat	rack
hop	that	back
	hat	bath
Can a sock get lost? Can you rest on a rock?	Can a bat do math? Could you trip on a rock on a path?	Could a sock get lost in a bath tub? Can a rat fit in a sock?

Quick Check			
Can student read?	rock	→	If no, repeat D1.
	that	→	If no, repeat D2.
	path	→	If no, repeat D3.

Lists D4–D6

Lists D4–D6 focus on the grapheme *sh*. List D4 presents words with *sh* in the initial position. D5 focuses on words with *-sh* in the final position. D6 involves words with the digraph *sh* in both the initial and final positions.

D4: *sh*	**D5**: *-sh*	**D6**: *sh*; *-sh*
sh, o, p, i, h, t, ck	m, a, sh, r, c, t, d, i, f	c, a, sh, d, i, w, p, o, h, f
shop	mash	cash
ship	rash	dash
hip	cash	dish
ship	cat	wish
shop	rat	dish
hop	rash	dip
top	mash	ship
shop	mat	shop
shock	rat	ship
shop	rash	hip
hop	dash	dip
hip	dish	dish
	fish	fish
Can you hop to the top of a ship? Can a ship hit a fish?	Can you eat fish on a red dish? Can a sick cat have a rash?	Would you wish to have a big dog or a thin cat? Would you brag if you had a lot of cash?

Quick Check			
Can student read?	shop	→	If no, repeat D4.
	rash	→	If no, repeat D5.
	ship	→	If no, repeat D6.

Lists D7–D9

Lists D7–D9 involve the digraphs *ch/-tch*. List D7 presents words with the grapheme *ch* in the initial position. D8 involves words with *-tch* in the final position. D9 includes words with both *ch* in the initial position and *-tch* in the final position.

D7: *ch*	**D8**: *-tch*	**D9**: *ch*; *-tch*
ch, i, p, o, h, t, b, a, c	d, i, t, ch, h, a, c, m, p	ch, a, t, h, c, p, o, r, i
chip	ditch	chat
chop	hitch	hat
cop	hatch	hatch
chop	hat	catch
hop	hatch	cat
hip	catch	chat
chip	cat	chap
hip	mat	chop
hit	match	hop
hat	patch	hip
bat	hatch	rip
cat	hitch	chip
chat	ditch	hip
Do you chat when you sit in a bath tub?	Can you catch a cat in a ditch?	Can you chop chips as you chat?
Can a dog chat with a cat?	Would you match a black sock with a red sock?	Would you rip a chip and toss it in a ditch?

Quick Check			
Can student read?	chip	→	If no, repeat D7.
	match	→	If no, repeat D8.
	chat	→	If no, repeat D9.

Lists D10–D12

Lists D10–D12 involve discrimination among various consonant digraphs in both beginning and final positions.

D10: *sh*; *ch*; *-tch*	**D11**: *sh*; *ch*; *-ch*; *-tch*	**D12**: *th*; *ch*; *-ch*; *-tch*
sh, i, p, ch, a, t, c, r, h, d	ch, i, n, p, sh, o, h, a, t	ch, i, n, th, t, p, d, a, b
ship dash chip dish chap ditch cap chap chat cat rat rash hash hatch hash	chin hot in hat inch hatch in pin pinch pin shin ship shop chop hop	chin batch thin bat tin bath pin pinch pitch ditch dip chip chap chat bat
Would a dish chip if you hit it with a bat? Can a rat eat fish on a dish?	Would you pinch a dog on the chin? Which could be an inch, a hat or a pin?	Can you pitch with a bat? Would you chat as you catch?

Quick Check			
Can student read?	chip	→	If no, repeat D10.
	hatch	→	If no, repeat D11.
	batch	→	If no, repeat D12.

 ## Administer Specific Phonics Assessment (SPA-D) (consonant digraphs)

If students have difficulty with one or more of the consonant digraphs, review appropriate Word Building lists. Consider supplementary phonics activities, additional dictation, and additional reading of decodable text.

Sequence E
Long Vowels/CVCe
Lists E1–E3

Lists E1–E3 introduce words with long *a* and silent *e*. All lists require discrimination between CVC words with short *a* and CVCe words with long *a*. Often this is the student's very first exposure to long vowels.

E1: C*a*Ce	E2: C*a*Ce	E3: C*a*Ce
m, a, t, e, n, c, r, k	g, a, p, t, e, c, k, m, d, n	r a, t, e, p, l, n, s, m
mat	gap	rat
mate	tap	rate
mat	tape	plate
man	tap	plane
mane	cap	plan
cane	cape	plane
can	cake	lane
ran	make	late
rat	made	slate
rate	mad	late
rake	man	mate
make	mane	mat
cake	cane	map
Can a rat make a man mad? Can a man run with a cane?	Can a pet have a cap and cape? Would you be mad if mom made you bake a cake?	Can a plane be late? Would you hit a plate with a rake?

Quick Check			
Can student read?	cane	→	If no, repeat E1.
	made	→	If no, repeat E2.
	plate	→	If no, repeat E3.

Lists E4–E6

Lists E4–E6 introduce words with long *i* and silent *e*. E4 and E5 require discrimination between CVC words with short *i* and CVCe words with long *i*. E6 also includes CVC words with short *a* and CVCe words with long *a*.

E4: *CiCe*	**E5**: *CiCe*	**E6**: *CiCe*; *CaCe*
l, i, d, s, e, h, r, m	f, i, n, e, v, d, m, t, r, p	h, i, d, r, e, a, m, n, p
lid	fine	hid
slid	fin	rid
slide	fine	ride
slid	five	hide
lid	fine	hid
hid	dine	had
hide	dime	mad
side	time	made
ride	tim	mad
rid	tip	man
rim	rip	mane
dim	ripe	mine
dime	ride	pine
Can you hide under a slide? Can you get rid of a dime under the rim of a pot?	Would you dine on fish all the time? Can the tip of a pin fit under a dime?	If a hog made you mad, would you hide, or go for a ride? Can a man hide a pin under a dime?

Quick Check			
Can student read?	hide	→	If no, repeat E4.
	dime	→	If no, repeat E5.
	mine	→	If no, repeat E6.

Lists E7–E9

Lists E7–E9 introduce words with long *o* and silent *e*. E7 and E8 require discrimination between CVC words with short *o* and CVCe words with long *o*. E9 also includes CVC words with short *a* and CVCe words with long *a*.

E7: *CoCe*	**E8**: *CoCe*	**E9**: *CoCe*; *CaCe*
c, o, p, e, s, l, t, m, r, b	h, o, p, e, m, c, d, r, t	c, o, n, e, p, a, t, m, h
cop	hop	cone
cope	hope	cope
slope	mope	cape
slop	mop	cap
stop	cop	tap
top	cope	tape
mop	code	tap
mope	rode	top
rope	rote	mop
robe	rot	mope
rob	cot	hope
		hop
Would a man rob a cop with a rope? Would a dog mope if it got a spot on Mom's robe?	Would you hope to hop to the top of a big rock? Would you mope if you had to mop under a cot?	Would a cop have a cap and a cape? Would you hope to tape a pin to a cop's cap?

Quick Check			
Can student read?	cope	→	If no, repeat E7.
	rode	→	If no, repeat E8.
	mope	→	If no, repeat E9.

Lists E10–E12

Lists E10–E12 introduce words with long *u* and silent *e*. E10 and E11 require discrimination between CVC words with short *u* and CVCe words with long *u*. E12 also includes CVC words with short *o* and CVCe words with long *o*.

E10: *CuCe*	E11: *CuCe*	E12: *CuCe*; *CoCe*
c, u, t, m, e, b, n	r, u, d, d, e, m, t, c, b	c, u, t, e, m, o, p, n
cut	rude	cut
mut	dude	cute
mute	dud	cut
mut	mud	cot
cut	mut	cop
cute	mute	cope
cube	cute	cop
cub	cut	cot
cube	cub	cut
cub	cube	mut
tub	tube	cut
tube	tub	cute
tune	rub	
Can a cute cub sing a tune? Can a bug and a cub fit in a tube or in a tub?	Would a rude dude make you mad? Would a cute cat play in the mud?	Would a cop play the flute on his bike? Would a cute cub rub a cut with mud?

Quick Check			
Can student read?	cute	→	If no, repeat E10.
	rude	→	If no, repeat E11.
	mute	→	If no, repeat E12.

Lists E13–E15

List E13 includes long and short forms of four vowels.

Lists E14 and E15 both involve words in which the *c* is followed by the letter *e* and stands for the soft *c* sound, as in *mice*. At the same time, the vowel sound is made long by the presence of the silent *e* at the end.

E13: *CaCe*; *CiCe*; *CoCe*; *CuCe*	E14: *ice*	E15: *ice*; *ace*
c, u, t, e, a, m, r, o, n, h, i, d	r, i, ck, c, e, n, m, s, p, t	p, a, n, ck, c, e, i, l, s, r
cute not	rick rick	pan span
cut hot	rice sick	pack pan
cat hit	nice trick	pace ran
mat him	nick pick	lace race
mate hid	nice rick	place rice
rate hide	mice	ace
rote	spice	ice
rot	mice	slice
not	price	spice
note	rice	space
Would a rat or a cat hide under a mat? Would a man hide a note under a cot?	Would you like spice on rice? Would five cats like to eat mice?	Should you race on ice? Can a man ride on a bike from place to place?

Quick Check			
Can student read?	cute, mate, note, hide	→	If no, repeat E13.
	rice	→	If no, repeat E14.
	pace	→	If no, repeat E15.

 **Administer Specific Phonics Assessment (SPA-E)
(Long vowels of the CVCe pattern)**

If students have difficulty with one or more of the four long vowels, review appropriate Word Building lists. Consider supplementary phonics activities, additional dictation, and additional reading of decodable text.

Sequence F
Long Vowels/CVVC
Lists F1–F3

Lists F1–F3 introduce the vowel digraphs *ee* and *ea*. List F1 contrasts *ee* with short *e*. List F2 contrasts *ea* with short *e*. List F3 contrasts *ee* and *ea* with short *e*.

F1: *ee*; short *e*	F2: *ea*; short *e*	F3: *ee*; *ea*; short *e*
m, e, t, ee, s, p, b, d, f, n	m e, t, ea, ch, s, h, b, d	s, ee, d, k, m, e, ea, t, n
met	mot	see*
meet	meat	seed
met	eat	seek
set	cheat	meek
pet	seat	meet
bet	set	met
beet	seat	set
beef	eat	sea*
beet	heat	seed
bet	seat	need
bed	set	ned
fed	bet	net
feed	bed	neat
need	bead	eat
seed		*explain difference
Have you seen a man with three feet?	Do you eat meat on a plate?	Would you like to meet a green bat on the street?
Can you feed seeds to fish?	Have you sat on a seat on a ship at sea?	Do you need a net to get a fish in the sea?

Quick Check			
Can student read?	beef	→	If no, repeat F1.
	heat	→	If no, repeat F2.
	neat	→	If no, repeat F3.

Lists F4–F6

Lists F4–F6 introduce the vowel digraphs *ai* and *ay*. List F4 introduces *ai* and contrasts it with the short *a* pattern. F5 introduces *ay* and contrasts it with the short *a* pattern. F6 includes words with both the *ai* and *ay* patterns and contrasts those patterns with the short *a* pattern.

F4: *ai*; **short *a***	**F5**: *ay*; **short *a***	**F6**: *ai*; *ay*; **short *a***
p, ai, n, a, m, r, t	m, ay, a, n, t, r, l, p	p, a, d, ai, ay, n, m
pain	may	pad
pan	man	paid
man	pan	pad
main	pay	pay
man	pan	pan
ran	pat	pain
rain	pan	main
train	ran	man
rain	ray	may
ran	lay	mad
pan	lap	maid
pain	map	main
main	may	pain
Can a train run in the rain? Would a man be mad if he did not get paid?	Would you pay a man to pat your pet? Can you lay a lid on top of a pan?	If you had a pain in your leg, would you lay it on a pad? Does the main man on a ship need to get paid?

Quick Check			
Can student read?	pain	→	If no, repeat F4.
	ray	→	If no, repeat F5.
	paid	→	If no, repeat F6.

Lists F7–F9

Lists F7–F9 introduce the vowel digraphs *oa* and *ow*. List F7 introduces *oa* and contrasts it with the short *o* pattern. F8 introduces *ow* and contrasts it with the short *o* pattern. F3 includes words with both *oa* and *ow* patterns along with the short *o* pattern.

F7: *oa*; **short *o***	**F8**: *ow*; **short *o***	**F9**: *oa*; *ow*; **short *o***
g, o, t, oa, r, s, d, l, c, b	l, o, t, ow, s, g, b, r	r, o, t, d, oa, ow, b, c, l, n
got	lot	rot
goat	low	rod
got	lob	road
rot	low	rod
rod	slow	row
road	glow	bow
roast	low	boat
boast	lot	coat
boat	blot	cot
coat	blow	rot
cot	low	lot
got	lot	low
goat	rot	loan
boat	row	
Would you like a goat or a toad as a pet? Would you like to eat roast meat and toast?	Can you row a boat on a lake? Can a slow goat run on a road?	Would you load ten toads and five snakes on a row boat? Can you lay your coat on a cot?

Quick Check			
Can student read?	boat	→	If no, repeat F7.
	row	→	If no, repeat F8.
	loan	→	If no, repeat F9.

Lists F10–F12

Lists F10–F12 introduce the vowel digraphs *ew* and *ue*. List F10 introduces the *ew* digraph. F11 introduces the *ue* digraph and contrasts it with short *u*. F12 includes both *ew* and *ue* words.

F10: *ew*	**F11**: *ue*; short *u*	**F12**: *ew*; *ue*
f, ew, s, t, d, r, n, c, sh, th	c, ue, b, l, p, g, s, d, u	b, l, ew, ue, g, r, c, ch, d
few	cue	blew
stew	blue	blue
dew	glue	blew
drew	blue	grew
new	clue	glue
few	cue	clue
screw	cup	cue
shrew	cue	crew
stew	sue	chew
threw	sud	dew
	sue	drew
Do you like meat in stew? Can a few men eat a cup of stew?	Can you fix a cup with blue glue? Should you fix a cup with glue or a screw?	Would a man chew stew with blue glue on it? Can a crew of men chew blue gum?

Quick Check			
Can student read?	stew	→	If no, repeat F10.
	cue	→	If no, repeat F11.
	crew	→	If no, repeat F12.

 Administer Specific Phonics Assessment (SPA-F) (Vowel Digraphs)

If students have difficulty with one or more of the vowel digraphs, review appropriate Word Building lists. Consider supplementary phonics activities, additional dictation, and additional reading of decodable text.

Sequence G
R-Controlled Vowels
Lists G1–G3

Lists G1–G3 introduce the *ar* and *or* graphemes. List G1 introduces *ar*; G2 introduces the *or* digraph. List G3 provides for discrimination between the *ar* and *or* graphemes.

G1: *ar*	**G2**: *or*	**G3**: *or*; *ar*
c, ar, t, m, f, d, k, p	s, p, or, t, f, k, c, n	s, t, ar, f, or, k, c, d
cart	sport	star
art	port	tar
arm	fort	far
farm	for	for
far	fort	fork
car	sort	stork
cart	fort	stark
dart	for	star
dark	fork	car
mark	pork	cart
park	cork	car
part	corn	card
	torn	cord
Do you use your arm in art? What can take you far—a car or a cart?	What sort of sport do you like? Do you use a fork when you eat pork?	Can a stork drive a car? What sort of a star can you see in a dark sky?

Quick Check			
Can student read?	cart	→	If no, repeat G1.
	fort	→	If no, repeat G2.
	stork	→	If no, repeat G3.

Lists G4–G7

List G4 introduces three new graphemes that stand for the same phoneme: *er, ir, ur*. In list G5, the *er* grapheme is used by itself and then contrasted with the *or* grapheme in G6 and *ar* in G7.

G4: *er*; *ir*; *ur*	**G5**: *er*	**G6**: *er*; *or*	**G7**: *er*; *ar*
b, ur, n, h, t, er, d, ir, f, s	h, er, d, p, m, t, k, j, c, l	p, or, k, er, t, c, l, s, f, n	p, er, k, ar, sh, j, c, l
burn	her	pork	perk
hurt	herd	perk	park
her	perk	pork	shark
herd	per	port	park
bird	perm	pork	perk
fir	term	perk	jerk
sir	perm	per	jar
stir	perk	perk	jerk
stern	jerk	clerk	clerk
fern	clerk	cork	clark
first	perk	stork	park
burst	per	fork	perk
	perk	fern	
Could you see a bird in a fern? If you had a burn on your leg, would it hurt?	Can a clerk act like a jerk? Have you seen a herd of sheep chase a bird?	Would a stork eat pork with a fork? Would a clerk sell pork to a bird?	Would you take a shark to the park? Would a bird nest under a fern in the park?

Quick Check			
Can student read?	burn	→	If no, repeat G4.
	perk	→	If no, repeat G5.
	fern	→	If no, repeat G6.
	clerk	→	If no, repeat G7.

Lists G8–G10

Lists G8–G10 focus on the *ir* grapheme, which represents the same phoneme as the *er* and *ur* graphemes. In List G9, the *ir* grapheme is contrasted with the *ar* grapheme. In G10, the *ir* grapheme is contrasted with the *or* grapheme.

G8: *ir*	**G9**: *ir*; *ar*	**G10**: *ir*; *or*
b, ir, th, d, s, t, f, m, k, sh	s, t, ir, ar, f, m, ch, d, k	f, ir, m, or, t, k, s, th, n, c
birth	stir	firm
bird	star	form
third	far	fort
thirst	fir	fork
first	firm	form
firm	first	firm
fir	fir	form
sir	far	first
stir	farm	thirst
skirt	charm	thorn
dirt	chart	corn
skirt	art	cork
shirt	dart	fork
shirk	dirt	form
irk	skirt	fork
Can girl go from first to third grade? Can a girl in a skirt sit on dirt?	Can you see a star from a farm? Should you throw a dart at a chart?	Do you use a fork to eat corn? Would a bird eat to stop its thirst?

Quick Check			
Can student read?	bird	→	If no, repeat G8.
	dirt	→	If no, repeat G9.
	firm	→	If no, repeat G10.

Lists G11–G13

List G11 introduces the *ur* grapheme on its own, and then G12 calls upon the reader to discriminate between the *ur* and the *ar* grapheme. G13 involves all five two-letter *r*-controlled graphemes in one Word Building list.

G11: *ur*	G12: *ur; ar*	G13: *ir; ur; er; ar; or*
h, ur, t, n, b, ch, l, f	b, ur, n, ar, s, t, c, d, h, l	f, or, ar, m, ir, s, t, er, n, ur, p
hurt	burn	for
turn	barn	far
burn	burn	farm
churn	burst	firm
burn	burn	form
burnt	bar	storm
hurt	car	stern
blurt	card	turn
blur	hard	turf
fur	hurt	surf
blur	blurt	sort
If you got burnt, would you blurt out for help? Would a hurt bird get the first turn to see the vet?	If a man hit a barn with his car, would he get hurt? Is it hard to wait for your turn?	Can a storm form near a farm? If you see a storm, should you hide in a barn or a car?

Quick Check			
Can student read?	burn	→	If no, repeat G11.
	hurt	→	If no, repeat G12.
	surf	→	If no, repeat G13.

 **Administer Specific Phonics Assessment (SPA-G)
(*R*-Controlled Vowels)**

If students have difficulty with one or more of the *r*-controlled vowels, review appropriate Word Building lists. Consider supplementary phonics activities, additional dictation, and additional reading of decodable text.

Sequence H
Diphthongs
Lists H1–H3

Lists H1–H3 introduce the *oi* and the *oy* graphemes, both of which stand for the same phoneme. In List H1, *oi* is introduced. In H2, *oy* is introduced. In H3, the words include both the *oy* and *oi* graphemes, and the reader is called upon to discriminate them from the short *o* grapheme.

H1: *oi*; short *o*	H2: *oy*; short *o*	H3: *oy*; *oi*; short *o*
c, oi, n, j, o, l, b	b, oy, l, o, p, c, j	c, oi, n, oy, b, l, f, g, h, j, t
coin	boy	coin
join	toy	coy
coin	top	boy
con	cop	boil
coin	coy	foil
coil	joy	fog
oil	job	hog
boil	cob	jog
coil	coy	joy
coin	cob	coy
join	cop	cog
job	coy	cot
	joy	coin
If you fix cars, do you need oil to do your job? Can two small coins join to make one big coin?	Do you feel joy when you get a new toy? Would a cop give a toy to a boy?	What would a boy want for a gift—a toy or a coin? Should a boy jog to his job?

Quick Check			
Can student read?	coin	→	If no, repeat H1.
	joy	→	If no, repeat H2.
	boil	→	If no, repeat H3.

Lists H4–H6

Lists H4–H6 introduce the *ou* and the *ow* graphemes, both of which stand for the same phoneme. In List H4, *ou* is introduced and contrasted with short *o*. In H5, the *ow* grapheme is introduced and contrasted with the short *o* grapheme. In H6, words with both *ou* and *ow* are included and are contrasted with short *o* words.

H4: *ou*; short *o*		H5: *ow*; short *o*		H6: *ou*; *ow*; short *o*	
f, ou, n, d, p, r, o, ck, m, th, s		b, ow, h, o, t, r, c, g, d, f, l		b, ow, ou, n, d, f, r, o, d, c, p, l	
found	sod	bow	howl	bow	now
pound	rod	how	how	bound	brow
round		hot	hog	found	bound
rod		rot		round	
rock		cot		rod	
round		cow		cod	
mound		how		cow	
sound		hog		now	
mound		dog		plow	
mouth		fog		plod	
south		fowl		nod	
Have you ever found a round rock? Which is more round—a rock or your mouth?		Who can growl—a hog or a dog? Could you see a cow, a hog, and a dog in the fog?		Have you ever found a round cow? Would you bow to a cow?	

Quick Check			
Can student read?	south	→	If no, repeat H4.
	cow	→	If no, repeat H5.
	found	→	If no, repeat H6.

▷ Administer Specific Phonics Assessment (SPA-H)

If students have difficulty with one or more of the diphthongs, review appropriate Word Building lists. Consider supplementary phonics activities, additional dictation, and additional reading of decodable text.

Specific Phonics Assessments
Administration and Scoring Guidelines

Administration

When a student has completed the word lists in a sequence and has had opportunities to read text that includes the phonics elements to be tested, the appropriate SPA should be administered on a one-to-one basis. For each SPA there is a Teacher Page for scoring and summarizing. The Student Page follows the Teacher Page. Students can read the words from either the Student Page in this appendix or from the computer screen on this book's website: *www.guilford.com/p/beck10*.

1. Ask the student to read the real words aloud. You may want to give the student a guide, such as an index card. Mark the errors on the Teacher Page by drawing a slash through incorrect letters and writing what the student said. Say something like:

   "Read these words to me. Take your time and be careful. You can read the whole word together as a word. Or you can read each sound by itself."

2. Move on to the nonsense words. Try the following script or something similar:

   "Now, it's time to read these words. We call these words nonsense words. They are not real words. They don't mean anything, but you can still read them. Read exactly what you see. Don't change anything. It is OK to sound out if you need to. [Point to the first example word.] I'll read this nonsense word: *mag*. The word is *mag*. The sounds are /m/ /a/ /g/. [Point to *ket*.] Now you read this nonsense word." If the student reads *ket* incorrectly, you read *ket* one more time.

   When the student is comfortable with reading nonsense words, the directions under (2) can be omitted or summarized.

3. Say: "Now it's time for you to read this list of nonsense words. Point to each word as *you* read it." Continue having the student read the nonsense words and mark the Teacher Page just as you did for the real words.

Scoring

1. If the student reads a word incorrectly but reads the target phonic element being assessed correctly, IT IS MARKED CORRECT. For example, in SPA-A and SPA-B, the

CVC assessments, if a student reads *pav* for *pab*, it is marked as correct because the short *a* is the phonic element being tested. Similarly, in the *r*-controlled assessment, SPA-G, because the *ar* is the target that is being tested, if a student reads *pars* for *park* it is correct, but if a student reads *pork* for *park*, it is incorrect.

2. For the real words, count how many are correct and enter that number as the numerator in the fraction listed across from the real-words category on the Teacher Page. The denominator is already provided.

3. Then calculate the percentage correct and enter it before the % sign. For those of us who sometimes forget the way to convert fractions to percentage, if the student had read five of the nine real-word targets correctly on the first SPA, the fraction correct is 5/9. To arrive at the percentage, divide the numerator by the denominator, 5 ÷ 9. The percentage correct is 56%, rounded up.

4. Across from the nonsense words, enter the number correct in fractional and percentage terms, as you did with the real words. For example, if the student had read nine of the 12 nonsense-word targets correctly, the fraction correct is 9/12, and the percentage correct is 75%.

5. In the recap section, notice that four of the nonsense words are reprinted for each vowel. They are the four words that contain a particular target grapheme. Calculate the fraction and percentage correct for the grapheme that is being targeted in the four words.

Note: Percentages are calculated because they enable us to make apples-to-apples comparisons, such as between real and nonsense words and in comparing accuracy among different graphemes.

Observations/Recommendations

Under Observations/Recommendations, briefly indicate any observations and recommendations that could be helpful to future instruction or intervention. You might indicate a specific grapheme that requires additional help, a possible consistent error, things that struck you during the assessment procedure but might not be captured by the numbers, or even that a student is proficient with respect to some or all graphemes.

Notations that have been written in the past could be as brief as listing the grapheme that a student struggled with, such as short *a*; *oa*; /y/ for *u*; /a/ for *o*; or more general comments such as "no consistent pattern," "slow," or "OK."

Teacher Page
Specific Phonics Assessment A
CVC /VC/ Short Vowels (*a, i, o*)

	# short vowels correct	% short vowels correct

1. Short Vowels Real

sit   hat   lot   pad   fin

rot   fit   sap   log

_____/9   _____%

2. Short Vowels Nonsense

kig   wap   lon   pab   nif   gop

pid   rak   poz   hib   jad   rog

_____/12   _____%

Nonsense Short Vowel Recap

short *a* (wap, pab, rak, jad)   _____/4   _____%

short *i* (kig, nif, pid, hib)   _____/4   _____%

short *o* (lon, gop, poz, rog)   _____/4   _____%

Observations/Recommendations

Name: _____

Student Page
Specific Phonics Assessment A
CVC /VC/ Short Vowels (*a, i, o*)

Sample: **mag** (teacher reads)

Sample: **ket** (student reads)

Real Words	Nonsense Words
sit	kig
hat	wap
lot	lon
pad	pab
fin	nif
rot	gop
fit	pid
sap	rak
log	poz
	hib
	jad
	rog

Teacher Page
Specific Phonics Assessment B
CVC /VC/ Short Vowels (*a, i, o, e, u*)

	# short vowels correct	% short vowels correct

1. Short Vowels Real

bug rip   pat   let   hot   _____/10   _____%

pit   tub   met   rat   cob

2. Short Vowels Nonsense

tig   nup lon   pab hef   geb   _____/20   _____%

duk rak   rop   hib   jad   laz   mik

tuv   toz   gub   sov   lek   rez   nif

Nonsense Short Vowel Recap

short *a* (pab, rak, jad, laz)   _____/4 _____%

short *i* (tig, hib, mik, nif)   _____/4 _____%

short *o* (lon, rop, toz, sov)   _____/4 _____%

short *e* (hef, geb, lek, rez)   _____/4 _____%

short *u* (nup, duk, tuv, gub)   _____/4 _____%

Observations/Recommendations

Name: _____

Student Page
Specific Phonics Assessment B
CVC /VC/ Short Vowels (*a, i, o, e, u*)

Sample: **mag** (teacher reads)

Sample: **ket** (student reads)

Real Words	Nonsense Words	
bug	tig	jad
rip	nup	laz
pat	lon	mik
let	pab	tuv
hot	hef	toz
pit	geb	gub
tub	duk	sov
met	rak	lek
rat	rop	rez
cob	hib	nif

Scoring for Consonant Blend

A student is given 0 or 1 point for every consonant blend read correctly. In all blends, the student must pronounce the following to receive one point:

- Read both phonemes correctly (ex: In *stop*, the student pronounces both /s/ and /t/)
- Read both consonants without any other phoneme (typically a vowel/schwa) in between. For example, if the student says, *sutop for stop, it is marked incorrect.*
- However, if the student pronounces both phonemes in a blend but makes a mistake with another portion of the word, it is marked correct. For example, *stip* for *stop is marked correct.*

The recap section asks that you do exactly as you have been doing on previous SPAs:

- Total the fraction and percentage for real words correct.
- Total the fraction and percentage of nonsense words correct.
  In the recap section, of the words indicated, total up the fraction and percentage correct separately for initial blends and final blends.

Teacher Page
Specific Phonics Assessment C
Consonant Blends

	# blends correct	% blends correct

1. Consonant Blends Real

stop	spit	band	pest	_____/8	_____%
gasp	blob	crib	felt		

2. Consonant Blends Nonsense

crob	spub	flup	blom	_____/8	_____%
kelt	tisp	rint	tand		

Nonsense Consonant Blends Recap

initial (crob, spub, flup, blom)	_____/4	_____%
final (kelt, tisp, rint, tand)	_____/4	_____%

Observations/Recommendations

Name: _____

Student Page
Specific Phonics Assessment C
Consonant Blends

Real Words	Nonsense Words
stop	crob
spit	spub
band	flup
pest	blom
gasp	kelt
blob	tisp
crib	rint
felt	tand

Teacher Page
Specific Phonics Assessment D
Consonant Digraphs

	# digraphs correct	% digraphs correct

1. Consonant Digraphs Real

that   shop   chip   rock   _____/8   _____%

mash   then   chat   pick

2. Consonant Digraphs Nonsense

thep   shov   meck   chiv   bock   _____/16   _____%

chob   shap   thum   rith   cheg   seck

thid   rish   shom   wuck   vetch

Nonsense Consonant Digraph Recap

-ck (meck, bock, seck, wuck)   _____/4   _____%

th (thep, thum, rith, thid)   _____/4   _____%

sh (shov, shap, rish, shom)   _____/4   _____%

ch/-tch (chiv, chob, cheg, vetch)   _____/4   _____%

Observations/Recommendations

Name: _____

Student Page
Specific Phonics Assessment D
Consonant Digraphs

Real Words	Nonsense Words	
that	thep	rith
shop	shov	cheg
chip	meck	seck
rock	chiv	thid
mash	bock	rish
then	chob	shom
chat	shap	wuck
pick	thum	vetch

Teacher Page
Specific Phonics Assessment E
CVCe Long Vowels

	# long vowels correct	% long vowels correct
1. Long Vowels/CVCe Real		
make bike cute ride	_____/8	_____%
code tape tune bone		
2. Long Vowels/CVCe Nonsense		
rike dobe gake dute mape	_____/16	_____%
zide roke lipe fune jate		
fane bome tupe bige zove vube		

Nonsense Long Vowel/CVCe Recap

CaCe (gake, mape, jate, fane)	_____/4	_____%
CiCe (rike, zide, lipe, bige)	_____/4	_____%
CoCe (dobe, roke, bome, zove)	_____/4	_____%
CuCe (dute, fune, tupe, vube)	_____/4	_____%

Observations/Recommendations

Name: _____

Student Page
Specific Phonics Assessment E
CVCe/Long Vowels

Real Words	Nonsense Words	
make	rike	fune
bike	dobe	jate
cute	gake	fane
ride	dute	bome
code	mape	tupe
tape	zide	bige
tune	roke	zove
bone	lipe	vube

Teacher Page
Specific Phonics Assessment F
Long Vowels/CVVC

	# long vowels correct	% long vowels correct

1. Long Vowels/CVVC Real

seat pay road pail row need   _____/12   _____%

feet soap ray gain heat tow

2. Long Vowels/CVVC Nonsense

geed zow tain poam tay tead   _____/24   _____%

kow leab faip kay loap weej

meag vay doat waip dow meeb

reat zay leep fow goan taid

Nonsense Long Vowel/CVVC Recap

ea (tead, leab, meag, reat)	_____/4	_____%
ee (geed, weej, meeb, leep)	_____/4	_____%
ai (tain, faip, waip, taid)	_____/4	_____%
ay (tay, kay, vay, zay)	_____/4	_____%
oa (poam, loap, doat, goan)	_____/4	_____%
ow (zow, kow, dow, fow)	_____/4	_____%

Observations/Recommendations

Name: _____

Student Page
Specific Phonics Assessment F
CVVC/Long Vowels/Vowel Digraphs

Real Words	Nonsense Words	
seat	geed	meag
pay	zow	vay
road	tain	doat
pail	poam	waip
row	tay	dow
need	tead	meeb
feet	kow	reat
soap	leab	zay
ray	faip	leep
gain	kay	fow
heat	loap	goan
tow	weej	taid

Teacher Page
Specific Phonics Assessment G
R-Controlled Vowels

	# *r*-controlled correct	% *r*-controlled correct

1. *R*-controlled Real

park	for	cart	perk	hurt	_____/10	_____%
bird	burn	cork	her	firm		

2. *R*-controlled Nonsense

nurt	terk	varm	porz	hart	_____/20	_____%
jarb	korv	tirk	pern	lurg		
nirm	forb	surk	herp	dirf		
larg	horp	verg	sirp	durm		

Nonsense *R*-Controlled Recap

ar (varm, hart, jarb, larg)	_____/4	_____%
or (porz, korv, forb, horp)	_____/4	_____%
er (terk, pern, herp, verg)	_____/4	_____%
ur (nurt, lurg, surk, durm)	_____/4	_____%
ir (tirk, nirm, dirf, sirp)	_____/4	_____%

Observations/Recommendations

Name: _____

Student Page
Specific Phonics Assessment G
R-Controlled

Real Words	Nonsense Words	
park	nurt	nirm
for	terk	forb
cart	varm	surk
perk	porz	herp
hurt	hart	dirf
bird	jarb	larg
burn	korv	horp
cork	tirk	verg
her	pern	sirp
firm	lurg	durm

Teacher Page
Specific Phonics Assessment H
Diphthongs

	# dipthongs correct	% dipthongs correct

1. Diphthongs Real

coin	cow	toy	foul	_____/8	_____%
how	boy	loud	soil		

2. Diphthongs Nonsense

foib	zow	foy	toud	_____/16	_____%
fow	roin	woy	houg		
gouk	moy	woit	kow		
gow	bouf	poy	goid		

Nonsense Diphthong Recap

oi (foib, roin, woit, goid)	_____/4	_____%
oy (foy, woy, moy, poy)	_____/4	_____%
ow (zow, fow, kow, gow)	_____/4	_____%
ou (toud, houg, gouk, bouf)	_____/4	_____%

Observations/Recommendations

Name: _____

Student Page
Specific Phonics Assessment H
Diphthongs

Real Words	Nonsense Words	
coin	foib	gouk
cow	zow	moy
toy	foy	woit
foul	toud	kow
how	fow	gow
boy	roin	bouf
loud	woy	poy
soil	houg	goid

Words and Syllable Matrices
for Syllasearch

There are four sets of words and syllable matrices for Syllasearch. Sequence A, the Easy Set, contains only two-syllable words. Sequence B focuses on open and closed syllables. Sequence C, the Medium Set, includes both two- and three-syllable words. Sequence D, the Hard Set, includes two-, three-, and four-syllable words.

Sequence A: Easy

Four phonics patterns are the focus of Sequence A: CVC, -y, -le, and r-controlled vowels. In most cases, students will have already learned these phonics patterns.[1] The primary goal of Sequence A is to have students appreciate how much they already can decode in terms of individual syllables and to practice synthesizing two syllables into a word.

At times during Sequence A, Teaching Tips are provided to point out upcoming patterns.

Teaching Tip: A1–A7

When a word contains two adjacent consonants, whether they are identical or not, the syllables usually are divided between the consonants (example: *fun-ny*).

Remind students that they already know how to read CVC words, both real words and nonsense words. Emphasize that the ability to read such short words will help them to read longer words (examples: *pup* in *puppy*, *fun* in *funny*)

Teaching Tip: A1

Write the word *silly* on the board. Tell students that when the letter *y* is at the end of a long word, it represents the long-*e* sound, as in *silly*.

A1: -y   Two *pen* syllable cards are needed.

funny	sap	ny
penny	pup	cil
pencil	hap	pet
happen	pen	py
puppy	fun	pen
puppet		
happy		
sappy		

(continued)

---

[1] A review of the major commercial basal series indicates that most, if not all, of these patterns are taught by the end of first grade.

Teaching Tip: A2–A3

When two identical consonants are followed by the letters *l* and *e*, the syllables usually divide between the two adjacent identical consonants. The letters *le* represent the phoneme /l/.

A2: *-le*   Two *pen* syllable cards are needed.

happy	gig	py
penny	pen	gle
happen	bot	pen
giggle	wig	tle
wiggle	lit	tom
little	bot	ny
bottle	hap	
bottom	bot	

A3: *-le*

bottle	bot	ble
bottom	lit	tom
little	rat	tle
cattle	bub	
rattle	cat	
bumble	bum	
bubble		

(continued)

Teaching Tip: A4–A5

When an initial syllable contains a vowel followed by the letter *r*, the syllable usually divides after the *r*.

Remind students that the *ar* grapheme represents the /ar/ sound as in *car* and the *or* grapheme represents the /or/ sound as in *for*. If students have difficulty with *ar* and *or*, it could be useful to review Word Building lists within the G Sequence in Appendix 1.

A4: *ar, or*

carpet	ex	pet
carport	sup	ner
partner	car	ty
export	part	port
support	ex	lorn
forty	for	
party	par	
forlorn		

A5: *ar, or*

market	tar	est
basket	for	ket
forest	bas	form
forget	mar	get
target	in	
inform	stor	
deform	de	

(continued)

Teaching Tip: A6–A7

Remind students that the *er, ir,* and *ur* graphemes all represent the same sound, the /er/ sound. If students have difficulty with *er, ir,* and *ur,* it may be useful to review Word Building lists within the G Sequence in Appendix 1.

A6: *er, ir, ur*

circle	tur	cle
circus	per	tic
plaster	plas	cus
plastic	cir	ter
perhaps		haps
perfect		fect
turnip		nip
turtle		tle

A7: *er, ir, ur*

perfect	pur	fect
letter	but	pose
butter	let	firm
infirm	thir	ter
thirty	con	ty
confirm	per	ple
purpose	in	
purple		

Sequence B: Open and Closed Syllables

Sequence B introduces open and closed syllables. In open syllables, the syllable ends in a vowel, and it is pronounced with the long sound of the vowel, for example, *pi* as in *pilot*. In closed syllables, the syllable ends in a consonant, and the vowel is pronounced short, for example, *pic* as in *picture*.

Teaching Tip: B1–B6

Write *basket* on the board. Explain that when there are two adjacent consonants after the first vowel, the syllables are divided between the two consonants. Write *bas ket* on the board.

Because *bas* ends in a consonant, it is called a closed syllable, and the *a* is pronounced short. Some people remember a closed syllable, as in *bas*, by noting that the *a* is closed in by a consonant on each side.

Write *bacon* on the board. When there is only one consonant after the first vowel, the consonant usually stays with the second syllable. Write *ba con* on the board. Because *ba* ends in a vowel, it is called an open syllable, and the *a* is pronounced long.

Ask a student to pronounce the *a* sound in *basket* and the *a* sound in *bacon*. When the correct response is provided, reinforce by saying, "The *a* sound in *basket* is the short-*a* sound: /a/. Let's say the short-*a* sound together: /a/. The *a* in *bacon* is the long-*a* sound. Let's say the long-*a* sound together: /a/."

"Why is the *a* sound in *basket* the short-*a* sound? [Because *bas* is a closed syllable.] Why is the *a* sound in *bacon* the long *a* sound? [Because *ba* is an open syllable.]"

It will be useful to review this teaching tip throughout Lists B1–B6 as it applies to open and closed syllables with different vowels.

B1: long *a*, short *a*

paper	ra	per
baby	raf	by
basket	rab	ket
bacon	pa	con
radon	bas	don
rabbit	ba	bit
rafter	ras	ter
rascal		cal

(continued)

Sequence B (page 2 of 4)

B2: long *e*, short *e*

recent	den	cent
return	de	turn
rental	les	gion
region	re	tist
legion	le	tal
lesson	ren	son
decent		
dentist		

B3: long *o*, short *o*

posture	pro	ture
possible	fo	ty
protect	lo	tel
motel	ho	tect
hotel	mo	cal
lofty	lof	si
local	pos	ble
focal		

B4: long *i*, short *i*

bisect	dis	mate	nect
biscuit	di	cuit	
pilot	pim	lot	
pimple	pi	ple	
pirate	bis	con	
dilute	bi	lute	
dispute		pute	
disconnect		sect	
		rate	

Sequence B *(page 3 of 4)*

B5: long *a*, short *a*, long *e*, short *e*

basket	den	bies
rabies	de	cent
rabbit	re	cue
baby	res	ket
recent	bas	by
rescue	ba	bit
dentist	rab	tist
decent	ra	

B6: long *a*/short *a*, long *o*/short *o*

later	ro	ter
label	rob	bel
lasting	lop	tion
lotion	lo	ting
local	la	cal
lopside	las	side
robber		ber
roman		man

Teaching Tip B7–B9

Syllasearch lists B7–B9 include open and closed syllables interspersed among other multisyllabic words.

B7

principal	ac	cue	pal
pilot	res	lot	
return	re	tion	
recess	pi	turn	
rescue	prin	cess	
nation	na	ci	
action			
access			

(continued)

B8

hollow	in	ter	tial
holiday	hol	bust	day
yesterday	ros	low	
robust	ro	i	
rodent	yes	dent	
roster			
indent			
initial			

B9

interrupt	pre	dle	view
interview	de	vent	rupt
invent	cra	mand	
prevent	in	ter	
cradle			
crater			
deter			
demand			

Sequence C: Medium

Sequence C contains a variety of patterns with gradually more irregular syllable patterns. Sequences C and D do not focus as much on particular patterns as do Sequences A and B. From this point on, the goal is regular repetition, decoding syllables as parts, and repeated practice applying the rules already learned and recognizing a few irregular syllables. There are no more teaching tips.

C1

become	a	come	tion
beware	se	ware	
income	be	lert	
aware	in	lec	
alert		date	
selection		cure	
sedate			
secure			

C2

family	hid	oth	mal
suddenly	help	i	er
sudden	an	den	ly
another	sud	ful	
animal	fam		
helpful			
helpfully			
hidden			

C3

picnic	nev	ture	ful
picture	vis	nic	tor
powder	pic	er	ble
power	pow	i	
powerful		der	
visitor			
visible			
never			

(continued)

C4: Two *mo* and two *tion* syllable cards are needed.

rotten	at	mo	tion
kitten	rot	tion	dance
attention	kit	chase	
attendance	pur	ten	
commotion	mo	sue	
motion	com		
purchase			
pursue			

C5: Two *per* syllable cards are needed.

person	per	tle	ous
perfect	gen	son	man
travel	tra	per	
shovel	sho	er	
gentle	pros	fect	
gentleman		vel	
generous			
prosperous			

C6

vacation	dis	yon	ment
improvement	can	prove	tion
improve	im	play	
immense	va	cel	
cancel		mense	
canyon		ca	
disprove			
display			

C7

discover	ver	cov	cal
distract	prac	tract	er
contract	re	sid	
consider	con	tire	
retract	dis	ti	
retire			
practical			
vertical			

(continued)

Sequence C (page 3 of 3)

C8

exam	can	tial	ple
example	par	am	lent
excellent	ex	lor	
excel		cel	
parcel			
parlor			
partial			
cancel			

C9

protective	re	ceive	tive
reverse	de	verse	ish
demolish	pro	mol	
detective		tec	
deform		form	
deceive			
reform			
receive			

C10

authentic	tra	then	ble
audible	gi	di	tic
capable	au	pa	tion
cater	ca	tumn	
autumn		ter	
gigantic		gan	
tradition		ant	
giant			

Sequence D: Hard

Sequence D contains a variety of patterns with gradually more irregular syllable patterns and inclusion of three- and four-syllable words. The goal is repetition and practice.

D1

conversation	in	ver	dent	tion
consult	fe	just	sa	
advertise	ad	fi	tise	
confident	con	vise		
advise		sult		
adjust				
fever				
insult				

D2

recreation	cav	re	fy	tion
rectangle	mod	tan	a	
simplify	rec	pli	lar	
similar	sim	el	ty	
model		i	gle	
modern		ern		
cavity				
cavern				

D3

addition	con	ven	ture
adventure	in	di	tion
constant	ad	form	
conform		stant	
invention			
condition			
convention			
inform			

(continued)

D4: Two *ti* syllable cards will be needed.

procrastinate	pos	duce	vi	nate
produce	re	bre	ti	ate
reduce	ab	cras	ble	
abbreviate	pro	ture	vate	
posture	cul	si		
possible		ti		
culture				
cultivate				

D5

enrage	sur	rage	pear
encourage	com	ap	age
discourage	dis	prise	
disappear	en	cour	
compress		press	
comprise		vive	
surprise			
survive			

D6

profile	ev	nounce	dent
protect	pro	i	due
evident	pres	file	
resident	res	tect	
residue	an		
president			
announce			
pronounce			

(continued)

Sequence D *(page 3 of 3)*

D7

inhabitant	de	hab	ish	tant
demolish	home	form	i	
forward	for	stant		
homeward	in	mol		
deform		ward		
inward				
instant				
inform				

D8: Two *i* and two *ty* syllable cards will be needed.

humidity	hu	i	i	ty
vanity	pre	mid	ty	
preserve	ex	serve		
extinct	van	tend		
extend	re	sume		
pretend		tinct		
presume				
reserve				

D9

remarkable	ex	mark	ler	ble
propel	re	cel	a	
propeller	pro	li		
remark		pel		
reliable				
repel				
expel				
excel				

The Word Pocket

A Word Pocket is simply a one-row pocket into which a child can place letters to make a word. To make a Word Pocket use a 12" × 9" sheet of tag board. On the 12" dimension, mark and score a line 1" from the bottom and fold along the line to make a pocket. Staple the ends.

The advantage of the Word Pocket is that it helps to show the earliest learners where the beginning, middle, and end letters in a word belong. Some teachers put a green dot (as a "go" sign) at the very left of the Word Pocket to show where the first letter of a word belongs. As children become familiar with building words, which they do quite rapidly, most teachers have found that they can simply build their words on their desks.

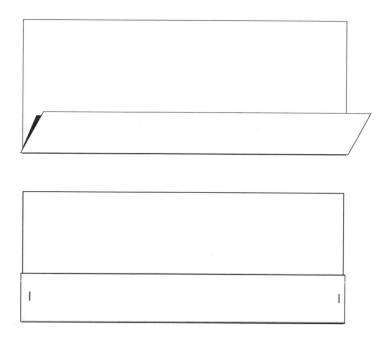

Lowercase letter cards that can be duplicated and are appropriate for a 12" × 9" Word Pocket follow.

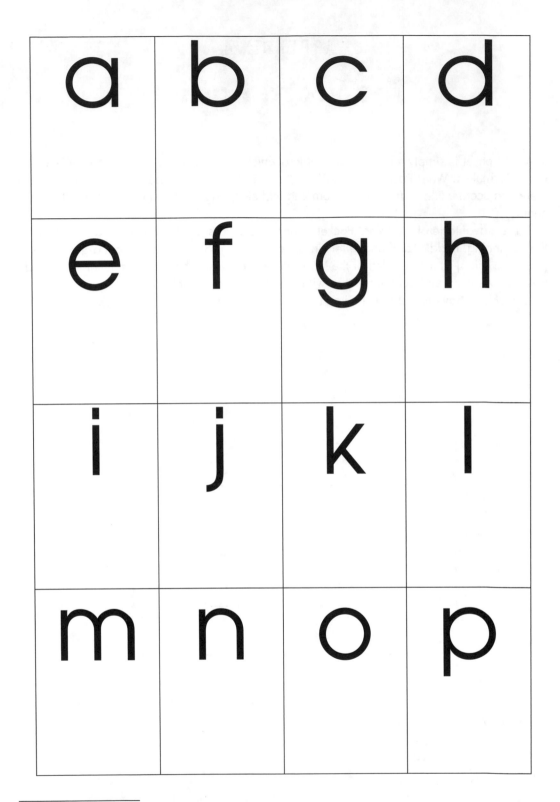

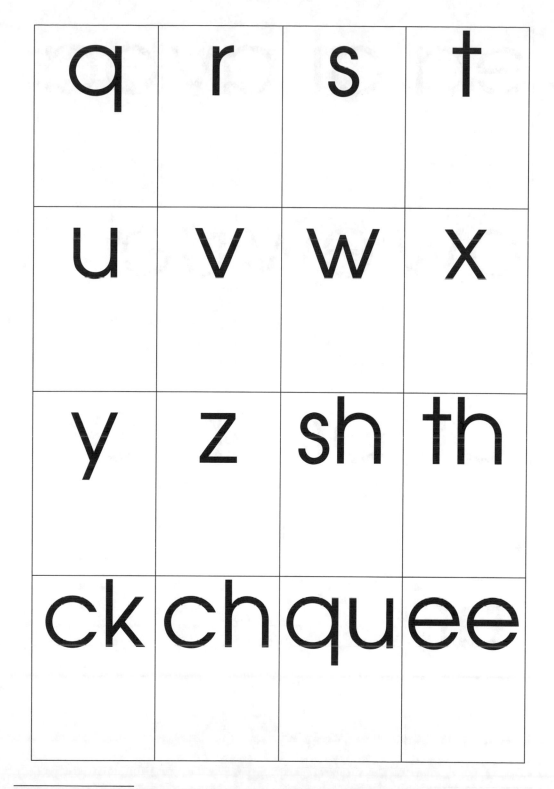

q	r	s	t
u	v	w	x
y	z	sh	th
ck	ch	qu	ee

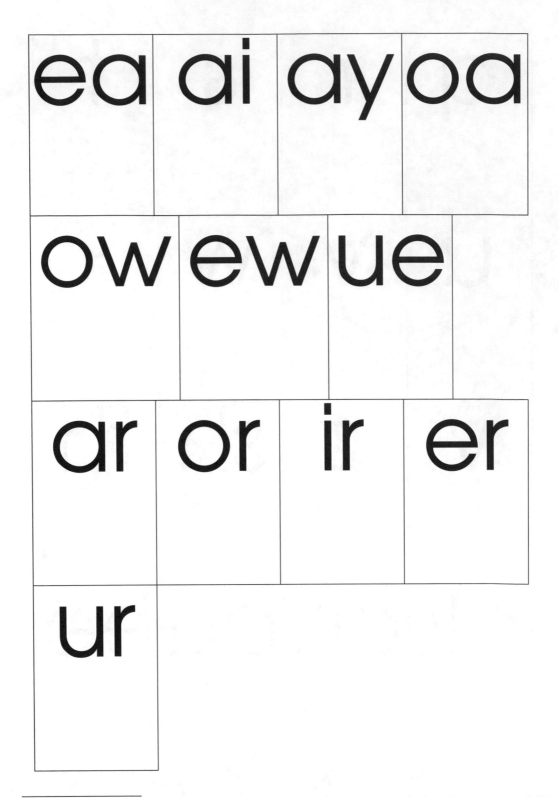

ea ai ay oa

ow ew ue

ar or ir er

ur

List of Online Teaching Resources

To assist teachers in conducting the assessments in Appendix 2 and the Syllasearch activities in Appendix 3, we have included several online resources as described below. Purchasers of this book may access the resources for downloading and printing or for use directly on their computers at *www.guilford.com/p/book10*.

SPA Word Lists

As an alternative to having students read the SPA words from Appendix 2, they can read the words directly on the computer, one word at a time. We have found that often students are more engaged reading the words from a computer screen than from a paper. Each of the files in this folder contains a word list that matches the corresponding Student Page in Appendix 2. For example, the file labeled SPA-A includes the same words in the same order as the Student Page for Special Phonics Assessment A in Appendix 2.

Syllasearch Word and Syllable Cards

Syllasearch requires displaying a number of word and syllable cards so that every student can see them. To reduce the time it takes to make the cards, we have provided enlarged versions of every word and every syllable in 35 separate files that correspond to the 35 Syllasearch lessons in Appendix 3. For example, the file labeled A1 includes all the words and syllables from lesson A1 in Appendix 3. Teachers can download and print the appropriate list of words and syllables for use in their classrooms. Printing them on card stock or laminating them enables repeated use of the same cards.

Syllasearch Stories

The 35 very short stories presented in these files correspond to the 35 Syllasearch lessons in Appendix 3. For example, the story labeled A1 (in Sequence A) features most of the target words from word list A1 in Appendix 3. These stories can be printed out and read in class at the end of every Syllasearch lesson. To add interest and help clarify the content, each story is illustrated with an original drawing by artist Patte Kelley.

Glossary

Alphabet. A set of written letters, with one or several letters together representing all speech sounds in a language.

Alphabetic principle. The understanding that sounds in spoken words can be represented consistently by specific written letters or symbols.

Automaticity. The ability to perform a task with little or no conscious attention.

Closed syllable. A syllable that ends in a consonant in which the preceding vowel is typically short (example: *mam* as in *mammal*).

Coarticulation. The act of pronouncing a phoneme in a word, while virtually simultaneously preparing one's mouth, tongue, and lips to pronounce the next phoneme.

Consonant. A phoneme that is not a vowel and is pronounced with at least partial obstruction of the airway.

Consonant blend. Two (or more) adjacent consonant letters that retain their phonemic quality but are pronounced together in a blended fashion (examples: <u>st</u>op, <u>tr</u>ain, be<u>st</u>).

Consonant digraph. Two consonants that, together, represent a separate and new phoneme, not represented by either of the individual consonant letters (examples: *sh*, *th*, *ch*, *ph*).

Cumulative (or successive) blending. An instructional practice for blending more than two phonemes, which groups phonemes in such a manner as to minimize taxing short-term memory.

CVC word. A one-syllable word that involves a consonant–short vowel–consonant pattern (examples: *cut, rib, mop*).

CVC*e* word. A one-syllable word that follows the consonant–long vowel–consonant-silent *e* pattern in which the first vowel is pronounced long and the final *e* is silent (examples: *cake, ripe, dude*).

CVVC word. A one-syllable word that follows the consonant–long vowel–silent vowel–consonant pattern in which the first vowel is typically pronounced long and the second vowel is silent (examples: *rain, meet, boat*).

Decode. The act of converting written language into speech.

Encoding. The act of converting speech into written language.

Explicit phonics. Teaching of letter–sound correspondences directly.

Full alphabetic decoding. The act of decoding an entire word, including all of its sub-unit parts, such as letters and syllables.

Implicit phonics. Letter–sound correspondences that are not taught directly but that need to be derived by the learner from whole words.

Long vowel. A vowel that sounds like its name.

Open syllable. A syllable that ends in a vowel, usually representing the long vowel sound (*ra* as in *radar*; *fu* as in *future*).

Orthography. The written spelling structure of language.

Phoneme. The smallest individual unit of a speech sound.

Phoneme segmentation. The ability to identify separate phonemes in a spoken word.

Phonemic awareness. The understanding that spoken words are composed of separate spoken sounds, or phonemes.

Phonics. An instructional practice that teaches the relationship between graphemes (letters) and phonemes (sounds) for use in reading and spelling.

Phonological awareness. The understanding of the overall sound system in language.

Phonology. The organization and use of speech sounds in language.

R-controlled vowel. When a vowel precedes the letter *r*, the pronunciation of the vowel changes from what it would typically be were it not followed by an *r*. For example, in a traditional CVC word such as *can*, the *a* is short. In an *r*-controlled word such as *car* the *a* sound is not the typical short *a* sound. Two-letter *r*-controlled examples: *ar, or, ir, er, ur*; three-letter examples: *air, are, ear, ore, our, oar*.

Rhyme. Repetition of the same sounds in the medial vowel and final consonants in two or more words.

Rime. The part of a syllable that consists of a vowel and any consonant sounds that come after it.

Short vowel. A vowel that represents its most common sound (*a* as in *pat*; *i* as in *lid*; *e* as in *red*; *o* as in *top*; *u* as in *bug*), typically taught before long vowels.

Short-term (or working) memory. That portion of memory that stores items temporarily and actively until such items are either lost from memory or moved into long-term or permanent memory.

Syllable. A sublexical unit of pronunciation within a word.

Syllasearch. An instructional activity that teaches and reinforces an appreciation for reading and spelling multisyllabic words.

Vowel. A phoneme that is not a consonant and is pronounced with no obstruction in the airway, the presence of which is necessary to any word or syllable—*a, e, i, o, u*.

Vowel digraph. Two vowels that together represent a single phoneme, typically the long vowel sound of the first letter (examples: *ee, ea, oa, ow, ai, ay, ie, ui, ue*).

Whole language. An instructional approach that emphasizes meaning, syntax, and semantics over letter–sound recognition.

Whole-word instruction (aka the **look–say method**). An instructional approach that teaches recognition of words as whole units without attention to subword units.

Word building. An instructional practice that teaches decoding through systematic, minimal changes in graphemes from one word to the next.

References

Adams, M. J. (1990). *Beginning to read: Thinking and learning about print*. Cambridge, MA: MIT Press.

Allington, R. L. (1983). Fluency: The neglected reading goal in reading instruction. *The Reading Teacher, 36*(6), 556–561.

Anderson, R. C., Hiebert, E. F., Scott, J. A., & Wilkinson, I. A. (1985). *Becoming a nation of readers*. Washington, DC: National Institute of Education.

Anderson, R. C., Wilson, P. T., & Fielding, L. G. (1988). Growth in reading and how children spend their time outside of school. *Reading Research Quarterly, 23*, 285–303.

Barr, R. (1972). The influence of instructional conditions on word recognition errors. *Reading Research Quarterly, 7*, 509–529.

Barr, R. (1974). Influence of instruction on early reading. *Interchange, 5*(4), 13–21.

Barr, R. (1974–1975). The effect of instruction on pupil reading strategies. *Reading Research Quarterly, 4*, 555–582.

Beck, I. L. (1981). Comments on the reading program. *Educational Perspectives, 20*(1), 20–22.

Beck, I. L. (1993). On reading: A survey of recent research and proposals for the future. In A. P. Sweet & J. I. Anderson (Eds.), *Reading research into the year 2000* (pp. 65–87). Hillsdale, NJ: Erlbaum.

Beck, I. L. (2006). *Making sense of phonics: The hows and whys*. New York: Guilford Press.

Beck, I. L., & McCaslin, E. S. (1978). *An analysis of dimensions that affect the development of code-breaking ability in eight beginning reading programs* (Learning Research and Development Center Publication No. 1978/6). Pittsburgh, PA: University of Pittsburgh, Learning Research and Development Center.

Beck, I. L., & Mitroff, D. D. (1972). *The rationale and design of a primary grades reading system for an individualized classroom* (Learning Research and Development Center

Publication No. 1972/4). Pittsburgh, PA: University of Pittsburgh, Learning Research and Development Center.

Berends, I. E., & Reitsma, P. (2007). Orthographic analysis of words during fluency training promotes reading of new similar words. *Journal of Research in Reading, 30*(2), 129–139.

Bergeron, B. (1990). What does the term whole language mean? Constructing a definition from the literature. *Journal of Reading Behavior, 22*, 301–329.

Bishop, C. H. (1964). Transfer effects of word and letter training in reading. *Journal of Verbal Learning and Verbal Behavior, 3*, 215–221.

Blachman, B. A., Ball, E., Black, S., & Tangel, D. (1994). Kindergarten teachers develop phoneme awareness in low-income, inner-city classrooms: Does it make a difference? *Reading and Writing: An Interdisciplinary Journal, 6*, 1–17.

Bloomfield, L. (1942). Linguistics and reading. *Elementary English Review, 19*, 125–130.

Bradley, L., & Bryant, P. E. (1978). Difficulties in auditory organization as a possible cause of reading backwardness. *Nature, 271*, 746–747.

Bus, A. G., & van IJzendoorn, M. H. (1999). Phonological awareness and early reading: A meta-analysis of experimental training studies. *Journal of Experimental Psychology, 91*, 403–414.

Carroll, J. B. (1964). The analysis of reading instruction: Perspectives from psychology and linguistics. *Sixty-third Yearbook of the National Society for the Study of Education, 63*(Pt. 1), 336–353.

Chall, J. S. (1967). *Learning to read: The great debate.* New York: McGraw-Hill.

Chall, J. S. (1987). *Learning to read: The great debate updated.* New York: McGraw-Hill.

Chard, D. J.,Vaughn, S., & Tyler, B. J. (2002). A synthesis of research on effective 12 interventions for building reading fluency with elementary students with learning disabilities. *Journal of Learning Disabilities, 35*(5), 386–406.

Coleman, E. B. (1970). Collecting a data base for a reading technology. *Journal of Educational Psychology Monograph, 61*(4, Pt. 2).

Cunningham, A. E., Nathan, R. G., & Raher, K. S. (2011). Orthographic processing in models of word recognition. In M. L. Kamil, P. D. Pearson, E. B. Moje, & P. P. Afflerbach (Eds.), *Handbook of reading research* (Vol. 4, pp. 259–285). New York: Taylor & Francis.

DeLawter, J. (1970). *Oral reading errors of second grade children exposed to two different reading approaches.* Unpublished doctoral dissertation, Teachers College, Columbia University.

Dewey, G. (1970). *Relative frequency of English spellings.* New York: Teachers College Press.

Diederich, P. B. (1973). *Research 1960–1970 on methods and materials in reading* (TM Report 22). Princeton, NJ: Educational Testing Service.

Dolch, E. W. (1948). *Problems in reading.* Champaign, IL: Garrard Press.

Drewnowski, A., & Healy, A. F. (1977). Detection errors on *the* and *and*: Evidence for reading units larger than the word. *Memory and Cognition. 5*(6), 636–647.

Ehri, L. C. (1999). Phases of development in learning to read words. In J. Oakhill & R. Beard (Eds.), *Reading development and the teaching of reading: A psychological perspective* (pp. 79–108). Oxford, UK: Blackwell.

Ehri, L. C. (2005). Learning to read words: Theory, findings and Issues. *Scientific Studies of Reading, 9*(2), 167–188.

Ehri, L. C., & Wilce, L. S. (1979). Does word training increase or decrease interference in a Stroop task? *Journal of Experimental Child Psychology, 27,* 352–364.

Elder, R. D. (1971). Oral reading achievement of Scottish and American children. *Elementary School Journal, 71,* 216–230.

Evans, M. A., & Carr, T. H. (1983). *Curricular emphasis and reading development: Focus on language or focus on script.* Symposium conducted at the biennial meeting of the Society for Research on Child Development, Detroit, MI.

Feitelson, D. (1988). *Facts and fads in beginning reading: A cross-language perspective.* Norwood, NJ: Ablex.

Felton, R. H., & Meyers, M. S. (1999). Repeated reading to enhance fluency: Old approaches and new directions. *Annals of Dyslexia, 49,* 283–306.

Flesch, R. (1955). *Why Johnny can't read.* New York: Harper & Row.

Gibson, E. J., & Levin, H. (1975). *The psychology of reading.* Cambridge, MA: MIT Press.

Gibson, E. J., Pick, A., Osser H., & Hammond, M. (1962). The role of grapheme–phoneme correspondence in the perception of words. *American Journal of Psychology, 75,* 554–570.

Goodman, K. S. (1967). Reading: Psycholinguistic guessing-game. *Journal of the Reading Specialist, 6*(1), 126–135.

Goodman, K. S. (1976). Reading: A psycholinguistic guessing game. In H. Singer & R. B. Ruddell (Eds.), *Theoretical models and processes of reading* (pp. 497–508). Newark, DE: International Reading Association.

Guthrie, J. T., Samuels, S. J., Martuza, V., Seifert, M., Tyler, S. J., & Edwall, G. A. (1976). *A study of the locus and nature of reading problems in the elementary school.* Washington, DC: National Institute of Education.

Gutman, D. (2012). *Ms. Beard is weird!* New York: HarperCollins.

Hanna, P. R., Hanna, J. S., Hodges, R. E., & Rudorf, E. H., Jr. (1966). *Phoneme–grapheme correspondences as cues to spelling improvement* (U.S. Department of Education Publication No. 32008). Washington, DC: U.S. Government Printing Office.

Harn, B. A., Stoolmiller, M., & Chard, D. J. (2008). Measuring the dimensions of alphabetic principle on the reading development of first graders. *Journal of Learning Disabilities, 41,* 143–157.

Hohn, W. E., & Ehri, L. C. (1983). Do alphabet letters help prereaders acquire phonemic segmentation skills? *Journal of Educational Psychology, 75,* 752–762.

Holland, J. G., & Doran, J. (1973). Instrumentation of research in teaching. In R. M. W. Travers (Ed.), *Second handbook of research on teaching* (pp. 286–317). Chicago: Rand McNally.

Johnson, D. D., & Baumann, J. F. (1984). Word identification. In P. D. Pearson, R. Barr, M. L. Kamil, & P. Mosenthal (Eds.), *Handbook of reading research* (pp. 583–608). New York: Longman.

Juel, C. (1988). Learning to read and write: A longitudinal study of fifty-four children from first through fourth grade. *Journal of Educational Psychology, 80,* 437–447.

Just, M. A., & Carpenter, P. A. (1987). *The psychology of reading and language comprehension.* Boston: Allyn & Bacon.

LaBerge, D., & Samuels, S. J. (1974). Toward a theory of automatic information process in reading. *Cognitive Psychology, 6*, 293–323.

Levin, A. (1994). The great debate revisited. *Atlantic Monthly, 274*(6), 38–44.

Levy, B. A. (2001). Moving the bottom: Improving reading fluency. In M. Wolf (Ed.), *Dylexia, fluency, and the brain* (pp. 367–379). Timonium, MD: York Press.

Levy, B. A., Abello, B., & Lysynchuk, L. (1997). Transfer from word training to reading in context: Gains in fluency and comprehension. *Learning Disabilities Quarterly, 20*, 173–188.

Liberman, I. Y., & Shankweiler, D. (1979). Speech, the alphabet, and teaching to read. In L. B. Resnick & P. A. Weaver (Eds.), *Theory and practice of early reading* (Vol. 2, pp. 109–132). Hillsdale, NJ: Erlbaum.

Lobel, A. (1970). *Frog and Toad are friends* series. New York: HarperCollins.

Logan, G. D. (1997). Automaticity and reading: Perspectives from the instance theory of automatization. *Reading and Writing Quarterly: Overcoming Learning Difficulties, 13*(2), 123–146.

Lundberg, I., Frost, J., & Petersen, O. (1988). Effects of an extensive program for stimulating phonological awareness in preschool children. *Reading Research Quarterly, 23*, 263–284.

Marino, J. M., & Ferraro, F. R. (2008). Reading rate and word unitization. *Psychology Journal, 5*(3), 140–146.

Mason, J. M. (1980). When do children begin to read: An exploration of four-year-old children's letter and word reading competencies. *Reading Research Quarterly, 15*(2), 203–227.

Massaro, D. W., & Taylor, G. A. (1980). Reading ability and unitization of orthographic structure in reading. *Journal of Educational Psychology, 72*(6), 730–742.

McBride-Chang, C. (1999). The ABCs of the ABCs: The development of letter-name and letter-sound knowledge. *Merrill–Palmer Quarterly, 45*(2), 285–308.

McCandliss, B., Beck, I. L., Sandak, R., & Perfetti, C. (2003). Focusing attention on decoding for children with poor reading skills: Design and preliminary tests of the Word Building intervention. *Scientific Studies of Reading, 7*(1), 75–104.

McGuinness, D. (1997). *Why our children can't read and what we can do about it*. New York: Free Press.

McPike, E. (1995a). [Editor's note]. *American Educator, 19*(3), 6.

McPike, E. (1995b). Learning to read: Schooling's first mission. *American Educator, 19*(2), 3–6.

Mewhort, D. J., & Campbell, A. J. (1981). Toward a model of skilled reading: An analysis of performance in tachistopcoptic tasks. In G. E. MacKinnon & T. G. Waller (Eds.), *Reading research: Advances in theory and practice* (Vol. 2, pp. 53–95). New York: Academic Press.

Moats, L. C. (2000). *Speech to print: Language essentials for teachers*. Baltimore: Brookes.

Morais, J., Cary, L., Alegria, J., & Bertelson, P. (1979). Does awareness of speech as a sequence of phones arise spontaneously? *Cognition, 7*, 323–331.

National Governors Association Center for Best Practices and Council of Chief State School Officers. (2010). *Common Core State Standards: Phonics and Word Recognition for K–2; Fluency for K–5*. Washington, DC: Author.

National Reading Panel. (2000). *Teaching children to read: An evidence-based assessment of the scientific literature on reading and its implications for reading instruction* (NIH Publication No. 00-4754). Washington, DC: National Institutes of Health.

Pearson, P. D. (1989). Reading the whole-language movement. *Elementary School Journal, 90*(2), 231–241.

Perfetti, C. A. (1985). *Reading ability.* Oxford, UK: Oxford University Press.

Perfetti, C. A. (1991). The psychology, pedagogy, and politics of reading. *Psychological Science, 2,* 70–76.

Perfetti, C. A., Beck, I., Bell, L., & Hughes, C. (1987). Phonemic knowledge and learning to read are reciprocal: A longitudinal study of first grade children. *Merill–Palmer Quarterly, 33*(3), 283–319.

Perfetti, C. A., Goldman, S. R., & Hogaboam, T. (1979). Reading skill and the identification of words in discourse context. *Memory and Cognition, 7,* 273–282.

Perfetti, C. A., & Hogaboam, T. W. (1975). The relationship between single word decoding and reading comprehension skill. *Journal of Experimental Psychology, 67,* 461–469.

Perfetti, C. A., & Roth, W. F. (1981). Some of the interactive processes in reading and their role in reading skill. In A. M. Lesgold & C. A. Perfetti (Eds.), *Interactive processes in reading* (pp. 269–297). Hillsdale, NJ: Erlbaum.

Pickett, J. P., et al. (Eds.). (2000). *The American heritage dictionary of the English language* (4th ed.). Boston: Houghton Mifflin.

Pikulski, J. J., & Chard, D. J. (2005). Fluency: Bridge between decoding and reading comprehension. *The Reading Teacher, 58,* 510–519.

Popp, H. M. (1964). Visual discrimination of alphabet letters. *The Reading Teacher, 17,* 221–224.

Popp, H. M. (1975). Current practices in the teaching of beginning reading. In J. B. Carroll & J. S. Chall (Eds.), *Toward a literate society* (pp. 101–146). New York: McGraw-Hill.

Rashette, C. A., & Torgeson, J. K. (1985). Repeated reading and reading fluency in learning disabled children. *Reading Research Quarterly, 20,* 180–202.

Raynor, K., & Pollatsek, A. (1989). *The psychology of reading.* Englewood Cliffs, NJ: Prentice Hall.

Roth, S. F., & Beck, I. L. (1987). Theoretical and instructional implications of the assessment of two microcomputer word recognition programs. *Reading Research Quarterly, 22*(2), 197–218.

Samuels, S. J. (1979). The method of repeated readings. *The Reading Teacher, 32,* 403–408.

Share, D. L. (2008). Orthographic learning, phonological recoding, and self-teaching. In R. V. Kail (Ed.), *Advances in child behavior and development* (Vol. 36, pp. 31–82). San Diego, CA: Elsevier Academic Press.

Share, D. L., & Stanovich, K. E. (1995). Cognitive processes in early reading development: Accommodating individual differences into a model of acquisition. *Issues in Education, 1,* 1–57.

Smith, F. (1971). *Understanding reading.* New York: Holt, Rinehart & Winston.

Smith, F. (1973). *Psycholinguistics and reading.* New York: Holt, Rinehart & Winston.

Smith, N. B. (2002). *American reading instruction: Special edition.* Newark, DE: International Reading Association.

Stanovich, K. E. (1986). Matthew effects in reading: Some consequences of individual differences in the acquisition of literacy. *Reading Research Quarterly, 21*, 360–406.

Stanovich, K. E. (2000). *Progress in understanding reading: Scientific foundations and new frontiers.* New York: Guilford Press.

Stanovich, K. E., Cunningham, A. E., & Cramer, B. (1984). Assessing phonological awareness in kindergarten children: Issues of task comparability. *Journal of Experimental Child Psychology, 38*, 175–190.

Stanovich, K. E., & West, R. F. (1989). Exposure to print and orthographic processing. *Reading Research Quarterly, 24*(4), 402–433.

Tan, A., & Nicholson, T. (1997). Flashcards revisited: Training poor readers to read words faster improves their comprehension of text. *Journal of Educational Psychology, 89*, 276–288.

Toward better teaching. (1995, September 18). [Editor's note]. *Sacramento Bee*, p. B6.

Treiman, R., Broderick, V., Tincoff, R., & Rodriguez, K. (1998). Children's phonological awareness: Confusions between phonemes that differ only in voicing. *Journal of Experimental Child Psychology, 68*, 3–21.

Treiman, R., Tincoff, R., Rodriguez, K., Mouzaki, A., & Francis, D. J. (1998). The foundations of literacy: Learning the sounds of letters. *Child Development, 69*, 1524–1540.

U.S. Department of Education. (2002, April). *Guidance for the Reading First program.* Washington, DC: Office of Elementary and Secondary Education. Available at *www.ed.gov/programs/readingfirst/guidance.pdf.*

Wagner, R. K., Torgesen, J. K., & Rashotte, C. A. (1994). Development of reading-related phonological processing abilities: New evidence of bidirectional causality from a latent variable longitudinal study. *Developmental Psychology, 30*, 73–87.

Index